THE MOON UNDER HER FEET

D0013505

THE MOON
UNDER HER FEET

CLYSTA KINSTLER

HarperSanFrancisco
A Division of HarperCollins*Publishers*

Grateful acknowledgment is made for permission to reprint the following:

Excerpts from INANNA: QUEEN OF HEAVEN AND EARTH by Diane Wolkstein and Samuel Noah Kramer. Copyright © 1983 by Diane Wolkstein and Samuel Noah Kramer. Reprinted by permission of Harper & Row, Publishers, Inc.

Translation of "Inanna's Descent to the Netherworld" by Samuel Noah Kramer reprinted from THE MASKS OF GOD: PRIMITIVE MYTHOLOGY by Joseph Campbell. Copyright © 1959, 1969 by Joseph Campbell. All rights reserved. Reprinted by permission of Viking Penguin, a division of Penguin Books USA, Inc. Reprinted by permission of Russell & Volkening as agents for the author. Copyright © 1959 by Joseph Campbell, renewed 1987 by Joseph Campbell.

Illustrations adapted from IN THE SHADOW OF THE TEMPLE by Meir Ben-Dov. Copyright © 1985 by Keter Publishing House Jerusalem Ltd. Reprinted by permission of Harper & Row, Publishers, Inc. and Keter Publishing House Jerusalem Ltd.

Excerpts from ORIENTAL CARAVAN edited by Sirdar Akbal Ali Shah.

THE MOON UNDER HER FEET. Copyright © 1989 by Clysta Kinstler. All rights reserved. Printed in the United States of America. No part of this book may be used or reproduced in any manner whatsoever without written permission except in the case of brief quotations embodied in critical articles and reviews. For information address HarperCollins Publishers, 10 East 53rd Street, New York, NY 10022.

FIRST HARPERCOLLINS PAPERBACK EDITION PUBLISHED IN 1991.

Library of Congress Cataloging-in-Publication Data

Kinstler, Clysta.
    The moon under her feet / Clysta Kinstler. — 1st HarperCollins paperback ed.
       p.   cm.
    Includes bibliographical references.
      ISBN 0-06-250497-5
      1. Mary Magdalene, Saint—Fiction. 2. Bible. N.T.—History of Biblical events—Fiction. 3. Jesus Christ—Fiction. I. Title.
PS3561.I584M66   1991
813'.54—dc20   90-49257
                                                  CIP

---

03 04 05 RRD H 20 19 18 17 16 15 14

To Joseph Campbell
Who awakened me to Mythology

To William Irwin Thompson
Whose insights are the bones of this work

To Barbara Walker
Whose research grew into its flesh

And to
Connie Warloe
Elizabeth Stewart
Theresa Enroth
Helen Mills
Gail Greenwood
Eleanore Wootton and
Nanci Lee
The Midwives who brought it to Birth.

TO MY READERS

While this book is a work of fiction, its many departures from familiar tradition, like those consistent with it, are based on much more than my own imagination. Many will prefer to enjoy it simply as a love story, but for those who may be more curious, I have provided detailed notes showing the mythological and historical sources, and a complete bibliography of books that influenced my work.

Contents

Key to Characters

Mari Anath Mari, the Mary Magdalene of Scripture from whose point of view the story unfolds, who becomes the High Priestess of Isis-Ashera, or Magdalene, after Almah.

Aethel Mother of Mari Anath, wife of Tammas.

Almah Mari The Holy Maiden of Israel, daughter of Anna, Magdalene or High Priestess after Anna. She is believed by Mari to be the incarnation of the Goddess Isis.

Anna The Magdalene, High Priestess of Isis-Ashera, Mother of Almah.

Antipas Herod Andipas, son of Herod the Great, half-brother to Philip Herod.

Claudius A retired Roman soldier, father of Aethel, grandfather to Mari Anath.

Deborah Handmaiden to Almah Mari.

Deidre Mari's friend, fourth wife of Philip the Tetrarch.

Geshtinanna "Nana," daughter of Joseph, stepsister to Yeshua, priestess-handmaiden to Mari.

Jason A Greek trader who becomes the husband of Nana.

Joachim Almah's father, a Persian prince.

John	A steward to Philip, later a disciple to Yeshua.
John	John the Baptizer, son of Zacharias and Elizabeth.
Joseph	Husband of Almah Mari.
Joseph of Arimathea	Distant relative, or "uncle" of Mari, a disciple.
Judas	See Seth.
Julia	Handmaiden to Almah.
Lazarus	Younger brother of Mari and Martha.
Lili	Mari's grandmother, wife of Claudius.
Lucius	A eunuch priest of Ashera, friend and bodyguard to Mari.
Lysander	Another eunuch priest, Mari's bodyguard and messenger.
Martha	Sister of Mari and Lazarus.
Matthias	A Zealot, one of the two crucified with Yeshua.
Mene	Son of Philip by Deidre.
Miriam	The famous midwife of Scarios.
Ninshubur	"Nina," a priestess, companion and handmaiden to Mari.
Peter	A Galilean, a Zealot, and a disciple of Yeshua.
Reuben	One of the Zealots crucified beside Yeshua.
Salome	Daughter of Mari by Philip.

Seth   Also called Judas of Scarios, adopted son of Miriam the midwife. Seth is also the name of the evil archon, creator of the world of matter and murderer of his brother, the god Osiris.

Shaher and Shalem   Mari's sons by Seth, named for the Morning and Evening Star.

Sharon   The Sacred King, bridegroom of Almah Mari, father of Yeshua.

Sita   Yeshua's beautiful Indian disciple.

Tammas   Mari's father.

Yeshua   The Christos, son of Almah Mari, also called Jeshouah, Joshua, and Jesus, and in this story, Osiris.

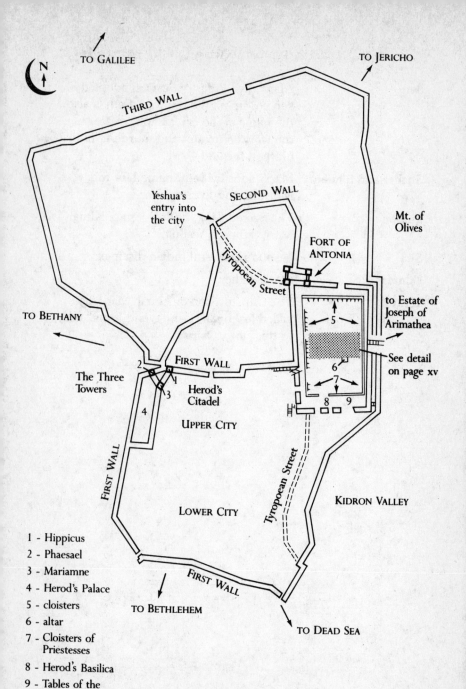

TO GALILEE

N

TO JERICHO

THIRD WALL

SECOND WALL

Yeshua's
entry into
the city

Mt. of
Olives

FORT OF
ANTONIA

Tyropoean Street

TO BETHANY

5

to Estate of
Joseph of
Arimathea

See detail
on page xv

FIRST WALL

6

2

The Three
Towers

1

7

3

8   9

Herod's
Citadel

4

UPPER CITY

FIRST WALL

Tyropoean Street

LOWER CITY

KIDRON VALLEY

1 - Hippicus
2 - Phaesael
3 - Mariamne
4 - Herod's Palace
5 - cloisters
6 - altar
7 - Cloisters of
    Priestesses
8 - Herod's Basilica
9 - Tables of the
    Moneychangers

FIRST WALL

TO BETHLEHEM

TO DEAD SEA

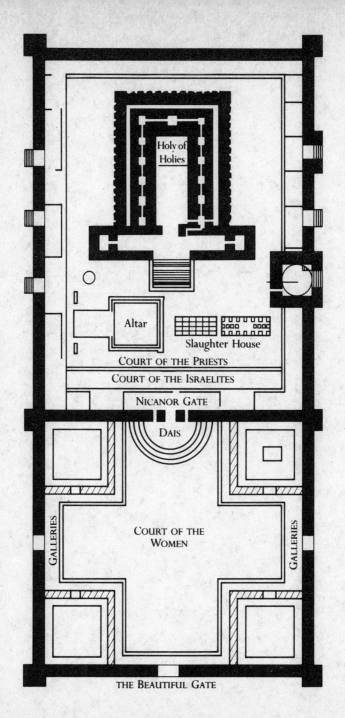

Holy of Holies

Altar

Slaughter House

COURT OF THE PRIESTS

COURT OF THE ISRAELITES

NICANOR GATE

DAIS

GALLERIES

COURT OF THE WOMEN

GALLERIES

THE BEAUTIFUL GATE

THE MOON UNDER HER FEET

Prologue

For now we see through a glass, darkly;
but then face to face: now I know in part;
but then I shall know even as also I am known.
I Corinthians 13:17, KJV

Mine is a story that must be told. And a story that must be heard, because those who presume to tell it do not know it. Or want to. Those who have taken possession of the story of Yeshua, the Christos, distort his record and mine, for one cannot be told without the other. I am Mari, the Magdalene, and I have set down the truth in this manuscript, trusting that the Goddess will bring it to light when the time is ripe.

I have always served the Goddess. I have served her in joy, in sorrow, and in rebellion; in anger and in love. Yet even when I raged against her, I loved her Law. The Law is greater than the gods. Even Yeshua, born of the Mother, reverenced the Law and died to fulfill it.

I was given to the service of the Mother when I was but five years old, and I became her High Priestess in Jerusalem in the reign of Herod Antipas and Pontius Pilate. The Goddess blessed me with intelligence and with beauty, but she could not give me wisdom. Wisdom is most often won through suffering, so she provided me much opportunity to gain it. Do not think I complain, now that I have earned some part of it—only a fool carps at the gifts of the gods. I count my suffering as light when I reflect on the blessings that came with it. Our earthly joys carry with them a measure of pain; this, too, is the Law. I love the Law, its balance of good and evil. My hope is not a Heaven of light, life, love, peace, joy, with no darkness, death, hate, strife or pain. The Mother sends both light and darkness, but she is not capricious. May her Law be written in my heart.

PART 1

The Temple of Ashera

Do not be ignorant of me.
For I am the first and the last.
I am the honored one and the scorned one.
I am the whore and the holy one.
I am the one who has been hated everywhere,
  and the one who has been loved everywhere,
I am the one whom they call Life,
  and whom you have called Death.
I am the one whom they call the Law,
  and you have called lawlessness.

The Thunder, Perfect Mind

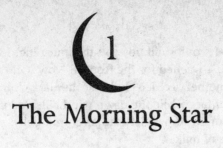

The Morning Star

And there appeared a great wonder in Heaven,
A woman clothed with the sun,
And the moon under her feet.
Revelation 12:1, KJV

On the day I was given to the Goddess I awakened before daylight, a strange fluttering inside me. The excitement that had wakened me combined with the cold, and I shivered, pulling my cloak around me. I went outdoors with the milking bowl and breathed in the sweet air. Hanging the bowl on Nadja's tether post, I faced into the dawn breeze and climbed the little rise behind our house. The sparse grass showed weak new growth at the crown of the hill where it lay open to the dew and light frost of the winter just past. There had been little rain this year or the one before, and though my parents worried about it in their talk, I thought little of it. I saw only that sunny days were better than rainy ones.

She was there—the Morning Star—just as Grandmother Lili had promised, brilliant in the brightening sky above the far roofs of Jerusalem, and beneath her, just rising over the dark shape of the Temple, the slimmest crescent moon. The cold wind flapped my cloak about me, but I did not feel it, overcome as I was by that heavenly sign. The Goddess was smiling her blessing on my special day, and the moon was under her feet.

Presently, chilled, I trudged down the hill and got the bowl. Nadja already stood expectantly on her milking bench watching me with soft eyes. I put two handfuls of oats in her box, and she chewed happily, moving her little jaws and flicking her long ears rapidly.

"I told you I would milk for you this morning, Mari, because your hair is just washed for the festival! Now you will smell like a goat," my mother scolded, holding the dark cloud of her hair away from her face while the dawn wind billowed it about her. I pressed my forehead against Nadja's round belly, stripping out the last drops of milk.

"Nadja smells good." A flash of unaccustomed anger eased the strange fluttering in my belly. Mother took the milk, and I untied Nadja, led her up the slope to the middle of the grassy mound, and pounded her peg securely into the earth with a heavy rock. I put my arms around her neck and dragged my clean hair over her brown back. She bleated sympathetically. There were tears in my throat.

The dawn had bleached the pale sliver of the moon to a bloodless white, but the Queen of Heaven still gleamed like a tiny candle in the blue morning. My sign. She would stay even when the sun rose and hid her light. Remembering that, I felt the fluttering ease.

I went in and Mamma pressed a steaming cup into my hand. She began to comb my hair. I drank Nadja's warmth with her milk.

"Let me do that, Aethel. You need to dress the little ones," Grandmother said, lifting the headband of gold links I was to wear out of her carved jewelry box lined with purple wool.

Baby Lazarus was still asleep. Mother combed Martha's black curls and put on her best gown while Grandmother struggled with the headband, which wanted to slide forward over my eyes. Martha was only three, two years younger than I, and she cried for a headband too. Mamma pacified her with a saffron-dyed ribbon and came back to me with her comb.

"Don't braid her hair, Aethel. It is a glory." Grandfather Claudius spoke from the doorway, his arms full of blossoming branches.

"You would tempt the angels, then?" Mamma said, sniffing handfuls of my hair for goat smell.

Grandmother Lili took the blossoms and began to weave them with linen strips into a garland. "The Pharisees would cover her for certain," she observed.

"Let the Pharisees veil their maids if they want," scoffed Grandfather. "The eye starved for delight is the one that strays."

"Hush!" admonished Grandmother. "The child is innocent."

Grandfather lifted me to match his height; my legs dangled. The fierceness of his blue eyes puzzled me, though I could never be afraid of him. He had taught me the names and hiding places of the wild birds and animals along the little streams between the hills, how to carve their wooden images without cutting myself, and how to keep from getting lost. He kissed me on each cheek, and I smelled apple blossoms. "Let the angels beware," he said.

Shocked, I saw tears brimming over in Mamma's eyes, but they embarrassed rather than moved me. I was not ready to forgive her for sending me away. She turned and began to braid her black hair into a plait as thick as her wrist. I knew she had guessed my thought and I was ashamed, but I could say nothing. The unfamiliar anger was a knot in my chest.

The Temple was blinding with the morning sun reflecting off its beaten gold and polished marble, more huge and grand than I remembered from the year before when my parents had brought me. There had been six maidens given to the Goddess then. Now, smallest and last in line, an insignificant seventh, I followed the heels of the maid before me, moving in procession between endless banks of people, keeping my chin high so the headband would not fall over my eyes. I could not see the top of the massive wall of the Temple Mount from the wide paved street bordering it along which we moved. The single stones that formed the wall were large as houses, and there were stones left out at intervals forming cavelike niches for the merchants' shops along the way.

Delicious smells from these stalls reminded me I had been too excited to eat breakfast. My stomach knotted, but I could not have eaten even then. The city was glorious with colored banners, music everywhere. The loud murmur of the crowd, like a great ocean, was frightening and strangely exciting. I feared, yet loved it, from that day.

We passed through the Beautiful Gate in the eastern wall of the Mount into the Temple courtyard, where the paving stones were polished smooth as the floor of a fine house. Great banks of steps led to the altar high above. Lifting the front of my gown as Grandmother Lili had taught me, I kept my head up as we climbed.

I was not an ordinary celebrant as my mother and grandmother had been. I was especially chosen for the line of the Magdalenes—the High Priestesses. I tried to imagine being a High Priestess, but could not. The daughters of former High Priestesses would rank before me, so I was only an alternate; even so, being chosen had cost me my rightful inheritance. My anger rose again, making me brave. I was no longer princess of Bethany, to own our lands after my mother. Martha would receive the honors that would have been mine, and I would be a priestess forever.

We approached the last bank of steps, and I was afraid the Mother would know my impious thoughts. Then I was angry with Her, too, as much as with my mother. If She is the "soul of kindness," whose love is "poured out on the whole world," I demanded to know, how can she ask so much of me? My life had been given away, and no one had even asked me. I had been promised to the Goddess before my birth!

Burning with indignation, I climbed the last step and looked up startled into the very face of the High Priestess, certain my flaming cheeks revealed my whole mind. I had glimpsed the lady at last year's festival, but she had seemed far off then, like a doll, more costume than woman. Now I stood before her on the great dais of the Temple, my head scarce higher than her golden girdle.

The High Priestess Anna was the Goddess-on-Earth, and her magnificent garments proclaimed it. Yet she outshone them. The jeweled crown she wore was less glorious than her red hair, flowing in abundance about her face and neck, catching the sunlight in a halo of fire. I had never seen such hair, nor such eyes, nor the amazing arts of painting them, nor such richness and grandeur of costume. I shrank before that living vision of perfection. Her gaze was kind, but so knowing, so stunning, that I could bear it for only a moment. Lowering my eyes, I caught my breath, for she held a snake whose perfect pattern of scales glittered like jewels. Then, as I stared, it moved and blinked its shining eye. I started, wanting to run, but the priestesses stood in a close half-circle behind us. I stared agape, my eyes on the serpent, as the lady stepped forward, gently placing it in the open basket another priestess held for her. I let out my breath. So we stood, trembling in our best white gowns, wreathed with flowers and heirlooms, each her own family's most precious offering to the Mother, and the Goddess-on-Earth came toward us.

Each small girl was like the queen of a great land, for our Lady took all the time in the world with us. She knelt in turn before each maid, glorious robes flowing, while the people watched in reverent silence. When it was my turn, she gently opened my clammy hands with smooth, jeweled fingers, and clasped them as she spoke, the kindness in her touch like cool water. Her voice was silver bells and angel choirs.

"Do you, Mari Anath, desire with all your heart and soul to serve the Mother as long as you live?"

"I do," my voice quavered like Nadja's bleating.

"Do you promise to follow in her service wherever she shall lead?"

"I do."

She dipped her ringed fingers into the oil that another priestess held for her, and placed them on my head.

"Welcome home, my daughter."

My anger and fear were borne away like foam on a great ocean that lifted and carried me with it. The waves and waves of people were part of it, and I was part of it, and we were all one in that ocean. The peacefulness that came over me then stayed with me for the rest of the ceremony, and I still felt it when I went to join my family for the feasting, and to tell them good-bye.

We picnicked beyond the walls of the Temple Mount on close-cropped grass beneath sycamores just leafing out, for we preferred our own company to the crowds. I was too excited to eat, and for once Mamma did not press me. It came to me that she would not be there urging me to do all the things that were good for me anymore. I found I was no longer angry with her, but what I felt now was more painful. My throat filled up and I couldn't speak, but then it was not our way to speak of difficult things.

Please, Mamma, don't let it be time for you to go, I wanted to say. I will eat a barley cake if you will wait a little longer.

I hid my face in the hollow of her throat. She smelled of hay and milk, and her tears were wet on my face. Grandmother Lili took me from Mamma and rocked me in her arms the way she had when I was very small. "Precious lamb," she crooned. I smelled the cedar shavings that perfumed her clothes, and she comforted me.

My father had a gift for me—the sharpest little carving knife, with a slender handle shaped to fit my hand. It meant that I was grown up and he trusted me to take care. He swung me round in a circle, and I laughed, but I knew he was telling me good-bye, and that he loved me. I would see them all often, I told myself, but I wouldn't live at home anymore, and we would grow apart. It was unbearable.

Then Grandfather carried me off to the border of trees, holding me up to see into a bird's nest, and he was telling me good-bye, too, without saying anything. Maybe the lump in his throat hurt as much as mine did, so he couldn't speak. I felt him stop, looking at someone behind me. I turned to see, and we stood still, caught in an endless moment I will always remember, like deer surprised in the forest before they suddenly spring to life and bound away.

A young woman in a pure white gown came across the grass. She was the vision of an immortal goddess, a garland of spring flowers about her neck, the blue of her eyes peaceful as the sky, her brown hair haloing the sunlight. Grandfather put me down, and I backed into Mamma's arms, staring at the maiden. All of us, even little Martha, stood gawking.

"My name is Almah Mari," she said, speaking directly to me instead of to my parents. "Are you Mari Anath? I am now your elder sister." She knelt before me stretching forth her arms. Mamma gave me a tender push, but I could not trust my voice and nodded stupidly. Almah Mari closed her arms, enveloping me in the scent of flowers and sandalwood, then she arose and led me away to my new life.

From that moment I loved her.

We entered the sacred cloister of the College of Virgins, passing through echoing marble halls and then an endless walled garden that looked like the setting for an Arabian fairy tale, fragrant with herbs and flowers I had never seen, and with arched galleries all around it. We entered a long passageway flanked on either side with rows of great cedar doors glowing with beeswax. I marveled at how much rubbing it must have taken to polish so many huge doors to such a sheen as we passed one after another, until Almah Mari opened one of them and we were in the room where I would sleep. I gasped to find already there the little chest from home that held my clothes. Two of the maidens who had marched with me that day were sitting together, still in their white dresses. They jumped up and came shyly toward us.

"This is Ninshubur," Almah said, taking the hand of the tallest, "and Geshtinanna. This is your sister, Mari Anath." We looked at each other afraid to speak, then gathered our courage and all started talking at once. Almah showed us the door to her own bedchamber just across the passageway, a few steps from our own. She left us briefly, returning with cakes and milk; there was no supper in the dining room tonight because of the feasting, she said. We rolled out our sleeping mats and pushed them close together. I wanted to talk, but the other girls fell asleep almost at once.

I lay awake, dreading the darkness, but it did not come. The shadows deepened, but yellow torchlight from the gallery shone through the high window and dimly illumined the room. After a long, anxious time, I realized it would grow no darker. I let out my breath and felt my body begin to ease, remembering the Morning Star as She had last appeared to me. She must be there still, watching. If I closed my eyes I thought I could see her, but her face was more distinct to me now. She looked like the High Priestess Anna, and like Almah Mari.

The Holy Maiden of Israel

And he placed her upon the third step of the altar, and the lord gave unto her grace, and she danced with her feet, and all the house of Israel loved her.

"The Protoevangelion"

I turned six at the autumn festival, and the elaborate preparations for the winter celebration began soon after. The Feast of the Winter Solstice was the most ancient of holy days, filled with wonder upon wonder—songs and dances, solemn pageantry, the wondrous voices of pipes and stringed instruments. We practiced our songs and dances and sewed our finery in great anticipation. All too soon it was over in a wonderful rush of excitement, and we began the cycle of preparations for spring, which would be observed by the celebration of the Sacred Marriage.

The drought continued during the usual rainy season, the third such year in a row. All the streams and wells dried up. The priestesses of Ashera watered their herb gardens from three deep wells within the Temple compound and fed their animals hay and grain laid by in the vast storage houses beneath its massive walls. Every day we gave grain, bread, and cheese to lengthening lines of people who filed through the gates of the Mount.

There would be no excursions into the foothills for herbs this year. The plants were too sparse and poor to risk weakening them further. No grass appeared on the brown hills, and the lambs that did not come too soon or stillborn were weak-legged and unable to survive. "Something must be done," I heard people whispering, and I wondered at what they said. What could anyone do about the weather?

Because his usual gardening tasks were set aside to conserve water, our favorite storyteller, Lysander, had extra time to spin his tales for us, and we were happy for that. Lysander was slight and graceful as a deer, with finely elegant features and astounding long-lashed eyes—black as jet. His skin was so black it was blue. In the snowy white of his linen tunic, I thought him one of the most perfectly beautiful creatures I had ever seen. I knew the young men who trained for the priesthood sacrificed their manhood to the Goddess, but I was not sure what that meant. They did not seem sexless to me. They attended us at our baths, scrubbing, massaging, and oiling, and their hands taught of secret pleasures.

Lysander did far more than entertain us; he was our principal source of news and our historian. We younger priestesses, who were never informed about anything by our elders, relied on what gossip we could overhear and on Lysander's willingness to explain to us the context of these tidbits. "Tell me what you heard exactly," he would insist. "Don't add what you think." We hardly realized that we ourselves were part of his amazing ability to know everything as soon as it happened, if not before.

Today, he had promised to tell us Almah's story. Not for the first time, for we had heard it before, but we never tired of it.

We all loved Almah Mari, but I idolized her, holding her above all others. I loved the sound of her name, rolling its soft syllables over my tongue. It meant "pure maiden," or "virgin," and the rest of it was the same as my own, Mari, the ancient name of the Goddess, a common and popular name among the people, but marked with awe and respect. My own second name, Anath,—I had learned this from Grandmother Lili—was that of the great warrior-goddess called by the Greeks Athena, known to our people as the virgin daughter of the Great Mother.

Common opinion supported our adoration of Almah by setting her in a place of high honor. So we listened eagerly to Lysander, trying to conceal our delight lest we be found remiss in our studies and assigned a less entertaining teacher.

"Our Lady, the High Priestess Anna,"—Lysander's voice was rich and smooth as cream, and his tone implied forbidden secrets—"is true princess of the Hasmoneans, the royal house of Israel. You can see her royal blood by her red hair and her blue, blue eyes. She is daughter of the High Priestess Mariamne, who was murdered by her jealous husband, King Herod."

"Our Lady cannot be the daughter of King Herod," I blurted, daring to say this time what I had thought before.

It was unthinkably rude to interrupt the story, and Lysander acknowledged this, rolling his eyes skyward, amazed that such ignorance could exist in his presence. "You are right about that, little sister," he derided, but his black eyes smiled.

My face felt hot. "My father has red hair," I said, regretting the words at once. Lysander crowed with delight.

"Little Miss Mari thinks she has royal blood, too?" He leaned forward and tweaked my brown braid. The others laughed. "I don't know where you come from, little mistress, with your white skin and pink nipples; your nose is freckled as a bird's egg. You are foreign here as me—half-bred at least—but you are not Hasmonean, be sure of that." He slapped his knee and crowed again, and the other children joined in. I was too embarrassed to look at anyone. Then he paused the way he always did to wait for us to pay careful attention.

"Listen," he commanded. "The world is full of beautiful things. Would you want all the flowers to be your favorite color? Or all the birds to look alike? When the Mother made everything, she didn't just want it to be good; she wanted it to be beautiful. Our Mother loves beautiful things, so she made beautiful flowers, all kinds, and beautiful animals with spots and stripes and curly horns and spiky antlers, and a rainbow of colored birds to sing different songs to her."

I forgot all about my foolishness listening to him.

"And she made beautiful people, too, all kinds, short and tall and round and square, white and red and brown and black. Red hair doesn't give Lady Anna royal blood; it just runs in her family." He pulled on my braid again, and I laughed with the others.

"Our Lady Anna was Temple-born, a sacred child not known to Herod," he went on. "Mari says true that he is not the father. A long time before, when he still loved his queen, the High Priestess, he named one of his great magdalas, the towers of his citadel, Mariamne, so the people called her Lady of the High Place, or Magdalene. Ever since, we call our Lady, the High Priestess, Magdalene."

"And Father Joachim was a prince," I put in. I wanted him to know I wasn't stupid.

"A prince of Persia." He marked this interruption with a long-suffering sigh. "A Magian, a worshiper of Ormazd. He took a Jewish name and forswore his god to wed our Lady." Lysander looked around at each one of us, his eyes and mouth triple circles of emphasis.

"King Herod would not recognize our Lady, because she calls no man her father, but she is royal through her mother's line, princess of all Jerusalem and Bethlehem." He lowered his silky voice even more, and we strained not to miss a word.

"Joachim was her true choice, and the people honored him too. He has the fierce blood of warriors, made noble by generous deeds. It pleased them he changed to their religion, but after a while they started talking against him.

"No child was born to them for a long time, and the people said Joachim was cursed by Jehovah. They wanted Lady Anna to take another husband in the Sacred Marriage, or divorce him.

"Father Joachim prayed with the elders to Jehovah, and Lady Anna prayed to the Mother. Who answered their prayers? Joachim prayed for a son. We say Almah Mari is sent by the Mother."

We all nodded in solemn agreement.

"But the priests and elders of Father Jehovah fell in love with our little princess too; they sent their wise men to see her." Lysander's voice was a joyful singsong. "All the sacred signs agree. Almah Mari is the Holy Maiden. She will be mother of the Messiah." He beamed angelically at our awed silence.

We had listened to talk of the Messiah ever since we could remember—the Holy One to come who would free our people from their enemies. Perhaps it was the familiarity of the title that made me think I understood its meaning. The Messiah would be majestically grand and wonderful; I was certain of that, and Almah—my Almah—was the Holy Maiden who would bear him. Lysander crooned like a doting grandmother.

"Our sweet little Almah Mari—she walked, she talked, she sang, she danced; no other baby could do this so young! Lady Anna and Father Joachim dedicated her to the Mother when she was three years old! Three years, three months!" He showed three ebony fingers twice. "You know what darling Almah Mari did on her dedication day?" His face radiated pure joy. "She danced! She danced right up the steps of the Temple, and all the House of Israel loved her!"

Later that day, I had reason to remember the story when we were all together in the spacious workroom where the women of Ashera gathered in the late afternoons before supper. I had learned to spin a little, a smooth thread without lumps or weak places, and was learning as well the pleasure of a useful task that leaves the mind free.

Ninshuber and Geshtinanna were dramatizing the story of Isis, Osiris, and Seth. Their players were clay dolls dressed in scraps of silk trimmed with colorful seeds and bits of glass. Combining legend and imagination, they wove their tale as the women's voices rose and fell in gentle waves and the fire crackled in the great hearth, leveling out the silences between their bursts of merry laughter. But Almah Mari was unusually silent, bent over her embroidery, so absorbed in her thoughts that she neglected her duty as our assigned "elder sister" and did not notice their play had grown unseemingly loud.

Watching Almah, I saw that her forehead was strained into unfamiliar lines and her mouth had shed its tender softness. She had been summoned earlier that morning by the High Priestess— her own mother—and had returned flushed and distant. I took a deep breath and opened my mouth to ask the cause of her unhappiness, when she turned to me, her eyes full of trouble.

"I am chosen for the part of the Goddess in the Sacred Marriage, come the full moon," she whispered breathlessly, as if she did not realize the import of her words before she said them.

"It is a great honor," I stammered. Foreboding descended on me like a cloud. Almah would be changed forever; it could never be the same for us again.

The Sacred Marriage, I already knew, was the yearly spring ritual renewing the king's right to rule as true spouse of the Goddess. But the king was Almah's own father. I could not understand why the High Priestess Anna would not perform the rite with him as she did most years.

"A Sacred King has come forward," Almah choked, "he has been found without blemish and will wed the Goddess as my bridegroom." Her beautiful eyes and her delicate nose turned red and streamed with tears as she tried to hide her face behind her embroidery.

I glared, furious at the wondering eyes of the others on Almah, who, no longer able to speak for crying, tried blindly to pick up her embroidery. Then, with an imploring look, she fled, dropping her precious bundle of purple threads and leaving behind her a silent circle of round eyes and mouths.

Almah never lost her composure. Never before this. Now I was crying too. She had been chosen for a great honor; why was she so sad? With a fierce glance warning my two friends not to follow, I went after her, picking up the scattered colored threads.

When I found her alone in the garden, the sunlight a glory in her hair, she was composed and silent. I could get nothing more from her. "You will understand soon enough," she said in a tight, closed voice. "We will speak no more of it."

That night my head ached unbearably, and I cried with the pain until I realized that crying made it worse. When I finally slept on the softly rustling pallet beside my two bed mates, I dreamed, and the dream began with a strange and sickening smell.

I was alone, wandering endlessly in some marshy, mossy land, searching for someone or something. Dripping moss dragged across my face, and gnarled branches clawed at my clothing. The urgency of my search was overpowering in spite of the smells of horrible things, living and dead, wet mouths stinging and sucking at me. Then when I thought I would find what I sought, dread rose in my throat, strangling me, and I cried out in a voice not my own, waking myself and my companions.

My head pounded with every heartbeat; my ears still rang with the eerie sounds, and my nostrils flared at the stench.

"I thought I heard Almah cry out," Geshtinanna murmured agreeably through a wide yawn, sitting up to hear me tell my dream. As Temple children we were taught to recall and understand our dreams by telling them to each other as soon as we awoke. Ninshubur—"Nina," at six years already long-legged as a young colt, turned on her side and propped her chin in her hand expectantly.

"I think I have dreamed someone else's dream," I stammered wonderingly, and felt my face turn dark with sudden awareness of the fast-cooling warmth in which I lay.

"It is no shame, Mari; your dream has given you a fright." Nina was up and rummaging through my clothes chest. She found what she sought and hurried to me with a clean gown. "Now put this on and don't be so silly." She dabbed at my embarrassed tears with the still-dry part of the wet nightgown. "Come into bed with me," and she bundled me into place beside her. "Tell us what was so frightening."

I tried to describe my vivid dream, while the others prompted me with prescribed questions, too sleepy to be really interested, dutifully playing their role.

"Maybe it was Almah's dream," Nina offered, dropping her round chin into the pillow. "It was her voice."

Certain Ninshubur was right, half-afraid to sleep again for fear the dream might return, I lay awake, stomach churning, head pounding. I had to slip out of bed and vomit violently into the chamber pot, and my head felt as if it would burst, but then the pain eased away as if I had vomited it out of my body.

My thoughts were all of Almah. I knew that custom allowed a lesser priestess to represent the Goddess in the Sacred Marriage if a substitute king was being crowned. Who was this "unblemished" stranger, and why had he "come forward" and for what purpose? Lysander had said that sometimes a substitute could take the king's place in the festival, but he had seemed unwilling to explain why, and I could not imagine why Father Joachim should decline so great an honor.

I slept at last, but awakened before the others, the thought of Almah instantly present. It was just dawn.

The stone floor was cold to my bare feet, but I crept from the bed, shivering, wrapped a shawl about me, and stealthily unfastened the heavy door. I tried to push it open just far enough to squeeze through, but the groaning sound it made roused movement beneath the blankets where the other two cuddled together in the morning chill. "It's all right," I hissed at them, "go back to sleep."

Nina's dark head appeared, eyes black in the half-light, instantly concerned. "It is not yet morning, Mari. Stay. Almah will come to us."

I made a face at her. How did Nina always know my thoughts? It was no use lying to her or trying to keep anything from her. And she did it without even trying! Worst of all, she was proving awfully good at it. It was embarrassing not to have one's thoughts to oneself.

The other dark head rose from the pillow, and Geshtinanna, daughter of Joseph of Nazareth, still recovering from the grief of her mother's death only a year ago, wound her arm about Nina's neck, pulling her down on the bed. "Nina, let her go. Let's sleep yet awhile."

Slipping out and closing the heavy door behind me, I thought it a great saving that I need never explain anything to these two. Geshtinanna never asked, and Ninshubur had no need.

The court on which our rooms faced was open to the sky, and the cold flagstones were damp as I moved to Almah's door and silently tried the heavy latch. It was barred. I dared not waken her, and I wondered why I had come. Nina would know, I thought to myself, turning down the empty gallery in the morning silence. The huge household was wakening; a purple-robed priestess crossed the long passage opening on the hallway, followed by two eunuchs. They were setting about the day's food preparations, sweeping, grinding, carrying water.

Lysander appeared in my path so suddenly we startled each other. He bowed graciously, and I bobbed my head in flustered acknowledgment. "My lady," he said with perfect courtesy, "how may I serve you?"

My voice trembled. I was determined not to miss this chance to learn the truth. "Tell me why there will be a substitute king in Father Joachim's place," I implored, "and why Almah is so sad."

His expressive face closed. "That is not for me to tell, Miss Mari," he said kindly. Then he echoed Almah's words. "You will know soon enough."

He would say no more. I sought again the shelter of my room, creeping close under the woolen blankets against Nina's back, my feet and hands cold as ice, my troubled spirit unsoothed.

3

Almah-Isis

Mistress of the gods, thou bearer of wings
Praise be to thee, O Lady,
who art mightier than the gods . . .
Hymn to Isis

The next part of my story is more about Almah than myself; it is her story, and to tell it properly I must speak of many things that I understand now but either had no idea of at the time or else saw dimly from the outside. That I can relate these things almost as though I *were* Almah, which should be impossible, is nevertheless a fact, which I will explain later at the proper time. Do not think, either, that Almah's entire life and thoughts have been opened to me in some magical way, for it is only of these things I am about to tell that I have intimate knowledge; the rest is as hidden from me as from anyone who knew her. I do not betray a confidence, since it was for this very purpose I was shown these things.

Almah refused to leave her "little sisters" even though she could not spend much time with us during her initiation period. We would be separated for good only too soon, so she continued to sleep with her two companions, Julia and Deborah, in the room close to ours, except on those nights when her meditative vigils lasted into the dawn.

Maidens in the special line of the High Priestess were taught to journey through the realms of the soul, ascending in imagination to the seven levels of Heaven, gaining the blessing of each guardian planetary power at the "gate" of that stage of consciousness, the key to a higher level of psychic ability. We committed to memory the powers of each level, for the mind creates reality; thus I can recite them to you:

The first gate opened the way to perfect recollection of dreams; the second revealed the knowledge of other minds, living, dead, or yet unborn. At the third level, the soul reclaimed memories of past lives. The fourth and fifth levels revealed the whole history and purpose of the universe. On the attainment of the sixth level, the unity, or oneness, of all things would be fully realized in perfect compassion, unconditional forgiveness, and absolute love for all beings, living, dead, or yet to be. The seventh level of awareness, if it could be achieved, would be past the powers of language to describe—the dissolution of the self in union with the One, perfect bliss.

Less inviting, but just as positive in its rewards, we were taught, was to descend by vivid imagery through the seven levels of Hell, past the seven gates of the Netherworld, guarded by the Seven Judges or Annanaki, each of whom must be bribed with the sacrifice of something precious to obtain passage. At the deepest level, most dreadful and dangerous to confront, sat the dark aspect of the Goddess, the terrible Queen of the Underworld— Ereshkigal, Nephthys, Persephone.

Almah Mari at fifteen years of age was already practiced within the first two levels of reality that were taught to all the priestesses. She had learned to apply dream knowledge to the problems of waking life and to enter into the thoughts of others. Now she found that her former knowledge had been only practice for a purpose she did not yet understand. With her mother, or sometimes with the old seeress Hecate, as a guide, she was led deeper and deeper into the hidden depths of herself. She relived her birth, then she became her own mother, remembering Anna's birth and life as vividly as her own, yet she knew it for Anna's life, not hers.

In the late afternoons, when Almah returned from her meditations to find her "little sisters" watching and waiting for her, she seemed distant and preoccupied. We were awed by what we understood of Almah's ordeal, but we missed her playfulness and attention to our needs. I sensed her twinge of guilt when she made an excuse to retire earlier than usual, as she often did now, but her need for sleep was overwhelming at times. She often gave in to my unspoken entreaty and invited me to share her bed. It comforted us both, and Nina and Geshtinanna expressed no jealousy or hurt feelings. I never pressed her with questions, but was alert to her every word, sigh, or change of expression. But Almah was not oppressed by my concern. I had touched her heart, and she loved me above all the others.

Almah's companions had been chosen with her unique destiny in mind. Julia and Deborah were daughters of Jewish nobility, and the circumstances of Almah's position pushed them toward the role of handmaiden—like the attendants of royalty. This they accepted as a great privilege. Julia was a handsome, large-boned girl of fifteen, with high cheekbones and shining brown hair, who excelled in gymnastics and dance. Deborah was small and slight, with black eyes and very curly hair. She sang like an angel and played the lyre and systrum.

But the most important gifts for which Deborah and Julia had been chosen were their loyalty and devotion to Almah and the holy child she would bear. Their special gifts would be essential, and each would do her part to shape the mind and heart of the promised redeemer. One of these two always accompanied Almah to her meditations, sitting in the background reading or sewing should she be needed, for the deep trances could be perilous to an initiate. Memories of former lives and deaths and insights of import and grandeur could be exhausting, at times terrifying.

On the twenty-third day, Almah had been sitting steadily, sinking ever deeper into trance. Every hour she arose briefly, walked about and stretched, then resumed her labors, moving further beyond the limits of space and time.

The past and future of the world reeled by her, but not as temporal events following one upon the other. She saw aggregates of forces and ideas in ceaseless combinations of relatedness and difference, moving into, through, and beyond one another. Her fragmented memories and dreams were suddenly whole. As if a closed door had opened, Almah knew with a strange calmness— yet exhilaration—with astonishment, yet without surprise, the mystery of herself.

"I am Isis, Queen of All the Worlds; Mistress of Heaven, Earth, and Hell; Mother of all things; eternal Wisdom, Truth, and Beauty; keeper and protectress of all who call upon me," she chanted ecstatically in girlish wonder—yet dignity—from the truth of her deepest soul, striking speechless those who watched with her. Pure bliss flooded her spirit, and she exulted in the terrible power of her being, the resourcefulness of her indomitable will, and the invincible strength of her love.

Almah-Isis watched the endless spiral of time wind away behind and before her as she searched—but for what? Whom? Then with remembering came anguish. She saw the open coffin where Osiris lay pale and bloodless, imprisoned in the corruption of mortal flesh, dying or dead. She fanned him to life with her wings, with her love. She kissed him and called him, but he could not answer her.

Then she felt it rise—his phallus rose to her. She caressed him and took him into herself, and he opened his glorious eyes in one long look of love—then he was gone. She could arouse him no more. She cried out, "Osiris! My brother, my spouse! Come back to me! Come, my love, come!"

The Magdalene Anna, present as witness and spiritual guide, sat with her eyes and mouth open wide in amazement. She could not doubt her daughter's vision, for Almah was transfigured by the rapture of her trance. The Magdalene, true priestess that she was, recognized the Goddess in her own child and wept to be so favored, prostrating herself, while little Deborah, wide-eyed, dropped her embroidery and fell upon her face.

The day of the spring festival arrived, but spring did not. The Judean hills were bare and brown. Even the red windflowers did not appear except in pots and tiny patches of ground where, hand-watered in honor to the dying god, they opened their scarlet petals for one day, dropping and scattering them the next. Some said the Goddess, in mourning for her spouse, had withdrawn fertility from the earth, seeking him in the underworld, but others said she had sent him down to death as a substitute for herself. The long shadow of famine reached out toward Judea, with her near-empty granaries and decimated flocks. The people did not speak of it, but their forced gaiety held an excitement, an expectancy, more than just the annual festival spirit. And it was all related somehow to the mysterious stranger, he who had "come forth," a "ram without blemish." Even the youngest priestesses in the Temple convent sensed the rising tension, but we put our own heightened interest down to Almah's involvement.

It was a rare treat to march out in our festival finery before the assembled people, and we younger girls tried to behave as if this were no special thing to us, while we furtively searched the crowd for the familiar faces of our families; we knew they were there, somewhere. The High Priestess welcomed six new five-year-old maidens into the College of Virgins, and when that part of the ceremony was finished, she stepped back, and Almah took her place.

An audible gasp greeted her, a simultaneous indrawn breath from the assembled witnesses, an expression of amazement and gratification, of incredulous satisfaction and adoration. She stood, the darling of her people, their princess become for this day their Goddess, garlanded and crowned, the spiritual power of her initiation radiant on her face.

Now the wedding procession reached the base of the steps, and the people tore their eyes from their priestess to greet her bridegroom. Dressed in ceremonial shepherd's attire, the staff of Dumuzi in his hand, came the Sacred King—the Ram Without Blemish, he who had "come forth"—escorted by a dozen young men in shepherd's dress bearing his sacred cup and churn. He moved slowly up the steps of the dais toward Almah, his eyes on her face.

A great sigh rose from the people, as though every mother saw in him her own son, and every father the child of his loins. Love and pride mingled with grief in that sound, but I understood only the sighs of the maidens who looked on his beauty. He wore the air of initiation and purpose, his preparation had surely been as thorough as Almah's. When he reached her side, the Lady Anna stepped forward, and taking her daughter's hand, placed it in his. As the couple knelt before her, she dipped her jeweled fingers in a golden cup with a serpent handle and placed them on the bowed head of the shepherd king. Her melodious voice intoned like temple bells, "In the name of the Goddess, Inanna-Ishtar-Ashera-Isis, I anoint you."

The pact was sealed. The people responded with a shout of relief and cheer, breaking the respectful silence that had reigned since Almah's appearance. The ceremony of the Sacred Marriage had begun. Almah and her bridegroom were carried in chairs on the shoulders of priests to the banqueting rooms, to preside over toasts and roasts, ceremonial awards, betrothal announcements, and naming of babies. Then they would be briefly separated and dressed in their bridal garments for the ceremony of the Sacred Marriage.

Everyone had forgotten about Joachim, Almah's father, who, of course, was not a king in any political sense, because Judea was ruled by a Roman procurator. But the High Priestess Anna belonged to the old royal family and was princess of Jerusalem and Bethlehem as well as High Priestess. As her consort, Joachim's title was a ceremonial and spiritual one only. The usually elegant King's Guard, now dressed in mourning, brought up the rear of the procession, leading the king himself, Joachim, at the end of a coarse rope, clothed in sackcloth, his head shorn. A crown of sacred thorn was pressed upon his brow; blood and ashes streaked his face, and a few people in the crowd threw handfuls of ashes on him as he passed. What could Father Joachim be mourning on this happy wedding day, I wondered briefly, but I was distracted by so much excitement. I did not yet understand that tomorrow he would be beaten with harmless but stinging whips to show his contrition for being spared by the sacrifice of his substitute, and if he did not weep the portent for the crops would be grave.

That afternoon must have been unbearable for Almah and her bridegroom, knowing what they could not help knowing, but I was blissfully unaware of coming events, caught up in the excitement and joy of reunion with my family. They came for me at the great doorway to the cloister of Ashera by the western wall of the Mount, and I led them proudly into the guest courtyard where all the families of the priestesses were entertained. My mother beamed with pride and pleasure, and the smell of grass and animals that clung to her was sweeter than any perfume. Father's red beard was curled in the handsome ringlets he wore on important occasions, and I almost felt jealous as he tossed little Lazarus to make him laugh. But he handed Lazarus to Mamma and hugged me long and hard, and my heart was appeased.

We sat on stone benches to eat our sweet cakes and cheese. Martha was enthralled by everything about my being a priestess—my clothing, my status, my privileged existence. I accepted her admiration half-guiltily, realizing that I now felt closer to Ninshubur and Geshtinanna than to my sister.

The afternoon passed all too quickly, and when it was time to say good-bye, I wept, but for only a moment. It was easier than before.

4

The Sacred Marriage

Then the people answered Jeremiah:
As for the word you have spoken to us in the name of the Lord,
    we will not listen to you.
But we will do everything that we have vowed,
    burn incense to the Queen of Heaven
    and pour out libations to her,
as we did, both we and our fathers, our kings and our princes,
in the cities of Judah, and in the streets of Jerusalem:
    For then we had plenty of food,
        and prospered, and saw no evil.
But since we left off burning incense to the Queen of Heaven
    and pouring out libations to her,
        we have lacked everything,
    and been consumed by the sword and famine.

Jeremiah 44:16–18, NEB

A full moon rose soon after sunset, illuminating the Women's Court of the Temple filled with people. I could not see my family, but I knew they were there, their eyes turned toward the marble dais before the Nicanor Gate. There the Holy Maiden of Israel sat enthroned beside her bridegroom beneath a shimmering canopy of purple and gold. The priests and maidens who had been her companions for twelve years had arranged themselves like a royal court in her honor, for tonight she was the embodiment of the Goddess on earth. We youngest priestesses sat beneath the elder ones on the steps below her right hand, all of us a chorus of women's voices that would recite the Goddess's part in the ceremony. On her left, the priests and their acolytes, eunuchs all, their voices only a little deeper than those of the women, chanted the part of the Sacred King. But I must tell you how it was for Almah, as she blended her clear, girlish voice with the women's chanting and Sharon, her bridegroom, joined with the priests, following the part haltingly, for he was not of the Temple and had learned the part for this day only.

The women began the song of the goddess Inanna, and Almah tried to concentrate on the words, but her mind raced and her heart pounded. She had never before set eyes on the young man beside her, this remarkable man who had come forward and offered himself for the people. Now he seemed not only known to her, but intimately. She felt as though a part of her had come to life for the first time.

> Make your milk sweet and thick, my bridegroom.
> My shepherd, I will drink your fresh milk.
> Wild bull, Dumuzi, make your milk sweet and thick.
> I will drink your fresh milk.

All the people who could crowd into the Temple court and its surrounding galleries sat or stood under the clear evening sky, their eyes fixed on the young couple, joining the chorus in the parts they knew, all the while gazing with strange fascination at Sharon, the Ram Without Blemish.

Zacharias, a priest of Jehovah, was notable by his absence, and Almah recalled how he had used his marriage to her mother's cousin to press the Pharisees not to prevent Sharon's purpose. "It is better that one man should die for the people," he had argued. They hoped that his offering might also move Jehovah, Lord of Storm and Thunder. The laws of the Jews officially forbade the sacrifice of a firstborn son, but the custom remained as plausible to them as it had seemed to Father Abraham, and they averted their eyes when it pleased them, so it continued. There was always a way to use the altar of another god, and Ashera, in her dark aspect as Ereshkigal, was a bloodthirsty goddess. So Zacharias had delivered the silent complicity of the Pharisees. Then he had taken his wife Elizabeth's pregnancy as excuse for a public show of humility, swearing himself to silence—supposedly in abject gratitude to Jehovah—and closeting himself until the promised birth. This left the High Priestess Anna alone to prepare and offer Sharon's sacrifice. Zacharias bitterly opposed the Goddess and her worship, as did the powerful Pharisees, whose favor had many times proved more necessary to him than the Lord's, but he had obtained for her a sacred victim. Let the blood-drinking Mother release her waters, or let this fool's blood appease Jehovah, her spouse, sender of thunder, lightning, and storm. Ancient custom decreed that only the High Priestess of Ashera could anoint and consecrate a victim through the rite of the Sacred Marriage. None but the beloved spouse of the Goddess could be an acceptable offering.

The Magdalene Anna abhorred sacrifice; she had never allowed it during her reign as High Priestess, and never would have, but the strange and beautiful young man had so moved her when he appeared out of nowhere to offer himself that she had seen it as the long-awaited sign from the Goddess. Surely this perfect being was the one chosen by the Mother to sire the Messiah! His appeal had filled the people with such hope that she had had no choice but to consider his petition. Now she would not flinch from her duty. Almah was certain of that. The Goddess's purposes, and Anna's, would be served. By this man and in the most auspicious of circumstances, her daughter would conceive the Hasmonean prince who would redeem her people from their enemies.

Almah knew her mother considered the patriarchs themselves the chief enemies of Israel, with their warrior kings and warrior god. They profaned the rites of the Goddess and subjected the people to endless war, taxed them beyond reason to raise armies, and took sons and fathers from their families. So the Pharisees did not attend the service in any official presence, disdaining the rites of the Mother, but Almah could see many of them in the crowd, their eyes all on Sharon.

He sat with marvelous composure beside her, his right hand closed around her left one, his fingers cool and steady against her own. She dared not turn to look at him. Her whole body felt unbearably aware, every nerve attuned to his presence, and she knew that the more she allowed herself to be drawn to him, the more she would suffer on the morrow.

Tomorrow. She could not bear the knowledge of what would then take place. With supreme effort she gathered her courage. She would not retreat from this holy purpose, nor hold back her feelings, nor spare herself in any way.

When she had made this resolve, Almah felt calmer, and let the music take her where it would; she felt her awareness expand and fill every level of her being until she became what she symbolized: the Goddess. The sacred song filled the four quarters of the earth, ringing through the realm of the blessed gods and the bleak silences of Hell. It was a hymn to life, to the love between woman and man that turns grief into hope, that dares to create life out of death, that fertilizes the barren soil with redemptive tears. Its power was of the earth, of the endurance of mortal flesh, of the life force to bring forth its own good forms, a celebration of the goodness of life under the sun and the delight mortal beings steal from the gods.

> Let the milk of the goat flow in my sheepfold.
> Fill my holy churn with honey cheese.
> Lord Dumuzi, I will drink your fresh milk.
>
> My husband, I will guard my sheepfold for you.
> I will watch over your house of life, the storehouse.
> The shining quivering place which delights—
> The house which decides the fates of the land,
> The house which gives the breath of life to the people.
> I, the queen of the palace, will watch over your house.

Sharon's hand tightened around her own as the priest's voices swelled with the reply of Dumuzi to Inanna:

> My sister, I would go with you to my garden.
> I would go with you to my orchard.
> I would go with you to my apple tree.
> There I would plant the sweet, honey-covered seed.

Now the women's voices chanted Inanna's reply to her beloved, and the air was charged with an energy that throbbed through the crowd, a mass arousal, sublimated to its sacred purpose, ecstatically shared by everyone present.

> He brought me into his garden.
> My brother, Dumuzi, brought me into his garden.
> I strolled with him among the standing trees,
> I stood with him among the fallen trees,
> By an apple tree I knelt as is proper.

> Before my brother coming in song,
> Who rose to me out of the poplar leaves,
> Who came to me in the midday heat,
> Before my lord Dumuzi,
> I poured out plants from my womb.

The women's voices rose an octave, pure and emotionally rending. The people participated without reserve. They opened themselves to the ecstasy of the ritual, for they believed their joyous participation was a true offering to the Mother, and her gift to them in return. The women's voices throbbed from throats husky with tears, and the hearts of the listeners thrilled to the sound.

> I bathed for the wild bull,
> I bathed for the shepherd Dumuzi,
> I perfumed my sides with ointment,
> I coated my mouth with sweet-smelling amber,
> I painted my eyes with kohl.

Here the chanting dropped to a tremulous whisper, intimate and suggestive as a lover's caress. The people barely breathed to hear.

> He shaped my loins with his fair hands,
> The shepherd Dumuzi filled my lap with cream and milk,
> He stroked my hair,
> He watered my womb.
> He laid his hands on my holy vulva,
> He smoothed my black boat with cream,
> He quickened my narrow boat with milk,
> He caressed me on the bed.

A little louder now, yet hauntingly slow and sweet, the voices of the priestesses made love to the body and soul of each hearer:

> Now I will caress my high priest on the bed,
> I will caress the faithful shepherd Dumuzi,
> I will caress his loins, the shepherdship of the land,
> I will decree a sweet fate for him.

The men's voices took up the refrain of praise to the Goddess:

> The Queen of Heaven,
> The heroic woman, greater than her mother,
> Inanna, the First Daughter of the Moon,
> Decreed the fate of Dumuzi:

The women's chorus was a fullness and resonance of her own voice as they chanted Inanna's response in measured martial tones. Almah turned to her bridegroom, expressing the words with her whole being as she held his eyes with her own:

> In battle I am your leader,
> In combat I am your armor-bearer,
> In the assembly I am your advocate,
> On the campaign I am your inspiration.
> You, the chosen shepherd of the holy shrine,
> You, the king, the faithful provider,
> In all ways you are fit:
>
> To hold your head high on the lofty dais,
> To sit on the lapis lazuli throne,
> To cover your head with the holy crown,
> To bind yourself with the garments of kingship.

They sat entranced in each other while a pause in the poem was filled with the harmony of string and wind instruments, led by plaintive shepherds' pipes. The men's voices filled in a line of narration:

> Ninshubur, the faithful servant of the holy shrine,
> Led Dumuzi to the sweet thighs of Inanna and spoke:

And the pure, full voice of a single priestess announced:

My queen, here is the choice of your heart,
The king, your beloved bridegroom.
May he spend long days in the sweetness of your holy loins.
Give him a favorable and glorious reign.
Grant him the king's throne, firm in its foundations.
Grant him the shepherd's staff of judgment.
Grant him the enduring crown with the radiant and noble diadem.

Now several female voices joined in, then more as each line was spoken, so that the chorus swelled to a greater and greater fullness. Almah felt as if it lifted her and Sharon, bearing them aloft on its wings.

> From where the sun rises to where the sun sets,
> From south to north,
> From the Upper Sea to the Lower Sea,
> From the land of the huluppu-tree to the land of the cedar,
> Let his shepherd's staff protect all the land.

The men's voices gradually joined in as the chorus rose in fervent desire for the restoration of the fertility of the land.

> As the farmer, let him make the fields fertile,
> As the shepherd, let him make the sheepfolds multiply,
> Under his reign let there be vegetation,
> Under his reign let there be rich grain.

Stirred to the heart, Almah tried to keep her mind from tomorrow. Whenever she looked at Sharon, his eyes were on her face. He was only a little taller than she, with softly curling dark hair and gentle eyes that held death in them. His determination to offer himself, and her own understanding of that purpose, could not keep her mind from searching frantically for some way to dissuade him, but it was futile; she knew their fate was sealed. How perfect he was; how fit to sow the seed that would become the Messiah! Had he been born for this as her people believed she had been?

Almah tried to resign herself, but she could not. She knew that no gods or demons would be appeased by his death. The people— the people and their priests would be appeased. Their hope and belief in the future would be restored by his blood. Her chest contorted harshly, heaving with protest even as she prayed the fervent prayer of the people:

> In the marshland, may the fish and birds chatter,
> In the canebrake may the young and old reeds grow high,
> In the forests may the deer and wild goats multiply,
> In the orchards may there be honey and wine,
> In the gardens may the lettuce and cress grow high,
> In the palace may there be long life.
> May the Lady of Vegetation pile the grain in heaps and mounds.

Then the people all arose with a great rustling and shuffling to stand facing the celebrants. During the final words of the prayer, they surged forward, surrounding the sacred pair, bearing them upon their shoulders without the intervention of chairs between their hands and the consecrated bodies of the blessed couple. As they were carried above the throng, Almah and Sharon were lovingly passed from hand to hand, as if every soul present had vowed to touch their flesh, to draw from them some blessing. Almah felt loved and protected, floating in a sea of people, still clasping Sharon's hand. He was smiling and laughing like any groom on his wedding day.

The bridal chamber was outside the Temple court within the western cloister that separated the Temple Mount from the rest of the city, and thither they were borne to the last lines of the marriage hymn.

> O my Queen of Heaven and Earth,
> Queen of all the universe,
> May he enjoy long days in the sweetness of your holy loins.

The people burst through the doors of the sacred chamber and placed the bride and groom on the great marriage bed, lavish with scarlet and purple. Then they filed past the two in a ragged line of men, women, and children, their sleeping infants in their arms, flushed with passionate participation in the rite and with the best of the wine, which had been held back for this day. It seemed to Almah the stream of people would never stop, but at last the procession ended, the doors closed, and the eunuchs who had taken their guard stations just outside intoned the last blessing.

> The king went with lifted head to the holy loins.
> He went with lifted head to the loins of Inanna.
> He went to the queen with lifted head.
> He opened wide his arms to the holy priestess of heaven.

For several minutes they remained as the people had placed them, the spell of the ritual heavy upon them. Then they climbed out of the high bed and stood facing one another. Almah unfastened the headband of Dumuzi from his forehead, shyly fluffing his short curls. In turn, he took the crown of Inanna from her head. They began to remove each other's garments. The tooled leather girdle that spanned his narrow waist was too much for her unfamiliar fingers, so he aided her with a strong jerk on the end of the strap. They laughed then, nervously at first, then gratefully, breaking the solemnity of the ritual, and hugged each other, overcome with sympathy and fellowship. They were alone in all the world. Only the sacred task that had fallen to them could have brought them together. Trembling, they accepted the price.

Naked at last, they touched each other's flesh with hands grown exquisitely sensitive. Sharon's brown hand spanned the slender column of her neck and Almah felt her blood throbbing there against his fingers. She could not take her eyes from his mouth. The upper lip was perfectly curved, like a bow, the lower a full, ripe berry. They drew together, breathing each other's breath, touching, then tasting; and their kiss bore them away on a vast and swelling sea, drowning the world with it's roaring, and cast them forth clinging together, breathless, lost to all save each other. Sharon dropped to his knees, pressing his face against the satin smoothness of her belly, embracing her thighs. Her hands stroked his shoulders; her neck arched backward as he arose, lifting her toward the holy bed of the Goddess.

Long after, when they had risen, half sitting, half lying among the pillows, still in each other's arms, Almah opened her eyes and smiled into his face.

"We have always known each other," she told him.

He kissed her lips, full and blood red, her throat and breasts, flushed with the rush of her passion. "Then it is true, for I feel it too."

"Dearest Sharon," she whispered, "surely you are my only love, for all time. Your body," she caressed him wonderingly, "is familiar and dear as my own. Have we not always loved each other, through many lives and other worlds?"

"Ever I hear you calling to me," he said slowly, his eyes far away, "calling and calling me, and ever I strive mightily to come to you." His voice vibrated deliciously against her throat.

"Who is your mother, beloved?" Almah asked him. "From whence come your people?"

"She whom I called my mother confessed to me before she died—that was six months ago—that her husband . . ." Sharon paused. "He is dead too, years ago. He found me in the hills, newborn, or nearly so. They took me and brought me up as their own. So I am a foundling, and I have no people."

Almah was nodding, as if she had expected as much. "I knew you were a child of the gods," she said, "borne by the Mother herself and placed where you would be loved and cared for."

"More likely an abandoned twin," Sharon said.

"But you were loved?" Almah persisted.

"My mother lived only for me after Father died," Sharon admitted. "They were shepherds, and I grew fat and ruddy on good milk and cheese. But now I am free and leave no one to grieve for me."

"I shall grieve for you," Almah cried. "Oh, Sharon, please! My people love you already and will be glad if you rescind your vow. We can live long together and have many children . . . Please, beloved, please," her voice dissolved into a wail, and she wept helplessly. He comforted her as a mother holds a hurt child.

When they had spent their tears, they breathed heavy sighs and dried each other's faces with kisses.

"You must save your tears for tomorrow," he said. "We shall take our joy tonight. I am as good as dead, for I have sworn it, yet my soul may take refuge in your womb."

"Oh, Sharon, beloved, that I might bring you to rebirth!" she moaned. "But how can I let you go?"

"You cannot. But I will go." They held each other silently, then Almah spoke.

"Are you afraid?"

"No. Yes! But it will be over quickly for me. Yours is the worse part, beloved."

Then Almah could no longer think of tomorrow, or of any other thing than of kissing his mouth, pulling him down upon her among the pillows. "Tonight I shall conceive," she vowed; "the Holy Virgin shall be gotten with child. The savior of my people you shall get upon me this night." She covered his body with kisses, as though she had always done it, always gloried in it. "Come into my womb, my husband; death shall not separate us—come into me, beloved, come!"

5

The Sacrifice

To one who knows, there must be no grief, for all things come out of an unmanifested state, and staying awhile in a state of manifestation, go back to the original unmanifested state.

Brihadaranyaka Upanishad

Almah Mari stood supported by her maidens in the place reserved for the High Priestess, facing the altar. The dozen acres within the walls of the Temple Mount swarmed with all the people who could crowd inside. The galleries of the Temple and the roofs of the cloisters were filled, and those who could not push within stood beyond the open gates, straining to catch a glimpse of the sanctified victim. Would he do it? Or would he turn coward at the last?

Banners unfurled for the celebration the day before still fluttered in the spring sunshine; the sight and sound was festive at first glance. But the blended smells of oxen, camels, and cooking food in the stalls of the street vendors could not mask the odor of death. There was a shamed expectancy in the talk and manner of the crowd, as if they realized their guilty compliance in this morning's work.

Almah Mari looked for her mother with the other Temple women, but the High Priestess Anna had been glad to relinquish her office to her daughter for this day. Almah was sure she would be watching from some hidden place; she could not be unfeeling for her daughter's pain, nor for that of her husband, Joachim, who would be ritually scourged to signify the contrition of his people for the life being given for them. When she sighted him in his sackcloth and ashes, proud head bowed and hands bound,

Almah felt a stab of pity, but she was too desolate with her private grief to think long of him.

It was Sharon, from whom she had parted at dawn, that she both longed and dreaded to see. She swayed for a moment, and was grateful for the firm hold of Julia and Deborah on her arms. Dropping her head to the steadfast shoulder of Julia, she thanked the Goddess for such friends.

Her throat caught when she saw him. He walked with easy grace, flanked by two eunuchs, priests before and behind him. His eyes found hers, and the pain in his face was for her, believing that glance the last they would have of each other. Then the priests turned him away to ascend several steps to the altar. They moved him around so he again faced the people, and one of them spoke something to him. He nodded and knelt unhurriedly, as respectfully as if to receive a blessing.

Behind him, one of the priests moved forward and Almah heard her breath stop in unison with that of the whole courtyard. The sunlight flashed on the polished metal of the sacrificial sword. It was short-bladed, sturdy, as the priest placed it in Sharon's hands. He took it and with deliberate slowness and care, turned and placed the tip against his breast. He raised his eyes and found hers, round with terror. Holding her gaze, Sharon pushed the blade with a strong movement into his chest. That same moment, the executioner struck, severing his head at a blow, and Almah's sense of time was so altered that Sharon's head seemed to hang suspended in the air, his open eyes surprised, his lips parted, as though about to speak. Then it lay over to one side, falling ever so slowly, and struck the stone floor face down with a sickening sound that started time again. The two eunuchs had grasped the arms firmly and braced themselves to hold the headless body lest its thrashing about should be unseemly; it righted itself in their hands and made as if to flee, blood boiling from the severed neck. The legs straightened themselves; the back arched convulsively; and then the body sagged in the priests' grasp. They laid it full length upon the altar stone and bound the head in place.

Almah Mari had dropped to her knees, which could not support her, and her ears were filled with a cry that she did not know came from her own throat. It rose, a sobbing, screaming wail, the lament of the Earth Goddess for the death of love and for the destruction of beauty. Then the other women began to keen, and the age-old ritual mourning of the Goddess for her slain son and consort had begun. But Almah knew no more; she had fainted and was borne away by her maidens, their tear-blind eyes causing them to stumble and shuffle like very old women.

The Seeker

Let her who seeks
Not cease from her search
Until she finds.
When she finds, she will be bewildered
And when bewildered,
She will wonder, and reign over the All.
Didymus Judas Thomas

As younger priestesses, Ninshubur, Geshtinanna, and I were not witnesses to Sharon's death. We had glimpsed him only from afar, during the anointing and the marriage ceremony. Our confusion and distress grew from the guarded and garbled accounts that reached our ears. Almah was so thoroughly undone that we could not question her, and Julia and Deborah were too concerned about her to bother with us. The sight of her suffering was our only real evidence of the enormity of what had happened.

We sought out Lysander, and found him like ourselves, in coarse mourning dress, ashes in his hair, his face streaked with tears and soot. "Bless me, what tiny old ladies are these?" he asked softly. "How can I serve you, little sisters?" The other two looked at me, but the question in my mind was so terrible I could not say it. He understood at once. "Come and sit awhile," he said gently, and led us outside into the kitchen garden. He settled us in a row on a stone bench and knelt across from us.

"You know the story of Queen Isis and her beloved Osiris?" His question was meant as a statement, because he himself had told it to us many times. "Remember after Osiris was nailed in the coffin by his evil brother, Seth, how Queen Isis never stopped searching until she found him? And then she hid his body in the swamp until she could bring back the funeral spices? Then Seth came along and cut Osiris up into little pieces and buried them all over the world, and everywhere a part of Osiris went into the ground, the barley grew for the people to eat. And when the people ate the bread from that barley, they became male and female," he grinned mirthlessly, "instead of like me. And they had children. And they got old and died. Birth and death came into the world together because of the terrible thing Seth did.

"But Queen Isis loved Osiris so much she searched until she found all his buried parts, and brought him back to life. Osiris went to rule the immortals, so she gave birth to his son, Horus, to be with her. The people missed what they had lost, so they called on Osiris to make them immortal again, too, and he promised that everyone who ate the bread and drank the ale from the grain that grew from his body would be immortal and live with him in Paradise."

He stopped, as if he believed he had explained something, but we stared at him, mystified. He looked into the distance, waving his expressive hands as though to gather thoughts from the air. "Some people believe," he said slowly, still looking away, "that the sacrifice of Osiris needs repeating, so the grain will grow again."

"Then was Sharon . . ." I gasped.

"Osiris? Yes, in a way. When Lady Anna anointed him, he became a Sacred King, so his blood would fertilize the earth just like Osiris's did."

"But Osiris was murdered!" I cried.

"Is it so different that Sharon offered himself?" Lysander asked.

Geshtinanna sobbed, but Ninshubur was shaking with rage. I stared at her. "You are saying our Lady does murder," she whispered between clenched teeth.

"Remember," Lysander said softly, taking her hand, "Almah Mari is the Holy Maiden who will bear the Messiah. No lesser man than a Sacred King can beget the Messiah."

"Then Almah is . . ." I couldn't finish this sentence either.

"With child? Let us hope so, little sister. Birth and death go together, remember? Especially where messiahs are concerned."

A drop splashed on my face. Then another. We looked up. At first we wanted to shout for joy, then we looked at each other half-ashamed and went inside.

I had much to occupy my thoughts while I honed my skill on a spinning wheel in the great room. A thousand angry voices raged inside me accusing the Lady Anna. I thought of how she had acted to do the will of the Goddess, and my courage failed me. I remembered how She had comforted me in her appearance as the Morning Star. I didn't want to be angry with Her, too. Perhaps the High Priestess had made a mistake. But I could not explain the rain.

After that first spring storm, we had another, and then another, not as much as a whole year's rainfall, but enough to plant and look for a reasonable harvest. The drought was broken.

Almah appeared again, pale and subdued. She had cared for us, and now we cared for her. Sometimes she was touched by our concern, and tears would fill her eyes, but most of the time, she seemed not to notice us at all. The more I saw how she was changed, the more the voices inside me raged at what had been done to her. I slipped upstairs to the roof of the cloister before dawn for almost a month of days, hoping for some comfort, some sign from the Goddess. The new moon appeared for a while, but the Morning Star was nowhere in sight. My alarm was so deep and so personal I could speak of it to no one. I could not guess whether the Mother was punishing me or if her absence heralded the end of the world. Each day I kept my vigil, but the morning sky was empty.

Then, just before the six weeks we were allowed so spend at home with our families, Almah was suddenly married to Geshtinanna's father, Joseph, who had been widowed for little more than a year. The ceremony was done before we knew of the betrothal, and even Almah had said nothing to us. When I went home to Bethany and Nana went home to Nazareth with Almah and Joseph, my outrage against the Goddess so consumed me that I could not even enjoy fishing with Grandfather Claudius.

My family understood my grief and were patient. Martha, now four, was devoted to me. I found her much more interesting as a companion than she had been a year ago. She was clever and sweet-tempered, and I made her my pupil, teaching her as much of my new knowledge and skills as she could grasp. She was so pretty, with her apple cheeks and curling black hair; her eyes were so dark and thick-lashed you had to get close to see they were blue—dark blue—like Mamma's with yellow lights in them. She looked as Mamma must have as a child. I loved to dress her up and fix her hair, and she suffered everything in blissful patience.

By summer's end, as the time approached for my return to the Temple, the morning sky was still empty, and my desolation was unbearable. I was ready to forgive the Mother anything, if she would only comfort me in her old way. I made continual morning sojourns to the roof and found only the waning moon, then nothing. I decided to confide my fears to Grandmother Lili, who was wiser than anyone, even the High Priestess.

I sought her in her sitting room in the middle of the day. Her white hair made a bright halo around her face as she turned from her task, though I had made no sound. Her fingers were busy sorting dry peas, but she set down the bowl and held out her arms to me. "What troubles you, precious lamb? Your face tells me you have a secret."

"Oh, Grandmama, She has gone, and I am afraid of what will happen."

"Nothing will happen, dear child. She will have a lovely baby and live happily with Joseph, for he is a good man."

"O, Grandmama, I do not speak of Almah."

"Who, then?"

"The Goddess, Grandmama. The Morning Star. I believed she would watch over me as you said, but she is gone . . ." I was crying.

"Child, child, dry your tears. She is not gone. The heavens are vast, and you must learn where to look for her."

The hope that sprang up in me at her words set my heart pounding. It must have shown in my face, for Grandmother understood at once how troubled I had been. She began to kiss me, laughing and crying all at once. "My poor, poor lamb! No wonder you have been so sad. Did you think she had deserted you? Deserted the world?" She held me by the shoulders and looked very serious. "Listen, Mari. Listen to what I say. The Mother will never turn her back on us, no matter what we do. When you have children of your own, you will understand that. Tonight, after the sun sets, I will show her to you."

"Tonight?" How could that be?

"You will see."

We took our evening meal on the rooftop, just before sunset. When Mamma rose to clear away our meal, I got up to help her, but she shook her head. "Today is your birthday, Mari. Sit."

The sun slipped below the Judean hills, and they turned to violet. The sycamore tree by the stable stood dark against the sky. No one spoke, and I strained at the sparkling blue above the glow, my heart pounding. Something twinkled, disappeared, then twinkled again. Then it shone steadily, growing brighter. The tears ran down my cheeks. There could be no other star like that. Grandmother Lili put her arms around me. "The Queen of Heaven," she said.

We sat quietly, needing no words, until the last sunset color had faded and the star had reached her full brilliance. "How can the Morning Star shine in the evening?" I asked at last.

"The Goddess rules the heavens as the Morning Star for part of the year, and part of the year she leaves to rule her other kingdom, the land of the dead. That is why you could not see her. When she departs from the Netherworld, she returns as the Lady of the Evening. In a few months she will visit the Netherworld again, and then return as the Star of the Morning."

I thought for a long time. "The same Goddess rules the living and the dead?" I asked.

Grandmother shrugged. "There is but one Goddess. Mother of all. How else can it be?" The hills and the stars were silent, and I felt that silence enter into me and quiet all the anxious voices there.

"She can watch over me wherever I am," I said at last.

"Yes, my child."

We were assigned a new "elder sister" after Almah left. She was a Hellene, with wheat-colored hair and gray eyes, like a painting in the grand audience room of the goddess Athena. Her name was Demetria, a name that means, she told us, an initiate into the mysteries of the Great Mother, Demeter. We were fortunate, for Demetria was both pleasant and wise, but she always seemed a pale shadow of Almah.

During the flurry of preparations for the winter festival, we heard that Almah was returning. Through Lysander, we learned exactly where and when she would arrive, and were securely hidden where we could see her. She had been carried from Nazareth in a litter, a sort of chair within a tent supported on the shoulders of four bearers, because the long ride in a carriage would have been too rough for her advanced pregnancy. When she was helped from the litter, she could scarcely stand, but she smiled and laughed as she greeted her mother. The Magdalene held her by the shoulders and would not allow her to kneel, because it would be too hard for her to rise again swollen as she was with the child in her womb.

"It must be twins!" Nina exclaimed.

"How could the Messiah be twins?" I scolded her.

"Maybe messiahs are just bigger," Geshtinanna suggested.

It was agony knowing she was so near, yet not being allowed to see her. Lysander said she was very tired and must rest so the baby would not come too soon. We were kept busy with the preparations for the festival, but we could think of nothing but Almah.

The next night Lysander knocked on our door after we had gone to bed. "Dress yourselves and come with me," he said. We flew into our clothes and followed his torch up the stairs and through the marble halls to the apartments of the High Priestess. We entered a door, and Lysander knocked on another. A woman answered, and I recognized Deborah. "She is waiting for you," Deborah said to us, and led us into the most beautiful room I had ever seen. Almah was sitting on a velvet couch, her face radiant. She held out her arms to us.

We forgot our manners and ran to her, kneeling before her couch as she hugged us and kissed us. She stroked our hair and examined the gaps where my baby teeth had fallen out. Nina had two great new teeth to show her. We marveled at her swollen belly, and she put our hands against her. The unborn Messiah moved under our touch, and we were amazed.

Almah had a gift for each of us, and we were ashamed because we had none for her. "Just seeing you is present enough," she said. "And now you must go, little sisters, for I have promised my mother I would not tire myself. Soon I shall bring you my baby son to kiss."

But she did not. Lysander said she could not help it, because she had to keep him hidden from King Herod. We hoped to see her at the festival, but she was gone and so was her mother. The old priestess Hecate filled Anna's place in the ceremonies.

Lysander always knew everything, but he told us only enough to comfort us. "She is safe, and so is her little child. You will see her again when old Herod is dead." Nana was not sent home to Nazareth for family visits, so we knew they were not there. I invited her to come home with me, and she came, but she missed her father and Almah and her big brothers. The next year her brothers came for her, and she went with them, but when she returned, she had not seen her father or Almah.

King Herod died the following year, and the war among his heirs became so dangerous for us all that we were sent home for a whole year. The trouble continued after Herod's son Archelaus was made ethnarch, ruling from his father's palace in Jerusalem, but we learned to live with the unrest and were seldom made aware of it.

We talked together of our plans and dreams—I would marry a great prince and make him my consort when I became Magdalene. Nana dreamed of graceful ships with colored sails and a heroic sailing master who would come for her from far across the sea.

"I shall never marry," Nina maintained, whenever we asked her, which we did regularly, convinced she would change her mind.

"Will you have your children alone then?" I scoffed one day, when she had repeated her resolve. I was instantly sorry to see her fighting against tears.

"I shall die if I try to bear a child. My Aunt Cleo says so. I am big like my mother. She died when I was born."

Geshtinanna and I sat dumb.

"I was so huge a babe, my mother could not birth me and live," Nina sobbed. We put our arms around her, realizing that we had never needed to comfort Nina before. She was always our comforter.

When Ninshubur, Geshtinanna, and I were twelve years old, Almah and Joseph came back to Nazareth. Almah brought her little son, Yeshua, to the Temple, and we fell in love with him. He was six, two years younger than my brother, Lazarus, but he seemed older. At times he was serious beyond his years, and he asked us many questions about our lessons, seeming to comprehend things we ourselves were only just beginning to understand and would never have thought of at his age. But he was playful, too, and full of pranks, with a merry laugh that made everyone laugh with him. When we played hide-and-seek, he always came for me, squealing with delight and hugging me when he found me. Wherever I hid, he found me at once, even in my most secret places. "You have been peeking," I accused him at last.

"Why?" he asked innocently. "I can see where you are without peeking." It was true. We tested him over and over and marveled that he thought it no great thing.

Gathering herbs in the meadow, we lay on our backs and made up names for the cloud shapes overhead. "That one is an ox," he said, "with a heavy cart behind."

"He is hungry, I think," Geshtinanna agreed. "He seems to be looking for something."

"What can it be, that he hurries so fast across the sky, searching?" I wondered. Yeshua broke into peals of laughter.

"He will never find what he seeks," he said, "because he will never stop and look in the cart he draws behind him."

The next day, as they departed for Nazareth, my eyes were red with my tears at parting from Almah. Yeshua brought me a red rose, and as I drew in its fragrance and bent to kiss him, I realized I would miss him as much as I would miss Almah. He put his arms around my neck. "I love you, Mari," he said, and went away. Mopping at my foolish tears, I saw that I had pricked my finger on the rose. There was blood on my white gown.

Queen Isis

i found god within myself,
    & i loved her.
i loved her fiercely.

Ntozake Shange, For Colored Girls Who Have
Considered Suicide When the Rainbow is Enuf

During the years I spent in the Temple, the Dream in which I struggled through a loathsome swamp, searching for I knew not what, returned many times, always with the sickening headache and an unbearable sense of loss. The only help I found for my agony was the Goddess, and I would lie prostrate and sobbing for hours before the little shrine in our room, while Ninshubur and Geshtinanna sat awake, watching over me. We believed it was the Goddess who sent the Dream, but though I related it in detail many times, we could not guess its meaning nor tell why it brought me such suffering. We even played at trying to predict its occurrences, but the headaches came as often without the Dream. My anger and rebellion grew against what old Hecate assured us was my "gift" from the Mother, suspending me between Heaven and Hell. She tortured me, yet only She could ease my pain.

When I was sixteen, I was summoned one day into the presence of the Magdalene and told that His Excellency, Philip Herod, Tetrarch of Batanaea, Trachonitis, and Auranitis, had asked for my hand in marriage. He requested an audience, at which we were introduced to each other, and I found him very handsome and gallant. But I was troubled, because I could not see how marriage to a tetrarch could have any place in my destiny as a possbile High

Priestess. I reminded myself that I was only an alternate, and that Almah would doubtless soon have a daughter whose birth would make my service as Magdalene unlikely. I was being offered an excellent marriage, and I had better take it, even though the thought of leaving the Temple was unbearable. Learning to trust and serve the Goddess had been fraught with struggle and doubt for me, and now that I had finally become happy in her service, it seemed she was turning me away.

Stinging with doubt and feeling rejected, I sought the comfort of my "sisters." "Mari, you must consult the Mother," Nina said, reading my every thought, my every doubt. "She would never reject your service to her. Go to her."

And I did, that very night.

Nestling my buttocks into the imprint in the soft lambskin before our little shrine, I unlaced the lid of a dyed reed basket and lifted the sleeping serpent, Nehushtan. His hooded eyes blinked like miniature moons in the pale light, and his liquid coils flowed up my arm as his forked tongue flickered.

"Come, Nehushtan, little love, give me your kiss," I crooned, grasping the snake. Startled, it sent its venom deep into my arm.

Exquisite pain, like flashing colored lights, brief as passage through a doorway, and then I freed the loosening coils, replaced the serpent, laced tight the lid. Settling myself before the little altar, I watched the dancing crisscrossed shadows thrown by twin lamps on the plastered wall, a double spray of jasmine in a double alabaster vase.

The effect of the venom was already heightening my senses, the night chorus of tiny frogs growing madly discordant. The whole surface of my skin was icy-hot, the moonlit room a whirling pool of liquid silver and black.

"Holy Mother," I prayed, "send me your wisdom. Show me the path that will serve you best."

The putrid smell of marsh gases heralded the recurring vision, and I could not stifle a groan as it overtook me. I gave myself up to it. Snakelike roots caught at my feet, and leeches fastened upon my skin as I searched through moldering moss and spider webs, rending branches and sucking mud. Eerie voices of demons or demon-possessed animals, weird and woeful calls of birds, hideous shrieks of hunter and prey raised the hackles on my neck, but still I searched, for what, I knew not.

A sense of unbearable loss returned with me to wakefulness, a gnawing ache in my stomach, a hard lump in my throat. The Dream came unexpectedly at times, but from my first inoculation with minute amounts of snake venom, Nehushtan's sting nearly always induced it. The Dream's aftermath of sorrow and grief became my means of summoning the Mother, for then she never failed to comfort me.

And so once more I fell prostrate before the little altar, cradling my face on my arms. The oil lamps glowed mistily rose red through my closed eyelids; my prayer beads of purple amethyst felt smooth and cool to my fevered touch. "Blessed Mother, help me."

But this time was not like the others, for presently, barely breathing, I *saw*, really *saw*, forming out of the mist before me, first dimly and then more clearly, a glorious figure, clothed with the sun and the moon under her feet. A crown of twelve stars was bound about her forehead with a coiled serpent of gold. Her magnificent cloak was the night sky, emblazoned with the moon and stars, bordered about with all flowers and fruits of the earth. Her divine face was the image of kindness, her smile more dazzling than the sun. I shook with the violence of my trembling, unable to speak or breathe; I pressed my arms against my eyes and heard the Goddess speak.

"Dry your tears, my daughter. I am come. I, the mother of all things, governess of the elements, firstborn of the worlds. My love is poured out upon the earth. I am the soul of nature, the life of the universe. From me all things proceed, and to me they return. I call upon your soul to arise and come unto me."

Perhaps I was dying, I thought. I was not immune to the venom after all. But if she was calling me home, I would go willingly. I lifted up my heart in joyful obedience, but I felt instead the soul of the Mother enter into my very being, and the mind and memory of the Goddess became my own. I lay enraptured, my bliss beyond the power of words to express, as the very thoughts of the blessed Mother became my thoughts, the love and compassion of the Mother overflowed in my heart. The gates of my understanding were opened, and I recognized the unbearable sorrow that always possessed me after the Dream was the bereavement of the Goddess for the loss of her beloved. These thoughts of the Mother flowed through me:

Long ago before the beginning, in the eternal stillness before becoming was, I have been. I, Isis, and my beloved Osiris, drifting in perfect bliss, eating only joy, ourselves the whole universe, coupled together in love and delight in the womb of the Sky-Mother.

But time began, and we were born, husband and wife together, knowing nothing of limitation or death, to rule over Heaven, Earth, and the Netherworld. Together we taught the peoples of earth, yet immortal, to till the land, grind grain, and make bread, and to offer worship to the immortal gods. We had joy in our labors.

But Seth, our brother, was envious, plotting how he himself might rule over the worlds. He was the one who churned together the divine elements with the darkness and dross of limitation and time into a world of matter and flesh, binding beings of freedom and joy to the endless round of birth and death.

He constructed a coffin, wondrously inlaid with precious woods and carvings. At a great feast Seth promised it to whomever it fit best, and Osiris laughingly lay down in it. Seth's co-plotters quickly nailed shut the coffin and cast it into the Nile, where the swift current carried it out to sea. Osiris was immortal, but now he was cursed with continual death and rebirth. We would be separated forever unless I could release him.

In my agony I tore my clothing and pulled out my hair, strewing it about, weeping and wailing to the earth and sky.

I became a falcon, flying over earth and sea. What power was in those wings and eyes! A hawk told me where the coffin had lodged, in the roots of a giant tamarack tree on the island of Byblos. The tree had grown swiftly, enveloping the coffin, but exuding such fragrance the king of Byblos chose it for the center pole of his palace.

Disguised as an old wisewoman, I, Isis, nursed the king's sick infant to health and obtained the tree as payment. When my woodworkers freed the coffin and opened it, my beloved Osiris lay at last in my arms, imprisoned in a mortal body. I fanned him with my wings; he revived for a little while. We held each other in love, then he slipped away from me into death. Sorrowfully, I understood that Osiris was lost forever in the realm of wandering ghosts. Only if I could perform the sacred rites to preserve his body and reunite it with his soul could we be together once more.

I hid the body of my beloved in the swamp at Buto until I could obtain materials for the embalming, but when I returned, my enemy had been there before me. Seth had cut the body of Osiris into fourteen pieces, burying each in a different part of the world. All my searching had been in vain, for now I must discover anew each severed part of that sacred flesh.

Overcome with the magnitude of the Goddess's task, swooning with the burden of her sorrow, I, Mari, mourned for that lost and perfect unity of being, fragmented by time and place into an endless cycle of little lives and little deaths.

I have searched for thousands of earth-years; I will not rest until you and I are reunited eternally. I call out to you, beloved; do not despair; I will find you again. I have searched the far ends of the earth, but the parts of your body have become the grain that nourishes humankind. I can no longer find them.

I felt the holy tears of the Goddess spilling down my cheeks, my heart rent open. I heard the Goddess say:

I cannot redeem you, beloved, from afar. I have taken a mortal body, and I myself have given birth to you in the human realm. I will teach you, my son, that you are Osiris, Lord of all the worlds. You must live and die in this sanctified mortal body; thus your soul, and all souls, will be freed of the bondage of birth and death. You and I shall be together again beyond death, beyond time. I have sworn it!

Slowly, I felt the Goddess leave me, but the sense of her presence remained, like perfume lingering in an empty room. My misgivings about the future seemed but the self-indulgent imaginings of a willful child. I wept to be so favored. I would follow wherever my destiny led and be thankful.

At the spring festival that year, I was married to the son of King Herod the Great, His Excellency, Philip Herod, tetrarch of Batanaea, Trachonitis, and Auranitis. He took me far northward to his capital at Caesarea Philippi.

PART 2

Caesarea Philippi

In the beginning was the Law,
   and the Law was divine,
   and the Divine was the Law.
Through the Law all things came into being,
   and without the Law, nothing can be.
                Adapted from John 1:1–3

8

The Harem of the Tetrarch

In the Law is life and light.
And the light of the Law shines in darkness
and is not overcome by it.

Gospel of John

I had been wed seven years to Philip Herod, and our daughter Salome was six years old—I was twenty-three—when I again take up my story at Caesarea Philippi.

One thing I loved there: Mount Hermon. The Mother Mountain, the Mountain of God, she stood above the city to the north and drew my gaze always. Beyond massive doors of carved cedar open to the cloistered portico, above the pointed, blue-tiled roofs of the palace she towered, resplendent in her perpetual garment of snow, eternal as the Law. The people worshiped the mountain as their mother, for there could be no life in this desert land without the springs that flowed from her icy crown. She had a dark side and a sunny one, they said, like any woman. From Hermon's slopes, the children of Seth in their innocence had been beguiled by the painted eyes and jingling bracelets of the voluptuous daughters of Cain. But from her inexhaustible source the river Jordan burst forth to nourish the arid world at her knees. Mount Hermon never cast a shadow, the people said, for she stood to the north, and we were forever in her favor. I rested my eyes on the Mother Mountain, straining to draw some measure of her serenity into myself.

Lamech must be crazy. Risking certain death sneaking into the harem to meet Deidre!

"Philip will have you both killed!" I turned from Hermon's eternal ice to Deidre's hot and defiant face, streaked with eye paint and tears.

"We are getting away from this place! We have planned it all!" I could see the red flames of Deidre's anger and frustration crackling about her. They will consume her, I thought. I tried to reason with this sister-wife, my dear friend.

"If Lamech cared for you, would he put you in danger of your life? He is only a merchant's son; how can he protect you from Philip?"

Deidre's head snapped back. She was surely the loveliest of my husband's wives, lithe and graceful, with brown, African skin, jewel-like eyes, a cloud of black hair. "I thought I could trust you!" she pouted. "I would rather die than stay here."

"Deidre, think of Mene. What will happen to your child? The queen has no son. Mene could become Philip's successor; think of that."

"Mene is his father's favorite; I know it," Deidre insisted. "Philip would never harm him."

"He will be fair game for these jealous women!" I grasped her by the shoulders, wanting to shake her.

Deidre hung her head. "What can I do, Mari?"

"Wait. Do not do anything yet. Promise me," I demanded.

"I promise." She sank into my arms. "Oh, Mari, you are my truest friend in all the world. What would I do without you?" Then she slipped out of my embrace and left the room, leaving only the grapelike fragrance of her hair.

"That poor child suffers more than she gains from love," Nina remarked with compassion as she entered. "There is a messenger for you." She spoke to my back, for I had turned once more to the mountain and pulled my eyes reluctantly from the vivid cold that loomed distantly desirable in the afternoon heat.

The boy came to stand before me. He was about twelve, dusky brown with velvet eyes and crisp curls. He knew all the royal wives and concubines, for he delivered many messages to the harem. I suspected I was his favorite. He made a little bow, smiling.

"What message have you for me today, 'Big Man' Lugal?" I teased, reminding him I knew the meaning of his name.

"My lady, His Excellency the Tetrarch"—he was supposed to state the names of Philip's three provinces: Batanaea, Trachonitis, and Auranitis, but he substituted a little shrug and grin, managing to finish his long sentence in one breath—"requests your presence at a formal entertainment in the great dining hall tomorrow evening."

It touched me to see his pleasure; he loved to bring good news to unhappy women. Boredom was the chief curse of harem life. Boredom and jealousy grew rank as weeds here, fostering intrigues and endless plotting. An invitation led beyond these walls, if only for a few hours. I slipped some coins into his hand and kissed him. "My grateful thanks to my lord Philip," I said.

"I will walk with you to the gate," Nina told the boy, and the two went outside. Nina would glean every bit of information in the child's mind without asking him a question. I indulged a deep sigh and looked around me. This beautiful temple at Caesarea Philippi, with its white marble and blue-tiled cloisters grouped about a stately courtyard garden, had never become a home to me. It reminded me little of the Temple at Jerusalem.

Herod, called the Great, father of my husband, Philip, had built this temple in honor of Julius Caesar, and when Philip came into his inheritance he renamed the town, long called Paneas, Caesarea Philippi. The greater part of the temple complex consisted of gardens, kitchens, workrooms, and living quarters intended for priestesses of the Goddess—vestal virgins, the Romans called them—but Philip, in a strange lapse of his noted piety, had usurped its facilities for his household. The lavish apartment intended for the High Priestess he gave to his queen, Alexandra, and his other wives he assigned in order of rank or favor to the lesser, still luxurious, quarters. The sacred altar and Holy of Holies were watched over by a few priestly caretakers, but the center of the Jewish religion was at Jerusalem, where festivals and holy days were observed. The worship of Isis-Ashera and the offices of her priestesses had been completely displaced at Caesarea Philippi, the facilities intended for them degraded into a harem.

This had enraged me from the first; I wove fantasies of myself as the instrument for reviving the Goddess's worship and honor. But warrior kings and hero gods were displacing the Great Mother even more rapidly here where Greek and Arabian culture prevailed than in the Jewish provinces of Galilee, Samaria, and Judea. The wise old seeress Hecate, who had been chief adviser to the Magdalene Anna, and my own grandmother, Lili—surely a seeress herself though she made no claims to having the sight—both claimed that time would bring the justice of reversal. But I had little patience for that; perhaps the fierce spirit of the warrior-goddess Anath, whose name I bore, kept me from being at home here. My home was the Temple at Jerusalem.

Not that we lacked comfort or luxury, for Philip prided himself on his indulgence; largess was considered a mark of kingship. I walked outside into glowing twilight. The sun had just set, and the sky was rose red above tiled rooftops, shading upward through violet to translucent blue, where the first star shone in silent brilliance above the slimmest crescent moon. Overcome by beauty and portent, blinded by sudden tears, I remembered that night in Bethany when the sight of the Evening Star had restored my faith in the Goddess.

I awakened next morning before dawn, the thought of Deidre so vivid I arose, careful not to waken Salome, and slipped across the dew-wet garden to her rooms. The maids were drowsing fitfully, and Mene slept peacefully in his mother's bed, but Deidre was gone. With a feeling of foreboding, I returned to my bed, hugging my daughter's warm little body to me, but I could not sleep. Trying not to think of Deidre, I turned my own relationship with Philip over and over in my mind. How was it possible that I feared Deidre's death at Philip's hands, yet loved and honored him as my husband?

I opened my eyes wide with the intensity of that realization. Could it be that I was as unhappy as Deidre with my own tiny share of our husband's affection and attention? Thoughts I had long pushed away came in a flood. My romantic dreams about Philip had surely been only wishes, not reality. Whatever love they once nourished was fast dying. I had clung to them like a foolish child and denied the evidence that showed them for cowardly fantasies. Nina was right that Philip had married me only to gain the endorsement of the Mother; I had always known that, because nothing save marriage to a priestess of the Goddess can grant divine authority to rule. I had even forgiven his contempt for the Mother, hoping that he would come to love me above the others, and the Goddess through me. He had used me to seek advantage with the people, and I had not swayed him. I flushed with shame in the half-light.

But to sit in the grand dining hall was not an opportunity to be wasted. At least it would be some contact with the world outside. I dried my tears on the bedclothes. I was sure to get another headache from being so wrought up. Perhaps Philip wished to impress some learned guest with my conversation, as he had before. The opportunity to talk of sacred writings and ancient teachings came to me seldom, for my husband had no interest in such things and often mocked my education as useless. Still, it pleased him to display my gifts to others, though he would enjoy my humiliation just as much, I was sure. Restlessly, I drowsed until daylight.

"There is a knot here," Nina's strong hands kneaded the flesh between my shoulders. Lucius's ebony body glistened as he lifted the cover from a steaming cauldron and produced a hot towel, tossing it from one hand to the other, testing the temperature. He plopped it in the center of my back.

I jumped, refusing to cry out. He loved to scold me for complaining about what was good for me. I wrinkled my nose at him and relaxed, the moist heat easing the anxious knot below my neck.

Deidre had not reappeared. No one mentioned her absence for fear of sounding the alarm. The more time before she was missed, the better. I lost myself in the pleasure of Nina's hands, half asleep as my feet were kneaded expertly, then the still-warm towel removed from my back.

"That's better," Nina said with satisfaction, probing my upper spine with skillful fingers, draining away the tension. She patted my buttock in the signal to turn over.

I turned on the warm slab in the center of the heated pool where Nina, Lucius, and Lysander were performing the ritual of my bath. Nina's magnificent breasts bounced as she kneaded and rubbed, while Lysander, keeper of the bottles and vials, poured scented olive oil on my skin, fast turning pink. The slab was not tall enough for Nina's height; she bent far over to do her work. She was the tallest woman I had ever seen. But then what of the world could be seen in this place?

We had been of a size seventeen years ago, at our dedication to the Goddess as five-year-old maidens: Ninshubur, Geshtinanna, and I. We had all grown taller and fairer with the years, but Nina had grown taller and taller. Now she had the bearing of a queen, never bowing her dark head or hunching her fine shoulders for shame of her great height, lowering only her eyes, gazing down on one and all. She excelled at gymnastics and dance and contests of strength and prowess practiced by men who train for war. She well fit the part of a warrior-queen, but though my own head was lower than Nina's shoulder, she had chosen to serve me. Old Hecate had read in our stars that mine would be a great destiny.

Nina finished her massage and moved around to my head, rubbing my wet hair with henna and aloes to make a foamy lather, while Lysander applied a paste of henna to my fingernails and toes. Lucius waited with a large jar of warm water to pour over my hair at Nina's command. Like Nina, he and Lysander had attached themselves to me by their own choice.

Both were priests, eunuchs dedicated to the Goddess. They had chosen to serve the Mother through their devotion to me, since I, after Almah Mari, who now served, was next in line to become High Priestess in the Temple at Jerusalem. They had come with me to Caesarea Philippi after my marriage to Philip, resolved that I live long and well as my destiny allowed.

Huge muscles rippled beneath Lucius's skin, blue-black as Lysander's. Even taller than Nina, he came from a gigantic and slow-growing strain, and his fruit had not ripened before it was plucked. His sacrifice to the Goddess had consisted of a man-sized male member, but an empty, infantile scrotum, preserving the source of his great size and strength behind a smooth scar.

"Nina, Nina! I want a massage, too!" Salome was straining to pull her hand from the firm grasp of Geshtinanna. The two entered the warm pool, deeper than Salome's height. Nana held her up and placed her on the marble beside me.

My daughter's dark hair was tied back revealing her small face and body aglow with health and high spirits. My heart swelled at the sight of her, and I sat up, mindful of Lysander's stern warnings to keep my hennaed toes out of the water. He had carefully stained each nail so that its white moon remained clear. I pulled Salome into my lap, kissing her fondly. "You are slippery as a fish! Thank you, Nana, for bringing her."

Geshtinanna was not taller than I, but long slender bones gave her a lissome look. Lovely as a nymph, she had small, shapely breasts and a narrow waist. The delicate bones of her face were prominent, the brown eyes set deep in chiseled sockets, showing the whole curve of the eyelid fringed with black.

"Salome has been so very good, and done her lessons so well, I could not refuse to bring her," she replied. Salome glowed.

"Please, Mother, can Nina do me now?" She climbed out of my grasp, stretching herself on the marble.

"I will do it for two kisses," Nina offered, and the bargain was made.

After, with Lysander's leave to wet my fingers and toes, Salome and I played like a mother otter with her little one, sporting and splashing until we were tired. We sat in the sun drying our hair while Lysander buffed each jewel-like nail. He spent an hour painting my eyes with colors from his collection of exquisite pots, while Salome offered advice freely. When he held up the mirror of polished silver, I saw my green orbs glowing between the dark lines of my eyelids. The sight of my own eyes always disappointed me; they were so unlike the dark ones I most admired. I thought them pale and uninteresting, but Lysander's work enhanced them and I was pleased.

Later, I dressed in a gown of fabric so transparent the rouged tips of my breasts showed through below a heavy collar of jeweled chains. Almah Mari had sent it from Egypt; Cleopatra, she wrote, had worn such a gown. Golden chains of many lengths swung from a jeweled girdle as I moved, revealing my pale thighs through sheer drapery. Nina brushed and bound my hair in a gold headband with a mirror-bright moon of pearl on my forehead. I placed about my neck the huge emerald Philip had given me at our wedding—the color of my eyes, he had said.

"I will go and see for you how it goes with Deidre," Nina said from the doorway, reading my thoughts, "lest you ruin your evening with worry." When she reappeared, her face was troubled. "She is not in her rooms. Perhaps she also had an invitation and has gone."

I willed myself to accept the hope Nina offered. Deidre was Philip's fourth wife, but younger that I, his fifth. She must have been only twelve or thirteen on her wedding day. I would look for her at dinner, I thought, as I turned to go.

The Stranger

Jesus said, "If the flesh came into being because of spirit, it is a wonder. But if spirit came into being because of the body, it is a wonder of wonders. Indeed, I am amazed at how this great wealth has made its home in this poverty."

Gospel of Thomas

Lucius and Lysander escorted me to the palace. Everyone, even the tetrarch, assumed these two eunuchs were my slaves, and the role fitted their own purpose. Custom prescribed cutting off the tongues of household servants to prevent gossip, so even those who had kept theirs thought it wiser to be silent; thus people treated the presence of servants like that of tables or chairs, ignoring their eyes and ears, making those of my guardians even more useful.

When we arrived in the anteroom where the members of the tetrarch's household waited to be called to the table, I saw that Alexandra, Philip's first wife and official queen, was already present with her full retinue of attendants and the ceremonial escort that was her due. All my foolish hopes for the evening were dashed; Alexandra, not I, would be seated at Philip's left hand. Realizing I had clutched at my heart, so palpable was my pain, I looked about nervously, stroking the enormous emerald that hung between my brave rouged nipples, now puckered tight with sudden chill.

Resolutely drawing a deep breath, vowing my pleasure in the evening would not be spoiled, I set about to discover what I could about the guests of honor. Deidre was not present. Alexas, deputy to the chief steward, in charge of the seating arrangements, had always been friendly, but he would surely be too taken up with details to talk with me now. Yet he winked when I caught his eye, and came to my side.

"Mari, how beautiful you look! Wonderful! Wonderful!" He steered me away from the knot of people in which I stood, ignoring the twin shadows that moved with us. "His Excellency," he purred, "is depending on you to entertain a most important guest this evening." He crowed in delight, arching his plucked eyebrows even higher. "His Excellency has as his guests the great lady Miriam of Scarios, and her son—or ward, I don't know which he is," he waved his hand effeminately. "He is no more than a boy, but so brilliant a counselor he has already done service to kings.

"And the lady Miriam, herself," he continued in an effusive tone, "you know of her, do you not? She is famous far and wide as midwife to queens and princesses. 'Tis said she is a sorceress, incredibly old—for no one knows of her birth—and keeps her youth and beauty through occult knowledge and charms."

He paused for breath, and I nodded, but he hurried on without allowing me to say that I did indeed know Miriam of Scarios. Philip's third queen, my dear friend Lois, was in her sixth month, and I had persuaded Philip to send for Miriam to attend her, since Lois had lost both her first two children through difficult births. Alexas was speaking of Miriam's son.

"He is said to be very learned, and that is why His Excellency has chosen you to entertain him. But wait until you see him! You will quite lose your heart, my dear, so be careful! Such eyes he has! And so handsome!" With a final enthusiastic squeeze of my arm, he turned away and was gone.

I stood where he had left me, wondering. He was joking, of course; both of us were well aware that for royal wives, adultery—or even the suspicion of it—was considered treason and carried the same penalty. Still, were I foolish enough to risk my life and those of my whole household for the fleeting pleasure of dalliance with one of my husband's guests—a mere boy at that—I would not be the first.

Thus, those of his household who had been favored by invitations from our lord Philip waited to be called forward and led into the lavish dining hall on the arm of the chief steward, who announced each guest loudly and paraded us to our places.

Philip's grand dining hall was considered modest and tasteful, in keeping with the whole palace at Caesarea Philippi. The pillars and lintels were of white marble, colored with streaks of blue and green. The plastered panels between them were painted with murals depicting the history of the city, with many noble portraits of Herod the Great and his son Philip. Herod was shown routing the bandits from the caves of Mount Hermon, defeating numerous and nameless armies, being crowned by Mark Antony and Julius Caesar, being feted at the table of Cleopatra, and accepting the charter of Paneas. In each mural, his son Philip, at first only a child, then a youth, and finally a young man, accompanied him, as though Herod had no other sons. Herod himself was shown directing the building of the temple with a mature Philip beside him, and there was a scene showing Caesar presenting Philip with his tetrarchy. Other panels depicted Philip's great works: nameless battles, the raising of the palace and public buildings, and so on.

Philip favored blue. The great draperies that served to absorb the hollow echoes of so vast a room were of deepest blue, and blue predominated in the floor mosaics and art objects. The enameled tiles that decorated the great hearth were blue, and the table service was of exquisite blue procelain.

Philip's table was not modest. There were a dozen kinds of fish and fowl and seven or eight of roast red meat. And there were dainties and pies made of the livers and brains and entrails, all of which disgusted me. I ate no flesh except of fishes, though my parents served meat at their table. The priestesses of Ashera abstained from meat, and I had lost my taste for it long ago. But there were breads, leavened and unleavened, and cakes from many grains, and sweets and fruit-filled puddings that I loved. And cheeses of every description, hard and soft, sweet and sharp. Oranges and dates and apples and figs were in abundance, and tropical fruits of great variety and color.

When Alexas came for me at last and we entered the great hall, I looked first for Philip. He did not look up when my name was announced, and the familiar dull pain throbbed in my breast. *She* was there, of course. Alexandra. He would not look at me in the queen's presence. His princely head was turned in the direction of one of the Roman senators who were also his guests.

I looked for Miriam of Scarios and found her seated opposite Philip and Alexandra. She was handsomer, I thought with pleasure, than either of them. She looked even more beautiful than when I had last seen her—when she visited the Temple twelve years ago after old Herod's death. The deep scarlet and gold of her gown favored her shining black hair, flattered her smooth, olive throat and shoulders, unlined and fresh as a girl's. Her breasts were high and full as a new mother's with her first nurseling. I marveled how the bloom of youth never left her. Could she be a witch as it was rumored? Did she know a secret she might sell for a price?

Then the lady turned and looked directly at me. Our eyes met, and a thrill of recognition passed between us. I had expected to like her, even to trust her, but I had not hoped to sense such deep friendship from this fascinating woman. I reached my place, on the same side of the table as my husband and his queen and within earshot of their conversation. Because I was across from the lady Miriam, I could see her better than the others, and as soon as I settled myself on the low divan, she spoke.

"My dear—Mari Anath, is it not? How beautiful you are, my child!" Her voice was husky and sweet, genuine with feeling. She turned to a young man just across the table from me, whom I had until then been too busy to notice. "This is my son, Seth," Miriam announced, with all the pride of the most indulgent of mothers, "Judas Seth, my little Hebrew prince."

The young man could not be twenty—sixteen, perhaps, no more, though tall and well developed for his age. His eyes were already on me, smiling. How had I not noticed him before? His presence seemed to eclipse all others in the room.

"Call me Seth, please." His rich voice belied his boyish face. He looked at me with startling intelligence, eyes golden brown, light and clear as sunlight on the sea. He had long, thick lashes of darker brown than his short-cropped curly hair, and his face was either clean shaven or he had not yet a beard. Without Miriam's protection, the boy would surely have been made a eunuch for his beauty. I felt distinctly pleased that he had been spared. But he was not so innocent. Something behind the boldness of his gaze made me wary. His eyes caressed my breasts, my throat, my thighs; it was not a boy who looked at me.

"Then you may call me Mari," I told him, "for that is what my friends call me."

"My mother," he said, with a respectful nod toward Miriam, "has told me you are Temple-reared, and will someday serve as High Priestess."

"I am an alternate only," I demurred, feeling a pleasant glow at his interest, "should Almah Mari, the present Magdalene, have no daughter of her own." I was about to add that I thought this unlikely, but the guest seated next to me was making signs of annoyance. He was Gallus, a Roman senator. He probably supposed I had been seated next to him for his own entertainment.

"I beg your pardon," he said coldly, "a High Priestess?" His tone betrayed he had thought me a concubine and had been pleased at the prospect. Philip often lent his concubines to favored guests, whereas wives were held to the strictest constancy.

"Is it possible your duties as wife to the tetrarch do not conflict with those to the Temple?" Seth asked, emphasizing "wife" with the lifting of an eyebrow. His words were intended for the senator, who choked on his food. When I looked at Seth, he winked.

"The terms of my marriage are secondary to my service of the Goddess, of course," I answered. Surely he already knew this, too. It was a time-honored custom, not to be broken.

Senator Gallus recovered himself and became very gracious. "You are very fair, my lady," he said. "Is it possible you are of our race?"

"Both my grandfathers were Roman centurions and came here in the service of Pompey," I explained. The Roman blood that had mixed with that of my Jewish grandmothers had not turned my skin a pleasing olive like that of my sister Martha and brother Lazarus. I was a throwback, my father said, fair and freckled, with brown hair and green eyes that Philip called his "most precious jewels." I supposed it was my fairness that made me blush so easily, and I hated it. The senator had blue eyes like Grandfather Claudius's, but unlike my grandfather, he clearly believed there was something superior in that. "My other grandfather died before I was born, but my mother's father, Claudius, has told me many things about Rome, which he loved," I said.

"But he chose to remain here." The senator raised his cup.

"In Bethany, my grandmother's inheritance, and now my mother's, where I was born," I corrected, raising my own goblet with a smile.

"And will it not then be your own, to be ruled by your husband?" Seth lifted his cup to ours, ignoring the senator, his eyes on me.

"My matrimony is forfeit to my sister, since I was chosen to enter the line of the Magdalene. My husband gained no lands by our marriage."

"But he gained the blessing of the Goddess, the rule of his kingdom by her authority, the Seat of Dominion, the Lap of the Mother—once given, not likely to be taken away." Seth's eyes were lightly mocking. "So what gains he by keeping you now, lady?"

I sat with my mouth open, unable to answer.

The senator sniffed at Seth's rudeness. He gallantly changed the subject, speaking to me with studied deference.

"Tell me of another Mari, my lady, she who became High Priestess after her mother, the illustrious Anna. Does she not enjoy even greater honor in relation to a secret king expected among the Jews?" His question showed interest, and knowledge as well. His gallantry in the face of my discomfort was in in his favor, but he could scarce appreciate how years of rivalry among the royal wives had toughened my sensitivity. Even as I favored him with a smile, little prickles of alarm raced along my spine. Did he think me foolish enough to speak of such things with a Roman?

Now it was Seth who came to my rescue. "Are you so interested in the Jewish religion, then?" he asked the senator.

"My interest is political, not religious," Gallus replied. "I have heard that royal Hasmonean blood flows in this other Mari and her son, and that he will lead a war for independence when he is of age."

"I know little of such things," I demurred, "but I do know that Almah Mari's son is a scholar, not a warrior, who studies with the Masters of the far East. If he were the expected Messiah, it could interest you little. He would but reenact the age-old sacrifice, shedding his sacred blood as the wine of immortality, giving his body to be broken as the bread of eternal life."

"Some hold he comes to shed other blood than his own," persisted Gallus darkly. "The Jews have outgrown your fertility ceremonies, my dear; it is political salvation they hope for."

"Nay, eternal salvation!" Seth bantered, and the lady Miriam inclined her head to listen, though the tetrarch himself was speaking to her. "The Essenes believe," Seth continued, "that when their Messiah comes, the earth and their enemies upon it will be consumed by fire. A new world, peopled only by believers, will arise out of the ashes to be ruled by him forever in the name of their God and Creator!"

Seth had turned the conversation away from danger. Gallus seemed willing to let the matter drop, for he opened a new subject. "Those teachers in Rome who follow the great Pythagoras hold that your 'Creator' is not the high god, but an evil archon who has foolishly trapped our souls in this foul flesh for his own glorification," he stated agreeably, watching to see whether either of his listeners would take offense. "So says the noble Plato, as well." He took a mouthful of roast lamb and chewed daintily, wiping his fingers on his linen, glancing from Seth to me. "They might see your Almah Mari," nodding in my direction, "as Sophia, Mother of the Truth, or Logos, the savior she has borne to redeem this fallen material realm."

"I think she is Queen Isis herself," I said outrageously, keeping to the same light tone, "still searching for her lost Osiris, to whom she has given birth in this world so she can bring him again to paradise with her." Seth's eyes widened, then narrowed again; something was in his face not there before. I felt my face flame at his look, and heard Miriam laugh throatily, pretending to be amused. I turned, stricken. Had I offended her? Miriam's eyes were black, inscrutable, but her voice was kind.

"You have a fine sense of humor, my dear," my ears heard her say. "Please go on." But in my mind I heard, "Your words are dangerous. Do not pursue this." I studied the jewel-like pomegranate seeds on my blue plate as though I found them extremely interesting.

Philip, who had been conversing with Miriam, realized he had lost her attention and said pettishly, "Tell me about your gifted son, lady. Is it true he has served as a counselor to the treasuries of certain kingdoms?"

"But, Your Excellency, you must ask him for yourself," Miriam said gracefully, with a glance toward Seth that both asked and commanded.

Seth bowed his fine head in acknowledgment. "It would be a pleasure to serve you also, Excellency, should you have need of me," he said with just the right combination of deference and self-confidence. Everyone waited to see if Philip would complain of doubting the honesty of his ministers, or if Seth would dare to suggest it.

But Philip said easily, raising his cup to his lips, "I have need for an accounting of my revenues for the year against my expenses, and a more reliable forecast than I have had until now."

"Excellency, I am at your service." Seth bowed his head again to my husband, and I was once more entranced. I remembered little of the rest of the dinner conversation, or of the entertainment. Philip never acknowledged my presence, though he had commanded it, but I was used to his being too taken up with important matters to think of me.

Long after, when the warmth of the wine had left me and I lay awake, I saw Seth's long-lashed eyes, dancing with mischief and ready laughter. But when I slept at last, it was Deidre's face that appeared before me, not angry and tear-stained, as I had last seen it, but grotesquely contorted in terror and pain.

10

Palace Intrigue

> Whatever any of us does, the same we in ourselves will find,
> The good one good: and evil those that evil have designed;
> And so our deeds are all like seeds,
> And bring forth fruit in kind.
>
> *Pali Jataka*

"Are you sick, Mamma?" Salome wanted to know.

"It's only a headache, sweetheart." I told her. "Mamma isn't hungry. You have it, darling." I pushed the chilled goat's milk laced with honey and carob toward my five-year-old daughter. We were all at table together, a custom we had kept ever since we had come here for my marriage seven years ago. My place was at one end of the low table, with Salome and Nana at my left, Lysander and Lucius on my right, and Nina at the far end, facing me. We sat on individual mats on the floor, our knees crossed tailor fashion beneath the table.

Salome tossed her black curls emphatically. "No, Mamma. I have some, too. This is for you. Nina says." She picked up the cup and held it out to me. I took it so it would not be spilled. "You are too skinny, Mamma. Nina says!" She stood on her knees, her elbows extended like fledgling wings, her black eyes fiercely demanding.

Helpless against my tenderness for her, I lifted the cup and drank. I must be a sight if my five-year-old could see it. And I had been horrible to Nina, Salome, and Nana these last few days. Worry about Deidre had kept me from sleep, restlessly pacing the boundaries of our prison—a prison of silken cushions and carved ivory, of jewels and exotic perfume, with no communication from outside and no way out except death.

"Nina says!" I parroted, setting down the empty cup. Nina looked pleased as Salome. She seemed incapable of anger against me, though she had plenty of ire for anyone who caused me a moment's trouble. I had been furious with her two days ago when my headache was worst and she withheld the poppy seed potion to regular intervals, no matter how I suffered.

Salome climbed into my lap, and I looked over her black head at my friends. Their devotion to me imprisoned them too, and added to my responsibility. Whatever I chose, I would choose for them, as well. My health was not my own to spend in worry or to languish away in unrequited love. They were devoted to me, but they depended on me for their very lives. The dark circles beneath my eyes and my hollow cheeks worried them. I had better listen to Nina and eat a little of everything. No need to feel guilty for daydreaming about Seth and plotting how to see him again, if it took my mind off Deidre and made me feel alive.

The isolation of the women's quarters was maddening—even the queen must have chafed under it. Alexandra would have been in danger of harm from the other jealous wives and concubines had she not kept a half-dozen bodyguards, eunuchs as big as Lucius but with none of his gentleness. The other women had cause to fear the queen, but she did not dare poison her rivals often, for fear of Philip. Even so, there were many mysterious deaths among the concubines, especially if they held his favor long or were foolish enough to flaunt it. But intrigue was tempered with feelings of sisterhood among the women.

There were friendships as well as jealousies among us. We were all in the same situation, and most of the time we had wisdom enough to know it. I fumed with frustration at being cut off from information that could have eased my mind and only the discipline of my meditations preserved my sanity. No messages except from Philip were allowed into the compound, so we had nothing but the palace gossip for what news we could glean or buy. Even this slender thread was subject to any manipulation Philip or his officers might find useful or amusing.

But Lysander found ways. He would not divulge his methods

even to me, but he knew everything that passed through Philip's official couriers. And more. But nothing of Deidre. He shook his head each day at my questioning look. But he had learned that the lady Miriam was indeed waiting upon Lois, and that both she and Seth would remain as Philip's guests until the time of birth, about two months from now. As for Seth, he was closeted long hours with the royal ministers, or with his accounts, and dining nightly with the tetrarch. If only Philip would invite me again! I tried to coerce him with the power of my mind, but nothing happened.

It came to me that afternoon as I paced the halls that if the lady Miriam was attending Lois, I might at least see her. Deidre, Lois, and I were the warmest of friends. Deidre and I had mourned deeply with Lois the loss of each of her infants. It was I who had gained our husband's ear and suggested to Philip—he had favored me mightily then for a time—that he send for Miriam of Scarios to attend Lois.

Nina sat bent over her sewing by the garden window, her brows laced in a scowl of concentration. Her vision was better for sighting from afar than for tiny threads. She had been as morose as I of late, so senstive to my thoughts and feelings that she often matched them mood for mood. She smiled as I entered and said, "The lady Miriam visits Lois at mid-afternoons."

It was still not too late for this afternoon's visit to be over. I caught up the wrapper I had been hemming for Lois's infant, but changed my mind; I would need no pretext to visit a friend.

Lois's apartments were across the garden courtyard, and I cut straight across to her side of the cloister facing the sun. Preoccupied as I was, I felt pleased to see Lois sitting in the autumn sunshine. She feared to darken her perfect nut-brown skin, aspiring to appear more fair. Languid with her advanced pregnancy, she sat with her feet up, the lady Miriam at the foot of her couch.

"How good of you to come, Mari Anath. I was about to seek you out," Miriam said in her warm, low voice.

I bent to kiss Lois's cheek and bowed to Miriam. "How may I serve you, lady?" The contrition I felt for being so absorbed in my own concerns made my voice eager.

"My apprentice has grown into a practice of her own, I fear, and I am in need of an assistant. You, with your training in the Temple, are obviously the most capable, and Lois will be pleased, since your friendship is so dear to her."

Lois nodded, milking my hand with both her own.

"Will you do me the honor of serving as my assistant and alternate at this most important birth?"

I was overwhelmed. I knelt before the midwife's knees. "Oh, lady!" I gasped as soon as I could gather my manners, "It is you who do me a great honor. If I can be of help to my dear Lois and to you, I shall be forever grateful."

Lois struggled heavily off her couch, giggling with delight, and together she and Miriam pulled me to my feet. "Darling child," Miriam cooed, laughter in the depths of her black eyes, "my son is quite out of his mind to see you again." I flushed darkly. The laughter came forth, yet it was kind. Lois stiffened in alarm.

"Mari! Have a care!" She turned angrily to Miriam. "Do you not know the danger in such words?" she demanded. "Philip would not hesitate to kill her!"

"Forgive me, lady; I spoke only in jest. Do not trouble yourself. How thoughtless of me to have upset you." And Miriam purred and cooed, patted pillows and draped blankets until Lois sat calmly again, but she looked meaningfully over the other's head into my eyes.

Here was the powerful ally I had sought! Surely the Goddess had sent her in answer to my prayers. I opened my mouth to confide my despair about Deidre, but thought better of disturbing Lois. She was resolved to believe Deidre had escaped with her lover and was well and happy. I would bide my time.

So it was arranged. Miriam told later how she had convinced the tetrarch that I would need to attend her in her rooms several hours a day for study and preparations. "It will be a great asset to Your Excellency's household," she point out, "since her training will serve you for a long time to come." But Philip had hesitated.

"Clearly your husband thinks you have already more knowledge than becomes a docile wife," Miriam laughed merrily, when she recounted the conversation. But her words must have warmed Philip's heart toward me. It titillated him—the thought of me as a priestess, especially as High Priestess, or Magdalene.

So Miriam's spell over Philip prevailed, and I, his fifth wife, was temporarily given a degree of freedom even his queen had never enjoyed. I was careful not to flaunt it, to remain as unobtrusive as the two silent bodyguards who followed me. Every weekday morning we walked quietly through the huge two-storied doors of the women's cloister, which miraculously opened for us, across the broad walk that curved through lush gardens, past still pools with snow white swans and stately peafowl strolling beneath towering cedars among the blossoming plants. Fountains splashed in cool forest glades, re-creations of untouched nature. I loved the gardens, the birds, and the bold squirrels that begged for my small offerings. It was difficult to hurry through this Eden, but the enjoyment of my studies—and the hope of seeing Seth—pulled me forward.

No news of Deidre came through Lysander or from Miriam, though I had confided in my benefactress at my first opportunity. I pushed my uneasiness away by imagining a meeting with Seth, but I dared not bring it up to Miriam.

Then one morning he was there. I had fantasized the event so often, I had difficulty believing I really saw him. How could I have forgotten he was so young? I stood embarrassed. None of the bright words I had rehearsed seemed remotely appropriate. I stood dumb as he came toward me. Miriam was nowhere in sight.

"Lady Mari, I have longed to see you again!" He wore a disarming air of worldly wisdom; his words were charming, courteous. Was it my imagination that read more in them? Feigning composure, I held out my hand. He clasped it in both his own. It was the first time we had touched, and the flood of sensation it aroused overwhelmed me. I was certain, in the long moment we stood there, that he felt it too. Yet the note of warning I had sensed before was present too, and stronger than ever. It cleared my mind a little, and I said quite calmly and pleasantly, "It is my pleasure! How go your labors for the tetrarch?" deliberately choosing not to refer to Philip as "my husband."

How could this boy-child have such a powerful effect on me? I made a motion to retrieve my hand, but Seth did not comply. Nor did his eyes, more spellbinding than I remembered, release my own.

"Let us not speak of paltry and petty things," he said softly. "Do you know who you are, Mari Anath? Do you know your destiny? What are you doing here as the sixth wife of a petty despot?" His tone was so searching I was again speechless. I started to stammer that I was the fifth not the sixth wife, but the foolishness of the words struck me before I could speak them. Seth managed to capture my other hand and clasped them both in his own, as though to dramatize my struggle against his suggestion.

After a long moment, I knew I had chosen to trust him. I stopped struggling to think of what to say or how to hide my thoughts and instead studied his face.

"What do you mean?" I whispered finally, my question a surrender.

"Your destiny is in Jerusalem, not here." The intensity of his manner held me fast. "You must return to the Temple, for you will be Magdalene." He turned my hands over in his own, examining my fingers. "These beautiful hands will do great works," he promised and began, deliciously, to kiss them.

I remembered that the Goddess always chose young lovers. I thought I understood why. I felt foolish for wanting to believe him. I did not snatch my hands away, however, but gently disengaged them. "How could I do that?" I asked impatiently. "Philip would never let me go. He would put me to death first; do you know that?" The question of Deidre's fate flashed before me.

"You yourself said that your vows to the Goddess precede those to your husband." He was unruffled by my scolding manner. "It is written into your marriage contract. If the Magdalene demands it, your husband is compelled to write you a bill of divorcement."

How did he know all this? Why was he saying it to me now? But he was right. Why had I not realized it? I knew the terms of my marriage agreement, but I had never really considered them before. "I do not believe Philip would honor the terms of our agreement," I said slowly. "He would kill me first."

Seth nodded in assent. "That is why you must be in a safe place when the demand is made. Let us take you away from here, Mari, back to where you belong."

Miriam's voice came from the next room tactfully announcing her presence ahead of her appearance. "Seth, dear, are you still there?" Then she appeared, calm and gracious as ever. "Mari, good morning, my child."

He bent and kissed Miriam warmly on the lips. "I'm just going, Mother." I felt a stab of jealous anger. Hardly a proper kiss for one's mother—perhaps he was a foundling, after all. But if so, then, what was their relationship? The possibilities threatened such turmoil I forced them from my mind.

A natural teacher, Miriam delighted in my aptness as her pupil. I had learned the discipline necessary to suspend my personal concerns, to apply myself single-mindedly to the task at hand. But later the same day, as I traversed the verdant park, my Ethiopian friends behind me, I found myself once more embroiled. If Miriam had deliberately set up my meeting with Seth, what could be her purpose? Since the danger to me was so great, surely the midwife was not lightly playing the role of benevolent go-between for a pair of foolish lovers. She must be suiting some purpose of her own, but what?

Miriam was like a cat, allowed to purr royally on the hearths of kings, made welcome wherever she set her foot. All my life I had heard tales of her skill, knowledge, and cleverness. She traveled all over the world, never at her own expense, living in the castles of nobles and the courts of kings. And it was not for lack of a home of her own, for she owned a palatial estate on the Greek isle of Scarios—doubtless the gift of a grateful patron—and lived there, mistress of her hearth and life, beholden to no man. She entertained royally and had been known to invite the heads of opposing kingdoms together and deftly arbitrate their disputes. Also rumored was that she took lovers as she chose, belonging to none. She was guardian of more than a dozen children of widely disparate ages and racial types, but whether any were her own was unknown. I wondered for the thousandth time whether Seth was Miriam's son, or—Holy Mother forbid it—her lover.

I slowed my steps, and Lucius and Lysander maintained their distance behind me. I hated to quit this lovely place for the imprisonment of the women's compound, reeking of despair and broken dreams. These pampered women, the envy of those who thought themselves less favored, were actually prisoners and had not the clarity of mind or courage of heart to realize it.

How different a life from this had Miriam of Scarios made for herself. I felt a pang of real envy. Still, Miriam lived with danger and intrigue and could hardly do just as she pleased. She dared not decline the "invitation" of a powerful ruler such as Herod, Philip's father, had been, and whom Miriam had nursed through his last illness. Even petty kings and princes thought their every whim a command. Part of her legend was how artfully Miriam walked a narrow line between their gratitude and their vengeance. She had made of herself a necessity even the powerful could not obtain elsewhere. Her intimate knowledge of the secrets and scandals clouding her patrons' households increased her power and her peril, but she had earned her reputation for keeping her counsel. Nevertheless, death at the hands of a hired assassin could appear accidental, with no one the wiser. How had she continued to thrive amid such danger? They all secretly feared her, I decided. They feared her powers might reach beyond her grave.

So though Miriam was entrusted with momentous secrets, she herself trusted no one. She allowed no one to question her integrity. Miriam did not ask, she commanded. Kings, queens, and princes were summoned and banned at her word, honored to fetch her boiled water or hand her her instruments. Her potions and nostrums had enabled barren queens to conceive, and safely aborted their mistakes. Royal wives and princesses who had repeatedly miscarried she steered through perilous pregnancies and delivered of living heirs. She was skilled with diseases of children, the curing of wounds, poisoning of the blood, and fevers. More than one crowned head owed life to her, and remembered the favor.

The huge doors in the high wall surrounding the women's confines closed behind us. I turned toward my own quarters, and Salome came running, her dark hair flying. Unlike Philip's tight curls, it flowed in waves like my own. Named for Philip's aunt, the sister and confidante of his father, my vivacious daughter was a favorite of the tetrarch. This had always pleased me, for the competition among the mothers of Philip's children was bitter beyond belief. Now I saw his affection for our child in a different light. Fearfully, I considered that even if forced to let me go, he would never give up Salome.

"Mamma, you are hurting me!" cried my little girl.

"Oh that was just a fierce hug," I laughed, "to show how much I love you."

"I'll give you a fierce hug too, Mamma," and Salome squeezed me with all her might.

"Oh, oh, you are hurting me," I pleaded. "Please let me go!" Salome would have continued the game, but I changed my tone. "Where is Nana?"

"I am here." Geshtinanna came onto the patio. She had taken charge of Salome's lessons during my sessions with Miriam. "Are you now a full-fledged midwife?"

"Much closer than I ever thought to be," I admitted.

Nana's heavy hair modeled her shapely head and hung in a thick black plait to her waist. Seven years ago Joseph, husband to Alma Mari, had betrothed his daughter to a young apprentice of his trade, a match of the heart, but Simon had died in Antipas's war with Arabia. Nana, staggered by the second overwhelming loss of her young life, had begged her father not to make her another match, so he still waited for her word that she was ready to marry. Nana would never wed a man she had not met, nor would she or Ninshubur ever meet anyone closed up in these women's quarters. I must get them away, I thought.

Nana did not affect the dress of a lady, but kept to her priestess's robes. They became her, a white linen shift tied with a twisted cord at the waist, and over it a long coat of purple. Only the outside garment changed with the seasons. The sleeveless coat Nana wore now was of linen, while the winter garment had sleeves and was of wool. Both were dyed the rich purple that came from Tyrian shellfish, considered fit only for royalty. But the priestesses of Isis-Ashera had status enough. No one questioned our right to the purple of Tyre. I should wear my own robes more, I thought, admiring their simple elegance on my friend.

Nina appeared from across the court, and we three talked for nearly an hour, playing with Salome. Then we prepared our supper of barley cakes, goat cheese, and figs, calling Lucius and Lysander to join us, choosing our own company rather than the rich, communal meal with the other women. But I was distracted, and Nina was as quiet, taking in my thoughts. The things Seth had said filled my mind, and I wondered if leaving here might really be possible. Could I invent some pretext to travel with my daughter and household intact? Philip would not hesitate to make Salome hostage to my good behavior. I must find a way to send Geshtinanna and the child away first. It would be quite proper for Salome to be dedicated to the Temple at Jerusalem in the spring as I had been. A plan began to form in my mind.

Each day after our lessons, Miriam would settle into the cushions of the elegant divan in her audience room and offer me dainty cakes or yogurt sweetened with honey. Then she would entice me to talk about my family at Bethany and my life in the Temple, and to open my heart to her. And she would tell me her own stories, which always involved famous and illustrious people and wonderful intrigues. I would be spellbound, for she was a practiced storyteller. I knew she entertained me to take my mind away from my worry about Deidre, and about the plans for my escape from Caesarea.

"Thoughts become real," she often reminded me. "Imagine your successful enterprise over and over, and it will come to pass. If you entertain your fears, you will bring them into being. Such is the Law."

She wanted to know the history of my people, though I sensed she had heard it before and was comparing my account with others. I told her that the worship of the Goddess had been banned by King Josiah long before I was born, and that afterward the most terrible times had come for our people. The Babylonians under Nebuchadnezzar destroyed the Temple that had been built by King Solomon, pushing down the great stones and squabbling over the sacred treasures. They burned and looted Jerusalem and carried away all the noble families that were still alive. My family is descended from those less noble, who were not important enough to be exiled. Our people took their sufferings as a sign from the Goddess, not that she was punishing them for taking down her image, but that she was reminding them of the Law. By turning to the ways of the warrior God, they had pulled down violence on themselves. When Cyrus of Persia defeated the Babylonians forever, he brought back the expatriates with money to rebuild the Temple and the city. They returned the Goddess to her rightful place in the Temple and worshiped her with Jehovah as her bridgegroom and consort, just as they had done since the time of Solomon.

"I had forgotten the patriarchs banished the Mother altogether for a time. They will do it again if they can, and deny her memory as well," Miriam said.

"Surely it could never happen again," I protested.

Miriam wanted to know the names of my mother and grandmother. When I told her, she repeated the names to herself several times, as if she were resolving to remember them, then she asked, "And were your mother, Aethel, and your grandmother, Lili, firstborn daughters like yourself and educated in the Temple as priestesses of the Mother?" When I nodded, she continued. "Since I am Greek, myself, it cheers me that their wisdom does not reject Greek influence altogether. We too revere the Law above all."

"My mother," I affirmed, "praised the wisdom of the Greeks in teaching that all gods, everywhere, are the same god by many names. We call her Mother, and the Pharisees call him the Lord, but the divine is One. This we believe from the Greeks."

"Nay, Mari, from before the Greeks," Miriam said.

"Alexander's Greeks did not persecute us; for that we honor them. The great sufferings our people endured the last two hundred years before the Romans came were caused by strife among ourselves." I looked out the open window over the lush palace gardens and, looming beyond them, Mount Hermon.

"I thought until you told me of your Roman grandfathers, that your family might be descended from the aristocracy—the tribe of Levi," Miriam said.

"We have no claim to Levite blood, nor has anyone," I told her. The Levites forbade intermarriage with the other tribes—the black-headed people—and died out from their own inbreeding, or so I was taught."

Miriam snorted. "The Levites deserved to die out. The mixing of blood makes the strongest and handsomest offspring. Men know of their horses and sheep what they will not see in relation to themselves. Pride in race or blood leads to all manner of evil, Mari Anath."

"But John Hyrcanus was tall and fair like the tribe of Levi," I reminded her, "and the Hasmoneans—the royal house—are like him."

"They are mixed—mongrels, as you say—which explains their extraordinary brilliance and handsomeness," Miriam said positively. "Is your father tall, also?"

"Not at all," I shook my head. "We are not noble, as I have said—I myself least of all."

"But you were chosen for the line of the High Priestesses," she reminded me. "You will be Magdalene."

"Oh, Madam!" I protested. "I am not worthy."

"Others have deemed you worthy, if you do not," Miriam reminded me. "Why do you say you are unworthy?"

"I—my heart is rebellious—full of questioning," I confessed miserably.

"Toward the Mother?"

"Or the Father. Or any gods. How could their grand designs ever outweigh their cost in human suffering?"

Miriam nodded her head. "So I have always asked myself," she said, and we sat silently. The restful sound of a nearby fountain came to us. Then Miriam spoke again.

"A High Priestess who cares about suffering is surely to be desired. You will serve the Mother better for your doubts."

When we had made our good-byes, and I went back to my luxurious prison, the doubt I had brought to life with my words filled my thoughts so completely that I passed through the vast garden untouched by its beauty.

Blessed Mother, I prayed, how is it possible to both believe and not believe? To feel rebellious at one moment and comforted the next?

My own mother's face appeared in my mind, and her love for me was like a presence. "You loved me enough to send me away, even when I cried. I love you, Mamma," I wept.

The hymn to Queen Isis sang itself in my heart:

Mistress of the gods, thou bearer of wings
Praise be to thee, O Lady, who art mightier than the gods . . .

The Holy Birth

Seek the Lord, the beloved of the Great Goddess.
When he is borne ashore, you shall find him.
When he performs great feats, you shall wonder.
When he reigns, you shall share his glory.
Hymn to the Savior

"And it is the present Magdalene, Almah Mari, who was your 'elder sister' in the Temple?" Miriam asked next day after lessons, dipping conserve of quince with a crisp bit of unleavened bread.

"I have adored her since we met," I confided. "She is like the Goddess to me."

"There is too little loyalty and devotion in this world," Miriam observed. It was the kind of statement Philip often orated in the Roman grand manner with overstated gesture and inflection—but there was true feeling in Miriam's tone. "You are fortunate in your love," she said, "and so is she. Tell me, did you see at once that she was extraordinary?"

"I thought I had never seen anyone so beautiful—the sunlight on her hair, long and darkly golden—she seemed to me like the Goddess herself." I flushed at having revealed so much.

"Do not suppose I laugh at your devotion to the Magdalene." Miriam's voice was sincere. "I, too, came under her spell as soon as ever I laid eyes on her." She wiped her fingers daintily, shook the crumbs from her lap, and settled herself. I saw with delight that I was to be treated to another of her famous stories.

"It was sixteen years ago—no, seventeen this month—" she began, "I had been summoned by your husband's father, Herod the Great, to nurse him through an illness that threatened to be his last. What a tyrant he was! Albeit a great man. In him the fatal flaw loomed larger than his virtue—but that is another story.

"He had gardens, you know," she said, with a sweeping gesture of her hand toward the broad window, "greater than these. Like the hanging gardens of Nebuchadnezzar, they were, fabulous! I sat in those gardens one day, resigning myself to not being allowed to leave Jerusalem until Herod either died or improved greatly—and the latter seemed unlikely, even impossible, at that time. He had sunk to such a state he trusted no one, and his vengeance was swift and terrible. Even the most faithful servant or dearest relative, if suspected of so much as a critical word about him, he put to torture to extract confessions of what he imagined. He was helping his relatives and friends out of this world so regularly that no one could feel safe. And he had placed his life in my hands! I dared not do anything to hasten his death, even should he so order me, for love of my own life. I have never been in graver jeopardy." Miriam stabbed the air with her hands for emphasis.

"But the gardens fascinated me. I welcomed the opportunity to learn more of the secret properties of plants, so I wandered with my notebooks and drawing materials, recording observations for my apprentices—at that time I had two. I have trained but one other besides—my standards are high, as you know. I am not willing my knowledge should be lost, but I do not choose to create competition for my services." She laughed her throaty laugh, and patted my hand.

And I was to be a third. Or if not, I had, at least, the privilege of this great lady's confidence.

"So as I thus sat," she continued, "occupied with my sketches, still troubled with thoughts of Herod, I perceived Salome, his sister, the only relative who had managed to retain his favor, coming toward me."

"My daughter's namesake!" I exclaimed.

"Yes. This Salome was no longer young. Her face had a cowlike look of sweet suffering that had probably saved her from Herod's wrath. I saw she was shy even with me; it could be no mere pleasantry that brought her.

"This timid sister of Herod bowed meekly in greeting to me and waited for permission to speak, as if she were not herself a princess. When I gestured a little impatiently, she said—here Miriam affected a tiny, mouselike voice—"'Madame, if you please, there is a messenger for you in my apartments. Will you be so kind as to come, or shall I send him away?'"

I giggled appreciatively.

"Of course I told her I would come and how kind she was to fetch me herself. We crossed the gardens to the apartments she shared with Alexas, her husband. She led me to a sitting room where waited a beautiful boy dressed in Temple robes—obviously a eunuch," Miriam stopped to curse under her breath. "Barbarous practice!" she snorted, "to take the manhood from the fairest of boys and keep them for the toys of other men!"

"But Temple priests choose the sacrifice themselves," I protested timidly. "It is never asked of them." I withered at Miriam's fierce look. "It is because the Goddess and her priestesses are female— they see their maleness as an impediment."

"Surely you cannot believe the Mother would desire such a thing," Miriam demanded.

"In truth, I cannot," I admitted honestly. Miriam seemed satisfied. She moved into her characterization of the young eunuch.

"He raised his eyes like a shy maid," she pantomimed, rolling her own skyward, fluttering her eyelids, "and waited for permission to speak. 'If it please you, Madame, my message is for your ears alone,' and poor Salome jumped like a guilty child and ran from the room, as if it were not her own.

"'I come from the Mother,' the boy said to me. I knew at once he spoke of the Magdalene, Anna."

Miriam changed to an informative tone, leaning forward. "There was enmity, you know, between the High Priestess and Herod, since Mariamne, the wife he had tried and executed, held that office at her death, and Anna was rumored to be her daughter, Temple-begotten."

I felt my skin prickle. Miriam altered her voice and posture to indicate her next words came from the young eunuch.

"'The Sacred Maiden of Israel, daughter of our Lady the Magdalene, is about to bear. She begs you to meet with her at once.'

"Herod usually slept two or three hours in the afternoon. But if he were restless and called for me, I might be missed. It would not be easy, and I told him so.

"'Madame must find a way,' he said. 'Our Lady commands you!'" Miriam threw back her head and laughed.

"'Our Lady commands you!'" she said again, parodying the eunuch. "Everyone is always commanding me! Didn't our-Lady-her-Highness-Anna-Magdalene realize that Herod could have my head in a minute if he flew into one of his rages? But I knew I would find a way.

"Herod was a late sleeper, so I chose the second hour before dawn to steal from his palace for my meeting with the Magdalene. No moon, only cold starlight, but I could see the Temple towering against the gray morning. Demius, one of my wards, led the way with a small lantern over the stone street, all an uphill climb. The eunuch who opened the door knew who I was; he bowed and blessed me for coming. Demius put out the lantern and stepped back to wait. I was led through the magnificent gallery, with four rows of stone columns in rose and white, gold and lavender, each as large as could be spanned by three men and so tall they looked pointed at their tops."

I nodded. "It too was built by King Herod."

"Aye, he did great works, for all his brutality! It is magnificent! The eunuch's bare feet made no sound on the marble floor, but my soft leather sandals sent whispers and echoes from one end of the gallery to the other. We passed beneath a high arch into a courtyard, and from there through a pair of tall doors into a gracious waiting room.

"I supposed so great a lady as the Magdalene would be sleeping, and I expected to wait while her maids dressed her to properly impress a visitor. But the lady Anna did not bother with impressions, which impressed me more. She appeared almost at once in the receiving room outside her bedchamber." Miriam gazed as if into the far distance, and I knew she was seeing the

High Priestess Anna as she had appeared that night seventeen years ago.

"She was dressed in a plain robe thrown over her nightdress, her long red hair unbound about her. I had not imagined her so tall, because of her delicate appearance. She was very beautiful. We two stood, each waiting for a sign or clue, some idea of where to begin. I believe the Goddess helped us that night to see each other as we truly were, to perceive our sisterhood.

"'Miriam of Scarios, welcome!' she said graciously. 'You do me great service to come at such risk to yourself.'

"'I am greatly honored, dear lady!' said I. 'The fame of your goodness and wisdom reaches the far corners of the earth.'

"'If that is true, you would be the one to know,' she answered me. 'Is there anywhere a royal house you have not seen? It is your wisdom and good works that are known to all.' So we admired and praised one another, until she drew me toward her couch, seated herself, and motioned me to sit beside her."

Miriam clasped her jeweled fingers together in joyful satisfaction. "I was deeply honored that she had called me and had decided to trust me," she exclaimed with great feeling. "And what delight to meet such a woman! I saw that she suffered the loneliness of all those who attain great heights, who know no peers, and she recognized in me a friend. That I shall always treasure."

Miriam touched the tips of her eyelashes with her handkerchief. "You see, even I am liable to weeping at the stirring of old memories! I had expected much of the Magdalene, and I had put aside danger to follow my strong feeling that to go to her would be momentous."

She leaned toward me. "I tell you, Mari, I felt the pull of destiny in that meeting. 'How may I serve you, Lady?' I said to her, and I was saying to myself, 'Whatever she wants, I will do it!'

"And so she told me the signs and portents all confirmed that the child her daughter was about to bear would be the long-awaited Messiah of the Jews, the deliverer of Israel.

"You remember rightly her voice had the tone and sweetness of music. She told me it is written in the scriptures that he should be born at Bethlehem, that thither we would take her daughter within the week, or sooner if her labor began—as it might. The journey from Nazareth had been difficult with her time so near. 'All must go well for her and the child,' she said to me. 'You are the most renowned of all your profession. I beg you to employ all of your skill and knowledge in her behalf.'

"I was thinking I would have to trick Herod. He would never willingly allow me to leave for such an errand. I would have to give him a powerful sleeping draught this time! She begged me take care, and not to endanger myself, and asked if it was true that Herod was dying.

"I told her I thought that he was, and then I warned her of what I knew." Miriam's black eyes flashed just as they must have then. "'You know that Herod has spoken of this child—his spies are everywhere!' I told her. 'Look to it that there is not one in your own household!' I warned her he had sworn to kill the King of the Jews, this grandson of hers who was to be born, just as he had killed all the house of the Hasmoneans. 'Look to yourself, Lady,' said I, 'if you are of that blood, as I have heard.'

"The lady Anna laughed like the sound of a golden bell. 'Herod cares more for begetting than birthing. He sees no blood in the line of the mother,' she said.

"A wise woman, that one! Then she told me she was proud to be the daughter of Mariamne, Temple-born, before her mother's marriage to her murderer. 'This is no secret, but a truth Herod chooses to ignore,' she said to me. 'He is one of those who deny the power of the Mother and who treat women as possessions, to be bought and bred like mares and dams and slaughtered or sold if they do not please! I have no doubt he will try to kill the holy child,' she told me. 'We shall take every care.'

"I told the lady Anna I should best invent some pretext to journey openly to Bethlehem, with my servants and retainers in attendance, but that in order to be believed and gain Herod's leave I would need to plan with the day in mind. I asked to attend upon her daughter to better ascertain her time.

"So Anna made a sign to a maidservant who stood just out of earshot, and the girl approached to do her bidding. 'Tell my daughter's women to prepare her to receive an early guest,' she said. As the girl hurried away, I heard that melodious voice follow softly, but clearly, 'Tell them to waken her gently!'

"When she led to me to her daughter's rooms, Almah's maid, Deborah, led us through the spacious sitting room into her bed-chamber. The other girl, Julia, was stuffing pillows behind her lady's back, then she bowed and stood back. I—" Here the story-teller's powers of speech failed her.

"I felt I should kneel, my dear," Miriam said softly, "for I swear it was a young goddess before me, there among the silken pillows like Aphrodite in the white sea foam, haloed in the aura of her shining hair, spreading and shimmering about her." Miriam paused, shaking her head. "I tell you, I am quite sensitive to spiritual things, and to my deepest soul, this marvelous being was no stranger. I recognized the Goddess more strongly in her than ever in any woman." She stopped dabbing at her tears, letting them fall, smiling to see that I also wept. Then she went on slowly and with deep feeling.

"I stood there like a child, abashed, captured by a helpless girl, her frail body so ripe with the godling in her womb she could scarce move herself about, but her spirit so powerful that to look on her was to want nothing in life so much as to serve her, in what-ever way might avail her purpose."

Presently, Miriam composed herself, straightened her skirts, and went on with her story.

"The place for the birth had been chosen by the Magdalene Anna with care for the safety of the holy child and to fulfill the scriptures—to assure his recognition and acceptance by the peo-ple. She had sent her servants to Bethlehem three months before—sparing no expense to obtain the necessary privacy—the lodgings were reserved only after she had inspected them herself. The time of the census ordered by Caesar was upon us, so the inns would be crowded with travelers and the quiet her daughter would need could never be had in any of them. Anna secured the use of a charming cottage—actually a refurbished stable—adjoining the best of Bethlehem's inns. It lay off to the side below a hill, away from the road. A place usually sought for its privacy, it would fulfill the description of the prophecy.

"She made certain my services would be available for the day I believed the labor would begin—the third following our meeting. I obtained Herod's permission to leave temporarily by showing him the papers of my foster child, Demius, who had been born in Bethlehem, and explaining that I needed to go there to register him.

"You know that Bethlehem is but a half-day's journey from Jerusalem. The Magdalene and I traveled separately, of course, planning to reach Bethlehem before Almah's party to set all in order. So it was that we moved unrecognized by those we met. Dressed in garments of common people, we appeared separately at the inn at Bethlehem and took the different rooms reserved for us. We settled ourselves and our baggage, then, blending into the crowds, walked the streets as if to sample the shops. We met at the cottage below the hill with a legion of men and maids brandishing brooms, mops, herbs, and brushes. They stored the innkeeper's bedding away and replaced it with clean sheets and robes from the Temple of Ashera. They laid a new fire and set water to boil in a clean vessel. They burned herbs in pans, carrying them through the rooms to purify the air and dispel insects.

"The lady Anna had covered her hair and darkened her face. She hoped the press of people converging for the census would make it less likely she should be recognized by Herod's spies. Certainly he was aware of the prophecy that a king of the Jews should be born at Bethlehem. He might already have word of Almah's return to Jerusalem—if he believed the rumors that she was the chosen maiden. Such rumors circulated time after time; he would have no way of knowing this one to be different than the others—unless the presence of the Magdalene here in this place betrayed the truth to him.

"As for myself, I stripped away my ornaments and put on the garish garments of a trader's wife, so Herod's spies would not follow me. I sent my maid, Dorcas, who was practiced at impersonating me, to wait with Demius in the long lines of people for the census takers. When I had supervised all the preparations, the lady Anna and I sent away all the servants except our personal attendants, who were absolutely trustworthy, and sat down to wait.

"On the road to Bethlehem, so overripe she scarce could sit, came our darling Almah, borne in the Magdalene's own palanquin, stripped of its colored silk and dressed in common tent cloth. She felt hourly more and more pains and feared the birth would take place before they arrived. Young Julia rode with her in the curtained litter, rubbing her back, wiping her face with cool cloths handed up by Deborah, who trotted beside the bearers as much as she rode. The poor husband was in a flurry of anxiety; he adored her so—as we all did—but he kept stopping the bearers to inquire about her comfort, until she begged him not to tarry but to hasten as fast as possible.

"Because of the census, the press of crowds made it easy for Almah Mari and Joseph to move unremarked and unnoticed. They reached the inn three hours past midday. Joseph dismissed most of his party to find their own accommodations and hastened around the hill to the cottage with his wife. The palanquin was set down, and Almah stepped out supported by Julia. Swollen she was, to amazing proportions, my dear, but serene as an angel.

"We women bustled about, preparing her bath, installing her in the spotless, sweet-smelling chamber, bringing her broth and cool water. She gave herself trustingly into our hands, and she fell asleep and rested herself."

Miriam paused, as if uncertain how she wished to proceed, and I waited expectantly. When she spoke at last, she had lost the sense of being actually present during the events she related. "She awoke only when overtaken by her pains and delivered almost at once,"she said, as if to hasten the ending of her story.

"And the child?" I asked, unable to restrain myself.

"A perfect boy, as you know."

The silence was suddenly awkward between us. Then Miriam asked, "You have heard of Herod's atrocious attempt on the child's life?"

"I have heard how he ordered all the boy babes under two years put to the sword," I admitted. I felt unwilling to let go of the story I had just heard, but Miriam's eyes had turned fierce with old sorrow and rage.

"His spies told him one who would be King of the Jews had been born; Herod believed some poor child of Mariamne's blood had escaped him—he ordered them all killed. His hired murderers—hardened warriors they were, and cruel—had to drink themselves insensible to do their awful work; they made a mad game of the slaughter. Swooping down on defenseless people, breaking through gates and doors, they slaughtered many a father who tried to save his child. They threw innocent babes into the air and caught them on the points of spears, dashed out their brains against a wall, or hacked them to pieces before their mother's eyes. The keening was heard from town to town, and few escaped. Herod was determined no Hasmonean should be left to bear the name."

I waited, the horror Miriam evoked filling my imagination. At last she released the memory and said in a lighter tone, "My darling Seth survived that obscene slaughter."

I was startled. "Seth? Why, where was he born, then?"

"The Goddess knows from whence he came," Miriam said. "My women found him in a basket floating in the rushes by the river. A perfect, comely child; I could not but take him as my own. Doubtless he was concealed to escape Herod."

"Like the baby Moses!" I exclaimed.

"Surely a child watched over by the gods," Miriam agreed.

Deidre

Terrible one, lady of the rainstorm, destroyer of the souls of men, devourer of the bodies of men, orderer, producer, and maker of slaughter, . . . devoted one, lady of the Great House, conqueror of hearts, swallower of them. . . . Knife which cutteth when its name is uttered, slayer of those who approach thy flame.

Egyptian Book of the Dead

My "accidental" meetings with Seth continued almost daily in the lady Miriam's quarters. Utterly charmed by him, I soon forgot he was six years younger than my twenty-three. He was an absorbing and delightful companion, surprising me constantly. He launched himself into the labyrinth of Philip's accounts—the work of a long series of clerks with different concepts of organization—as he did everything, with playful ease. Frustration was unknown to him; everything was a game, a challenge to his growing powers, a delight. I would never have accused him of seeking only pleasure, but that is what he found in everything that crossed his path. He had none of the painful self-consciousness that distracts most young people; he was relaxed and at ease, totally present in the experience of the moment. The past was done, the future not yet. He saw and heard everything with his whole attention, not merely pretending to be interested while he planned his own speech. He spoke his thoughts as they came to him, cutting to the heart of things with the bluntness that had disconcerted me that first evening. I do not mean that he was careless or rash. He would spend hours planning strategies, as though he played an entertaining game, with backup plans for every conceivable circumstance—as we did now, laying plans for my escape from the harem—but he spent not a moment that I could see in anxious worry.

Seth loved life. He was at home in the world, no weary pilgrim, passing through. He saw himself the honored guest of life, expecting the best of everything, radiating that feeling to everyone around him. There was no place for patient suffering or resignation in his presence. He exploded my martyrdom with his outrageous question before I had known him one hour. "What gains he by keeping you?" What indeed? And what did I gain by staying? Nothing. Less than nothing.

Between our trysts, I searched for a way to put our slowly forming plan into action. It all depended on Philip's willingness to send Salome to Jerusalem for the winter festival, but convincing him would be a tricky business. Only with my daughter and Nana under Almah's protection in the Temple could I safely attempt my own flight. I needed Philip's ear. Even then, there was no certainty I could persuade him, but he was so enamored of his newest bride—blonde, gray-eyed Phoebe—he had forgotten not only me but his other women as well.

I still longed for some word from Deidre—even gossip about her. Each morning I resolved anew to put away my fears, to visualize her well and happy, but her anguished face still appeared in my dreams, and I could not shake the sense of disaster that crept upward from the earth into my very bones.

Then gray-eyed Phoebe was taken ill for several days with the malady of new brides, painful urination and fever. I remembered my own experiences and was sympathetic. Philip was secretly known as "the Bull" among the wives who dared to speak of such things, not for his size, but for his lack of skill. The lady Miriam attended Phoebe and reported daily to the concerned husband, spicing her conversation with little asides about her excellent pupil, Mari Anath. Perhaps her praises of me aroused a jealous twinge, or perhaps the daily reminder of my existence combined with Phoebe's incapacitation worked together, leading him to desire my company himself. But he did not send me a dinner invitation; he sent for me to come to his bed.

I was distracting myself from one of my interminable headaches by thinking and dreaming of Seth when the summons came from Philip. My headache seemed suddenly a selfish consideration I ought to ignore. Perhaps I had been unjust to harbor such cruel thoughts against poor Philip. Had he not always treated me with kindness and consideration—as he did all his wives? Perhaps he had even allowed Deidre's escape, knowing she was unhappy, and made only a show of pursuit to save face.

I toyed with the thought and rejected it. Still, Philip was often very kind—even indulgent. Though he kept seven wives and a changing number of concubines—as was customary—he was praised for his moderation. He was never known to abuse, debauch, or publicly humiliate his wives. He was scrupulous about seeing each of us separately, allowing us as much dignity as was needful for wives, even going so far as to maintain with each the polite fiction that she was his only one. Admittedly, this fed the jealousy of the younger women and became a bitter joke for those made wiser by experience. But if Philip wished to carouse with his friends, or enjoy more than one woman at a time, he sent for his concubines instead. All this had earned him the reputation of a considerate husband.

I saw Nina's raised eyebrow, questioning. Just for a moment, in annoyance, I closed my thoughts to her. At this, she rose from her seat and laughed with undisguised scorn.

"Tell him you have a headache," she suggested.

Chastened, I laughed with her. Better to laugh than weep, my mother always said. I had been ready to forget all the pain I had felt about Philip because he had, after months, finally thought of me! Nina stopped laughing and warned, "You must be careful, Mari, do not let him see any change in you."

When Lucius and Lysander escorted me to the door of my husband's bedchamber, where they would remain until I reappeared, Philip's old attendant, Menos, who had cared for him since childhood, let me in. He did not apologize for his master's absence; I was to wait, and it might be long. I settled in a carved chair by the small fire Menos lighted for me. The autumn evenings were growing cooler. The lamp of burnished bronze was too dim for the sewing I had brought, so I laid it aside and sat silently, trying to relax so the headache would leave me, allowing my consciousness to seek what level it might.

The first stages of meditation flooded my being with repose. Years of training and habit kept permanently unlocked for me the doors that Nehushtan's venom had first opened. Presently I felt weightless, without the limitations of space or time. In imagination—or in reality—I left the still form before the fire in its robes of white and purple. Thin and fluid as a vapor, I imagined myself floating out of the opulent bedchamber right through the narrow space between the closed double doors. Outside in the pillared gallery sat the patient giant, Lucius, and graceful Lysander, silent as the massive columns, ears and eyes open to every sight and sound. But they did not see me.

Large portions of the cloister were open to the sky, and the polished floors of colored stone shone like luminous pools in the darkness. In imagination, I hung above the tall roofs of the palace with the silent stars. I could see towering Mount Hermon to the north and, below it, shrouded in dark cedars, the deep, hidden caves hollowed out of the rock by centuries of gushing water. For hundreds of years, bandits and robbers had hidden there to prey on traders filing across the high desert from Arabia. Herod, later called the Great, had routed the bandits when still a young general and gained the lasting favor of Antony in Egypt and Caesar in Rome by establishing the fortress at Paneas to guard the trade routes from the East. When they made him king of the lands on both sides of the Jordan from the high desert on the east to the sea, Herod built the temple at Paneas in honor of Caesar.

After his death, when this northern part of his kingdom was given to Philip, the new tetrarch increased the size of Paneas, renamed it Caesarea-Philippi in honor of Caesar and himself, and imported settlers from every direction, offering them homes, work, and land.

Below the city to the south, I could see the river Jordan, where it began its hundred-mile journey to the Sea of Galilee, fed by the underground springs that honeycombed Mount Hermon and the ground beneath the city. Swiftly as thought, I entered a huge cave whose hidden mouth lay just above Caesarea to the north.

Though no moonlight found its way into the cave, so my bodily eyes would have availed nothing, I nevertheless could see clearly, and from all sides at once, the massive limestone columns, far taller than those of the Temple at Jerusalem, formed like thick honey dripping from the comb. As I moved in wonder through a labyrinth more magnificent than any palace, dazzled by colors I could not name, I came to the edge of a vast pool. It stretched before and to either side through the darkness, its still surface unbroken by the slightest ripple, though the sound of rushing water filled the cave. The purity of the water moved me to drink, and though I had no body of flesh and bone, I stooped to break the shining surface with cupped hands, finding it not still, but swiftly flowing. It splashed up high behind my hands, and how this could be I cannot say, for who can explain the reality of a dream? It pulled on my hands, my dream hands, as if to take me on its long journey south to the Dead Sea. I laughed aloud with delight. The sweet, cold draught refreshed me as though it were the water of life.

Gazing into the translucent pool, I could see nothing below, nor fathom its depths with my mind; wherever I cast my thought, no bottom was there. Legend said that here and all down the path of the river that flowed from its inexhaustible source was a seam, or fault, in the earth. The primordial sea above and below the world seeped through and would one day rend apart the seam and take back the earth again into itself.

I shivered, for the cold of the waters filled the cave and chilled me to the bone—though bones I had none. Swift as my wish, I stood in the columned gallery before the gracious banquet hall where Philip dined with his guests. I passed like smoke between massive carved doors and saw them lingering in conversation, the meal long since cleared away. I had a mind to summon my husband, but he did not respond to my thought. Uneasiness tugged at me. I should be seeking something, someone. Seth and Miriam were facing Philip, their backs to me, but Miriam turned on her velvet couch and looked at me with a smile of recognition. Then Seth saw me too—I had moved closer—and looked straight into my eyes. Startled at being discovered, I needed all my concentration to maintain my dream state. Again I sensed I should be somewhere else. Then I saw that Miriam was telling me something. She was framing the words with her lips, "Deidre. Find Deidre."

"Deidre? Of course." Quickly as my mind framed the question, I stood within a cavern not unlike where I had drunk the fresh water of the Jordan. But hand-wrought columns were here. Some of the water-stained walls appeared carved out of the limestone, others were made of huge rough-hewn blocks of the same stone, befouled with soot and mold. Disoriented in the flickering orange light, like that of torches, I passed a turn in the long gallery and saw them, burning weakly in the foul air. On one side ranged a long row of heavy doors with barred openings. Hesitantly peering through one, I saw only rags heaped in a corner, but the moan I heard was human. Feeling the hair rise along my neck despite my bodiless state, I resisted an impulse to flee, certain now I would find Deidre in this horrid place. I smelled the stench of filth, blood, and vomit, and I felt spider webs and the brush of horrid furry creatures past my feet. I had not imagined even hell could be like this.

At last, in a foul, stinking cell to which the door stood open— there was no need to close or lock it—I found what I knew to be Deidre. I hovered close over her broken form, shaking with grief and rage. I tried to embrace her, forgetting I had no arms of flesh and bone. Deidre's once lovely face was hollow, bloody and bruised, her eyes sunken and empty; she was not asleep. Neither was she awake. Unaware of anything, she did not respond to my thought. Both her arms lay bent unnaturally, broken. Her legs, too, had been broken; the marks of the rack were on her wrists and ankles. I moaned at the sight of her once lovely hand. One finger, the smallest, and the thumb remained, the nails pulled from them. The others had been cut off, at various joints, as had her toes. Most of her thick, black hair was pulled out, and her naked flesh oozed with cuts and burns. Her breathing, labored and shallow, brought a bloody froth to her bruised lips. I hoped she might already be dying; death was the greatest blessing I could imagine for her now.

I looked for something I could do, some way to be of comfort or aid; I could think of nothing. Maddened with rage, I struggled to comprehend that Philip must have ordered—even participated in—the atrocity before me. No other explanation was possible. I swore a silent oath. The Goddess had led me here. I would protect Deidre from more harm. I would not return to my body until I could find a way to help Deidre die.

It was then that one of Philip's jailers or torturers, a huge man, gross in his leather breastplate and shin-guards, staggered into the long gallery, humming in a hoarse monotone. Frantic to vent my rage, I turned on him in blind fury. Then I knew the Goddess had sent him. Here was the help I sought.

"Holy Mother, thanks be to you," I sobbed. "Make me strong and give me courage." In my thought I arose from Deidre's poor broken body and moved behind the unwary guard. Measuring my weightless form against the unsuspecting man, arm against arm, thigh against thigh, I pressed through his solid flesh and overwhelmed his careless and unwatchful spirit. The gross body did not fit me very well, but it would have to do. I flexed the powerful, hairy arms, and straightened the heavy shoulders. I turned on trunklike legs toward the helpless form of Deidre. I did not weigh in my mind whether it would be right or wrong to kill her. Philip was her torturer and her murderer; I was acting only to protect her from more harm. She was maimed and she was suffering. There was no other choice.

Leaning over her, I wanted to take her in those powerful arms and hold her to that barrel chest, but I knew the slightest touch would bring more pain; the pain was what I must end. Could I strangle her with these strong hands? If only Nehushtan were here, his boon to Deidre would be a painless death! I explored the heavy leather belt about the huge middle of my borrowed body. There were keys on a brass ring, an empty flask, a set of ivory dice rattling in their inlaid case—and here! An evil-looking pointed dagger. I examined it carefully. It was one of the type called sicarii, viciously sharp. The rugged, grimy hand that held it shook uncontrollably.

"Holy Mother, help me," I prayed.

Steeling myself to thrust true, I plunged the weapon into Deidre's stubbornly beating heart. The vacant eyes of my sister-wife opened wide, the horror left them, and she was for an instant self-aware.

"Oh, Mari, it is you," she said, in a tone of great relief, and died.

That same instant I started in my chair before the burned-out fire in Philip's bedchamber, my heart pounding so loudly in my ears I feared it would be heard in the next room. I stared in horror at my right hand, incredulous to see it clean. I had felt in it the hot blood from Deidre's heart but a moment before. Grief like a knife in my own heart doubled me over, and I hid my face in my hands.

"Holy Mother, help me," I prayed. If Philip should find me grieving, all would be lost. At the thought of Deidre's murderer my heart chilled, and the hot tears froze in my throat. Philip would not hesitate to reward me in the same coin. Resolutely, I quieted my racing heart while my head throbbed with its every beat.

The far-seeing alertness of the mind that sees its survival at issue moved uppermost. I could grieve and rage later. Now I must play my part so faultlessly Philip would suspect nothing. Better to protect myself, should he sense something amiss. I reached beneath the coils of yarn in my sewing basket and drew forth the deadly little snake whose venom was to me both blessing and protection. It undulated up my arm, instinctively seeking warmth, and I hid it in my bodice where it nestled beneath my breasts. Philip's voice and that of his gray-haired attendant sounded from the adjoining chamber, causing me to rejoice. I was eager to be done with this bit of business. Steeling myself that I might not draw back at his touch, I stood to smooth my purple robes and the heavy knot of my hair. Then I reseated myself, that I might rise decorously and bow low before him as a well-trained wife.

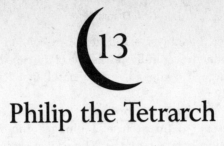

Philip the Tetrarch

It is the Law of heaven to make fullness empty, and to make full what is modest; when the sun is at its zenith, it must, according to the Law of heaven, turn toward its setting, and at its nadir, it rises to a new dawn.

I Ching

"Rise, Mari," Philip said in a peevish voice, "come and massage my neck and shoulders, as you do so well." He climbed heavily into his tall bed by three steps of elaborately carved cedar and dropped his robe off his thick shoulders. When I moved to follow him, he said with pained annoyance, "No, no, girl! Leave your robes there!" and motioned imperiously with his hand. Then he realized I had worn my priestess's robes especially to please him, and he amended in a pained tone, "It pleases me that you are wearing them, my dear."

Philip had not the massive frame of his father, Herod, but he was a stoutly built and heavy man. He had done his share of soldiering, necessary for any man of power, but he had found no need to war of late. His bulging muscles had softened and turned to fat, while rich food had extended his deep chest downward into a belly of unseemly proportions. Still, in his prime now at thirty-seven, he was a handsome man with the dark, heavy features of the Herodians and a thick growth of hair and beard that left no need for wigs or false curls.

I unwound my braid and shook out my waist-length hair. I began to undress without ceremony, knowing he wished to watch me, but I could not tear my mind from its vivid rehearsal of his death. Then, amazed at my own daring, still in my light undershift, I turned to face him, and began to sway rhythmically, drawing Nehushtan from his warm shelter beneath my breasts. I exulted as Philip's expression of haughty boredom changed to one of considerable interest. His eyes bulged, but he sat passive, watching. My hatred was to him unimaginable. He could not conceive that I might desire his death, even kill him, with the pretty serpent I was enticing to coil around my throat.

I dropped my shift and danced toward him, naked, Nehushtan reaching down between my breasts, seeking the warmth he had just left. I caused the snake to twine around my forearm, and extended it, nearly touching Philip's face. He rewarded me by throwing aside the bedclothes to reveal his erect phallus.

"Ah, Mari," he grunted appreciatively, innocent of the dark fury within me, "my little Magdalene. You delight me beyond words."

I had excited only his lust. Stung and humiliated, I wanted to punish him with some measure of the terror Deidre must have suffered. And the pain. But Nehushtan's sting was too good for him.

I closed my eyes for a moment and bade my sanity return. I could not buy my revenge at so dear a price; I must keep my own life to protect those I loved. Surely the Goddess had sent me this opportunity. I must not waste it. Slowly, I withdrew the serpent from where he could have slipped his deadly fangs into my husband's throat. Philip exhaled heavily, unaware that he had held his breath for some time. Swaying seductively, I retreated to the chest where I had laid out my clothes. I placed my hand in the open sewing basket and Nehushtan's forked tongue seemed to kiss my flesh for a moment as he hesitated, then he shot forth like whip beneath the coils of wool. I secured the lid and went to my husband, who awaited me wet-mouthed, with extended arms. He had forgotten the requested massage, and when I tried to move behind him, he grasped me roughly, pushing me down on the bed. "Now!" he panted, "I will have you now!" And he mounted me without ceremony, thrusting like a bull into my body, crushing me with his weight.

I was grateful for his urgency because it spared me the need of feigning tenderness for him. I knew I would be sore tomorrow, that he had cracked my ribs again, but I prayed it was for the last time.

When he rolled off me, and I had drawn a long, painful breath that he heard as one of passion, he had spent himself so completely he seemed about to fall asleep.

This was the moment I had awaited, paid dearly for, and now he was so drugged with either weariness or drink that he would not listen to my petition. It was usual for Philip to inquire how our daughter was, so I held my peace, not bringing it up myself, fearful he might not. Despairing, I began to massage his heavy neck and shoulders. At last, barely roused, he remembered his manners and asked long-suffering, "How is my darling Salome?"

"Wonderful, my lord." I took care my sigh of relief was not audible. "She looks forward with delight to her dedication to the Goddess in the spring," I tried the waters cautiously.

"This spring?" Philip was becoming more awake. "Certainly not! She is much too young."

"She will be five in two more moon-changes, and she is clever beyond her age," I said gently. "It is time her education is begun."

"I should think you would be as loath as myself to send so young a child away from her home," he grumbled peevishly, fully awake. "Surely you would miss her, as she would you. And I should miss her terribly!" My head throbbed. It was not going well at all.

"Even a child has her duty, my lord, as you had yours. I have heard how bravely you sailed for Rome when only four, while Antipas, older by three years, wept and stormed for his mother."

"We had different mothers," Philip explained, now sufficiently involved to affect the manner of overdramatization he had learned in Rome. "I was very close to my mother, but she did not make a baby of me for her own sake as that Samaritan woman did of Antipas and Archelaus. She cared not for their welfare so much as for her own!" He stopped to consider what he had just said.

"You are right, Mari," he announced after a long and dramatic pause, with a martyred air of renunciation. "It is I who am being selfish. We must do what is best for the child." He patted my thigh in approval.

"You are most gracious, as always, my lord," I praised him, straining not to reveal my excitement. "It is painful for me to think of separation from her," I confided in an intimate tone, "as I know it is for you, your love for her is so great." I let forth a deep sigh, finding it easy to display the huskiness of unshed tears in my voice. Philip put his arm around me, pulling my head over on his shoulder. The thick hairs on his chest threatened to make me sneeze, so I placed my hand beneath my cheek and nestled against him.

After a little, I ventured carefully, "Perhaps if Salome could see Jerusalem first, for a short visit, her fears of going to live there would be eased. It was this my parents did with me."

"Well," he said, absently fondling my breasts, "perchance we could send her for the celebration of winter solstice. It would be good for Mene to go too. Your woman, Salome's nurse—what is her name?—could take them both. What say you, little Magdalene?"

My heart leapt. I had only begun to search my mind for some way to protect Deidre's son from the jealous plotting of the other wives, who would find a way to eliminate the motherless rival of their children for Philip's favor. At least here was a beginning.

"Why, of course, the winter holiday is a perfect time. Why did I not think of it! Salome would have only pleasant memories of the Temple to bring back with her. How wise you are, my lord!" I managed the restraint necessary to show him I was pleased without letting him see that I was elated.

Next morning for my meeting with Seth and Miriam I arrived sick and shaken, headache raging, eyes swollen with weeping, my body gaunt and trembling for need of the food I could not keep down. The courage that had sustained me the evening before was quite used up, and my grief for Deidre was as physical as death. From the safe haven of Seth's arms, I told them stumblingly how Deidre had died and of my conversation with Philip. Then I waited, desperate for reassurance, for comfort.

"Holy Mother!" he exclaimed softly, at last, "you are magnificent! What a High Priestess you will make!"

Sensitive to the needs of lovers, Miriam had waited for him to speak first. She came to me and held me. "Dearest child," she crooned, rocking me in her arms, "you have suffered a bitter loss and taken a courageous step from which you cannot retreat. We are ahead in our lessons, so rest here and let us minister to you today. You are in grave need of our succor, and none will be the wiser."

I must have crumpled up completely in Miriam's arms. She passed me back to Seth while she arranged a place among the pillows, where they enthroned me. She brought me herbs that eased my headache and delicious soup that did not come up. When it was my usual time to leave, she presented me with a small packet of dried herbs.

"Drink strong tea of this night and morning until your moontime, without fail," she instructed firmly, "if you wish not to bear another Herodian."

Strengthened by hot broth, encouragement, and love, I hastened to Deidre's rooms to relieve Ninshubur or Geshtinanna, who sat in turns with prayers and lighted candles. Word from an unknown source of Deidre's death by torture was all about the women's quarters. Lysander had been determined to let the manner of her death be known before an "official story" could be invented. The disposal of our sister's abused and mutilated body was out of our hands; whether it would be burned or buried we did not know, but here where Deidre had lived nearly half her young life, three priestesses of the Goddess kept vigil with her spirit for three days, to guide her on her journey to the Netherworld.

A few days later Miriam related that the tetrarch had told her in passing that he intended to send two of his children, Mene and Salome, to Jerusalem for the winter festival.

"How wise you are, Excellency," Miriam's tone implied meaning beyond her words, "to remove your son from the jealousies of the women's quarters. You have no doubt some plan to educate him safely away from here until he is of age?"

The tetrarch had not, but her manner convinced him he ought to have been as farsighted as she suggested. He replied at once, dramatically overplaying the concerned and thoughtful father, "Illustrious madame, I am prepared to humiliate myself by begging of you a great favor."

"Sire?" Miriam waited, ignoring the opportunity to assure him that any favor to him would be a privilege past describing.

"The excellent education your son has received fills me with admiration and desire, so that I can imagine nothing so fine for my Mene as he could attain under your guidance. I implore you to find in your heart for me a measure of that great kindness for which you are everywhere praised and allow me to endow you with whatever moneys you would require to undertake his care and education until he is of age."

It was a long speech, and rambling, but commendable on the spur of the moment, and he waited expectantly, knowing that her refusal was unthinkable; his request was both an honor and a command. Miriam surprised him by replying somewhat sharply.

"Your Excellency, it is not my practice to steer children in the paths chosen by their fathers, be they royal as yourself. I believe a child's own gifts and talents, whatever they are, should determine the area and degree of his education. Mene may be fitted indeed for mathematics and music, as is Seth—though few are so gifted—and he may not. It is certain he is a very bright and talented child—he has extraordinary beauty as well, with his dark skin and fine features." She looked challengingly at Philip, and he flushed hotly. Miriam wondered if he had tortured Mene's mother by swearing to castrate the boy and use him as a slave. "I would agree to undertake such a responsibility only on the terms I have stated," she said.

"Dearest lady, I could wish for nothing else than what you have described. I trust your wisdom absolutely. Will you do it then?" Philip was effusive in his eagerness, doubtless visualizing himself being presented ten or twelve years hence with an accomplished Seth-like transformation of little Mene.

"You may have your scribe draw up the papers for my approval," Miriam agreed. Only then did she thank the tetrarch for the singular honor he had conferred on her. "It is a great privilege to be of service to Your Excellency," she bowed.

Thus it was Miriam who informed me that all these arrangements had been made. Miriam herself would be journeying hence soon, if all went well with Lois's child, for she planned to spend the winter in the milder climate of Jerusalem, where rain could be expected but little snow. The winter storms would not allow safe embarking for Scarios before spring. So as Seth and I met almost daily with Miriam's blessing, the plans were carefully laid. Besides myself, we intended to smuggle out Nina, Lucius, and Lysander, for no hostages must remain in Philip's hands when he discovered my flight. Lois would know nothing of our plans, so no harm would come to her.

One morning, as I came into Miriam's quarters hoping Seth would be there, I found with him my husband's steward in charge of his flocks. I recognized the curly hair and mild eyes of John, for we had met several times during morning audiences Philip often held in his bedchamber. I had liked him at once; he seemed near my own age. He came from Capernaum, and Philip valued his knowledge and skill greatly, often calling on him for advice.

"See, here is your lovely shepherdess!" Seth announced in a low voice that would not carry outside the room, full of high good humor.

John turned to me and bowed graciously as he had in Philip's presence, "Good morning, my lady. Will you, then, drive the tetrarch's prize yearling lambs to Jerusalem for the festival of the solstice?"

I was mystified by the question, and incredulous to find an ally in Philip's steward. Then I understood they had a plan for our escape.

"How can you do this without bringing disaster on yourself?"

"Lady, my people are of the soil. I serve the Mother. I have had my fill of the intrigues of a royal house. I will not return to Caesarea Philippi, and the tetrarch will receive word of my accidental death. Failing that, and his arm be long enough to reach me, I have chosen for what I am willing to die." He knelt and reverently kissed the hem of my gown, in the traditional gesture of homage to the Magdalene. It was the first moment I believed I would wear the robes of the High Priestess.

14

Nazareth

To everything there is a season, a time for every purpose under heaven.

Ecclesiastes 3:1, KJV

From the day of my first meeting with John, the time until Lois's delivery had dragged endlessly, until, only a week before the winter solstice, after an exhausting labor that spanned two days, she was successfully delivered of a great and lusty curly-headed son.

"Blessed be the midwife of Scarios!" the women said. Without Miriam, Lois had surely died herself this time, with her infant. When she was certain all would be well with the mother and child, Miriam and her son, the counselor, departed with their considerable retinue for Jerusalem. All was then in order for our flight, since there could be no suspicion we were concealed in Miriam's party.

It had all been so easy, when it finally happened. I cuddled deeper into blankets smelling of cedar, hugging Salome close. She was trying not to wake up, because our morning snuggles were her favorite time. She had fallen asleep almost at once, tired from her long journey with Nana, but I had been too overwrought to sleep.

Nana and Salome had been two days on their journey when Nina, Lucius, Lysander, and I, in rough shepherd's clothes, passed through the gates of Caesarea Philippi with written orders from Philip's steward of flocks, John. Outside the city, in a copse of cedar trees, we met the four real shepherds attired as peasants on the road to Jerusalem in a hay wagon. We exchanged clothing with them, trading Philip's lambs for the wagon, and continued to Capernaum, resting that night at the home of John's parents, Patricia and Sebedeh. Next day, yesterday, following the shore of the Sea of Galilee, we reached Nazareth and were reunited with Nana and Salome at the home of Joseph.

Our gentle host divided his time between the peaceful village life in his home at Nazareth—ably managed by Sarah, wife of his eldest son, James—and the palatial apartments of his own illustrious wife in the Temple at Jerusalem. Joseph suffered with painful knots on his hands, so he no longer did woodworking, but his two elder sons, James and Jude, still plied their carpenters' trade from the shop adjoining the house in Nazareth.

"Do not suppose my hospitality can protect you from Herod Antipas," Joseph had warned me as we sat before his hearth last evening. "Galilee is full of unrest, spies and treachery. The rebels—Zealots—command these hills; they raid and disappear at will." He leaned earnestly forward from his seat before the fire. "Antipas is trying to play both sides against the middle. It profited him for a time because his position gave him an in with both the Romans and the rebels, so he played them off against each other, to his own advantage. But when Caesar replaced the officer of Palestinian affairs who was taking his bribes in Rome—Sejanus was his name—Antipas found the tables turned on him as well." I could see this had not displeased Joseph, as he went on. "The new minister let him know that he would be held to account for the unrest in his domain, and if he could not put down the rebels and maintain the peace, a Roman procurator would."

"But Antipas hates Philip!" I protested.

"True, they are bitter rivals since childhood. But neither is so foolish as to let his feelings undermine their alliance. I wager Philip has already asked Antipas to search for you. Antipas will rush to aid his brother. The ownership of wives they agree upon."

"Philip may not have missed me so soon." My optimism was based on months with no contact from my husband except court gossip. "When I told my friend Lois good-bye—she would never have forgiven me otherwise—I warned her not to ask after me and to discourage others who might, as much as risked not her own safety."

"You are too hopeful, Mari," Nina warned. "There is enough spiteful jealousy about that place to make sure the alarm was raised the first moment."

I knew Nina was right, and we decided to leave the next morning for Jerusalem. The sooner we were quit of Antipas's territory the better.

Joseph agreed. "Remember, Herod Antipas travels often between Tiberias and Jerusalem; his men are everywhere coming and going." He snorted in disgust. "That fawning lap dog of Caesar has bled the people dry to raise his capital at Tiberias, filling it with hot baths and whatnot to attract the rich for the summer season. He has spared himself no comfort or delight there, yet he yokes the people besides with that Babylonian monstrosity at Jerusalem!"

"Philip and Antipas learned their extravagant ways in Rome," I agreed. "Philip also slavishly seeks the favor of Caesar, just as Herod did. Antipas will doubtless move to Jerusalem for the winter festival, as you say. But I had rather meet him in Samaria or Judea than in his own lands. Even if he has Herod's palace in Jerusalem, he is not tetrarch there. We will be careful, I promise."

I kissed the brown cheek above his white beard. He looked worn and tired beyond his fifty-odd years. I recognized unwillingly the mark of the Dark Goddess upon him. I wondered about Almah Mari, more than twenty years younger than her husband. Almah must be getting older too. I tried to imagine signs of age on that perfect face.

When Salome and I arose we found the others busily preparing for our departure. Our late breakfast of bread, cheese, and figs was interrupted by a commotion in the courtyard.

"Where is she?" The voice was unmistakable. I dropped my bread on the floor in my haste to gain the doorway.

"Almah! Almah, Almah!" We were clasped in each other's arms. Laughing and crying, I tried to ask why Almah had made the long journey from Jerusalem just as we were about to go there. "I didn't know—Joseph didn't say—why did no one tell me you were coming?" Nana was waiting to embrace her stepmother, so I gave Almah up to her and hugged Nina in celebration. But I could not take my eyes off Almah, as radiant with life and youth as her husband was aging and worn.

Almah disengaged herself from the happily chattering women and went to her husband, to bow before him in the formal Jewish tradition, which allowed no open display of affection between husband and wife. But Joseph stepped forward and interrupted her. "Nay, Mari, bow not to me, nor any man, for none is your master." His gnarled hands on her shoulders, he greeted her as brothers greet each other, with a warm kiss on each cheek.

"Soldiers, madame!" Lucius's alarm was a command. Hoofbeats and the clanging of armor were followed by harsh voices of men outside. Three men in the Romanized gear of Antipas's soldiers tramped across the courtyard to the doorway. I saw no more because Lucius picked me up like a small child and bore me swiftly into the back rooms of the house. "Stay, madame!" he commanded, and I obeyed, straining my ears to listen. All I could hear over the loud beating of my heart and Lucius's guarded breathing were muffled voices in a conversation that went on for some time.

"Where is Salome?" I demanded, suddenly afraid that Philip might be seeking her rather than myself. "You must go and find her!"

"She is with Nina, hiding as we are," he told me softly. "Listen, madame! If we cannot escape and you are taken with the child, Lysander and I have a plan—" He was interrupted by Joseph, who came into the small storeroom looking anxious but relieved.

"They are gone, but we must leave at once." He smiled into my worried face. "My wife has filled them with fear and awe, but they will be back."

Everyone came crowding into the little storeroom, still whispering, though the soldiers had gone. Quivering with excitement, Salome fastened her arms around my neck. "What did the soldiers want, Mamma? Why are we hiding?" I could not think how to tell my child we were hiding from her father. I wanted to ask Almah what she had told Antipas's men, but dared not frighten Salome further.

"We must go on to Jerusalem, or we will miss the great festival," I told my little girl. "Go with Nana and Mene and make your things ready."

During the flurry of preparations, I was puzzled to see Almah giving earnest instructions to two purple-robed attendants, who accepted a sealed scroll from her hand, mounted black horses with Temple livery of purple and gold, and sped back toward Capernaum and Caesarea. Alone with Almah in her carriage at last, I was able to ask, "May I know, please, where you have sent yonder priests, and with what message?"

Almah's eyes were dancing with mischief. "Oh, do you mean Raphael and Gabriel, my guardian angels?" Then, suddenly contrite, she patted my hand. "Dear Mari, I cannot bear to tease you. You have gone through enough already. No, they are Japheth and Matthias. I have sent them to your husband demanding he release you from your marriage vows."

I was speechless. "How did you—? What did you—? Why? I didn't tell you. How did you know?" Then I realized none of this was beyond the powers of Miriam of Scarios. "Miriam! Of course!" I cried. "How did she smuggle the message to you? It must have taken more than one to make all these arrangements. How did you acomplish it?" I stopped. Almah was listening curiously and would not offer to speak unless I stopped. I felt ashamed at having assumed so much.

"Darling Mari, I trust you are not too unhappy to leave your life at Caesarea Philippi? As your High Priestess, I have the authority to request your presence at Jerusalem when it is needed. I asked Miriam to arrange for your secret departure from Philip's court because I did not trust him to let you go, though he was sworn to obey the terms of your marriage agreement." She patted my hand again and said with great tenderness, "I am sorry for what happened to your friend Deidre." Her eyes were gentle and all-knowing. It slowly came to me that Almah had reasons of her own for wanting me back in Jerusalem.

I held my tongue, bursting with questions, until Almah spoke again.

"I have decided to retire. Yeshua will be studying in Egypt for several years, and it is time for me to be with him." I stared into her face, scarcely believing what I heard. "I shall spend one year teaching you your duties as Magdalene; then I shall go."

"Why did Miriam not tell me this?" I managed finally, trying to calm my racing thoughts. I dared not ask why Seth had played on my feelings, raising my hopes that we might be together if I would leave Philip. I had always suspected that Almah read my thoughts as easily as Nina did, but if it was so, as always, she chose not to let me know.

"I asked Miriam only to ascertain for me that you would be willing to leave Caesarea Philippi. I did not want you to come out of duty if your happiness lay with Philip."

"So she could not tell me your plans and be sure I was leaving of my own will?" I nodded slowly, wishing to be convinced. Seth had almost told me, I thought. He had made doubly sure I would leave willingly, with his flattering words and his charm.

I shook my head, half disbelieving. I would be Magdalene, as John had said, as Seth had known. But the more I puzzled about it, the more I wondered. Miriam and Seth, not just together, but separately, had worked to bring this about for purposes I did not understand. Each had been willing to serve Almah's wishes, I was sure, because doing so furthered plans of their own.

But surely I was being foolish, I thought again, looking into Almah's beloved face. I would have come at once had she simply asked me. I would do anything for Almah, anything.

15

The Temple

The Law was the tree. It had power to give knowledge of good and evil. It neither removed them from evil, nor set them in the good, for it created death for those who ate of it. For, "Eat this and do not eat that," became the beginning of death.

Gospel of Philip

Since childhood, I had thrilled to the bright banners bearing the lion, sign of the solar god, the son of the Great Goddess. The festival of the birth of the Sun, or Son, was a celebration of nativity, a time of special attention to children and honor to mothers. My earliest memories of the festival were its commemoration in my parents' home. We always went to Jerusalem for the sacred rites, taking our gifts for the holy child, and returned home to feast with our relatives. We children were given small gifts, a tool or implement to mark some milestone in our growing abilities—a spindle, knife, or leather pouch. We had celebrated the festival in the dance and song of sacred ritual during my childhood in the Temple and kept it among ourselves in Caesarea Philippi. Now we kept the sacred time once more in the Temple, with my little daughter and Deidre's Mene. Watching the wonderful preparations through their innocent eyes made me a child again. Caught up in the freshness and delight of their vision, I was almost able to keep from thinking about Seth—except when I was alone or trying to sleep. He and Miriam were guests at the palace of Herod Antipas, and there was little commerce between the palace and the Temple, so I had not seen or heard from them since their departure from Caesarea Philippi. I daily composed messages to him in my mind and each day persuaded myself to wait until after the holiday.

"You will need your own apartments now, Mari," Almah told me. "You will be studying and meditating constantly in preparation for you new office."

The cloister of the priestesses of Ashera was in all respects a large and well-appointed palace with several suites of spacious, elegant rooms for ranking priestesses and honored guests. Almah had chosen her mother's former apartments for me. The rooms had been empty since Anna's unexpected death from a fever two years before. She had remained in the Temple after Joachim died, though she had passed her office on to Almah some years before. She was always happy to fulfill the duties of High Priestess during her daughter's frequent travels to Egypt. Since her mother's death, Almah had felt imprisoned in Jerusalem; that was why she chose to forfeit her high position with its many obligations to me, next in the line of succession.

The elegant quarters now my own included a spacious sitting room opening on the great hall in front and bordered in back by a private garden. Through the garden danced a sparkling stream common to the other gardens in that part of the palace. Bordered by green ferns and moss, it was inhabited by jewel-bright fish and tiny frogs that sang joyfully. They fascinated Misha, the gray kitten Joseph had given Salome. Each sleeping room was a prayer room as well, with its own shrine, but the largest, where Salome and I slept, had a separate prayer room with soft rugs, where I could meditate undisturbed.

On the eve of the celebration, after many hours of practice and preparation, Salome and Mene had attained that height of excitement and exhaustion that children strive for on such days, resisting sleep with such zeal that they wore down Geshtinanna and me, even Nina. We bathed with my daughter and her half-brother in the opulent bath built by Herod, where pools inlaid with colored tiles varied from cold to hot. I soaked in the hottest one until I was pink and limp. We rubbed each other with perfumed oil and bound our wet hair in linen towels, then ran barefoot and laughing through the chilly galleries, lifting the children between us by their hands over the cold marble floor.

Still warm from the perfumed water, I spread my damp hair over the pillow and snuggled into bedclothes smelling of sandalwood and lavender. Salome fell asleep almost at once, with Misha purring in the curve of her neck. I tucked the blanket over her shoulders lightly—she perspired if she was too warm—and sighed heavily. Ever present thoughts of Seth took possession of my mind and senses. I scolded myself for being so foolish many times a day, but I could not deny myself for long. The thought of him was dearer than sleep. I sighed again, a long sobbing breath, exquisite with suffering love.

"Ah, Mari, that such sighs might be for me!" His low voice, scarce more than a whisper, not two steps from my bed, brought me upright, face to face with him in the dark.

"What are you doing here?" Even in my surprise I had the presence of mind not to waken Salome. How dared he presume? But his breath was warm against my neck; his hands, cool and strong, pulled me from my bed so I stood before him in my nightdress. My head just fit beneath his chin. I embraced his waist, his beating heart against my cheek. Our joy seemed to expand and fill the whole earth, as if our delight were one with everything—home and family and friends, the Temple, the city, the world, the seven levels of Heaven and of Hell.

"Mari." He took my face between his hands, kissing my forehead, my eyes, and then my lips. But Salome was in my bed.

"Wait." I put my finger to his lips, went around the bed, and scooped up my sleeping daughter. She nestled against me, warm, innocent. The kitten's eyes were golden slits in the darkness, questioning. I lowered Salome again and tucked Misha into her arms, then I carried her into Nana's room and placed her on the child's pallet beside Mene. Nana sat up, her face gently curious in the light from the window. "It's all right," I whispered, covering the children.

I left them and returned to my lover, opening the neckline of my gown as I went. Seth reached out his arms to me as I closed the door of my chamber. I let my gown fall around my feet. He dropped his long robe. I pulled gently at his tunic until he unfastened the wide band holding it at his waist.

"You smell wonderful." He kissed my throat, shed the last of his clothing. I pulled him into my fragrant bed.

It was my first experience with the true pleasures of love. My romantic imagination had prepared me to enjoy making love with Philip, but he had always finished before my passion was fully aroused. I knew there was more to be expected, and the talk of the other wives confirmed his lack of skill, but I suspected the delights of the marriage bed were romantically overrated. I had never lacked for pleasure from my own wise fingers, and I supposed all men to be as insensitive as my husband had been.

I should have known that Seth, who drew the last drop of delight from every experience, would match the lover of every romantic tale. I did not know how or where he had learned the arts of love—Aphrodite herself must have taught him—but I did not care.

"How did you come here, past the guards, from Herod's palace?" I asked dreamily, after a long time. We lay full length against each other, our flesh singing.

He laughed low. "There is a hidden passage from Antonia into the Temple. I bribed a guard to show me." I knew he smiled in the dark. "I can do it as often as you like."

I caught my breath. "Why should you take such risks to be with me? I am no longer wife to Philip Herod. I can take you as my consort if we both wish it."

He murmured with his lips against my forehead, "Would you wish it, Mari?"

"To take you as my husband?" I leaned over him, my damp hair a fragrant tent around our faces. "Oh, dearest Seth, would you? Will you be my husband?"

"Your Tammuz?" he chuckled softly. I saw the flash of his white teeth in the darkness. "Your Dumuzi? Nay, sweet Mari. I am not the husband for the Magdalene."

"You are most fit of all men to be husband to the Magdalene!" I persisted.

"You do me too much honor," he protested. "Brave, beautiful Mari, your destiny is not with me." He pulled my face down to meet his lips, stopping my words with kisses, driving all thoughts from my mind.

We slept little that night, and he left before morning by the same hidden passage. I spoke no more to him of marriage, but I asked breathlessly as he left me, "Will you come again?"

"Nothing could keep me away!" I lay back on the rumpled bed, a lovely weariness in my limbs. Surely he would wed the Magdalene. What man would not if he could? It would be unthinkable to refuse such an honor. He was just teasing, tantalizing me. I had forgotten to ask him all the questions that had been in my mind since I talked with Almah that day on the way to Jerusalem. Somehow, now they seemed less important. I vowed I would take Seth as my husband, or I would take no husband at all.

But he continued to put off my questions about marriage, first gently, and then obstinately, though he came nightly to my bed, and our rapture was such as the gods might envy. When the spring storms abated and Miriam made preparations to sail, I begged him to stay, and he consented, though he would not agree to wed. I would not take his refusal seriously.

By this time, the whole household knew of his presence, and their amusement at his strange taste for secrecy was a good-natured joke even I shared. Certain we would soon be married, I was eager to present him to Almah, confident she would like and approve of him.

"There will be plenty of time for that later," he said, and he put me off as the weeks passed. When I pressed him, he would disappear for several days, and I was so glad when he returned I would say nothing. I swallowed my growing hurt and anger, unwilling to spoil our pleasure in being together.

Spring passed into summer, and I was overworked training for my new duties and preparing for my coronation. Being with Seth eased my apprehension about the heavy responsibility I was to assume, so I was reluctant to drive him away again. I invited him to move openly into my rooms, to live as my consort without the ceremony of marriage, certain he would offer to wed as a gesture of equal generosity. He would think about it, he said, but he would wish to come and go freely, to travel as his profession demanded, when, where, and for however long he might wish. He went to Egypt, then, for nearly six months, to organize a partnership between two wealthy merchants.

The elaborate preparations for my installation as High Priestess of the Goddess intensified during those months Seth was gone, and I became more and more uneasy. My inability to accept the decrees of the gods—even the Mother, though she had appeared to me—made me increasingly certain I was unfit to assume office as her representative. I longed for another reassuring talk with Miriam, but she was gone. I began to notice that my doubts seemed to manifest themselves as the headaches that plagued me for three or four days at a time several times every month. Almah had reassured me when I spoke to her earlier, so I did not want to worry her again, but my resolve was worn down by my suffering, and at last I could bear it no longer.

"Please, dear Almah," I sobbed—I had broken into tears the moment I tried to speak my heart—"can you not see that I am no fit priestess to serve as Magdalene?"

Almah's lucid gaze was undismayed. "Because you have sometimes felt anger against the Mother?" she demanded. "Mari, answer me. Do you think Salome has ever felt anger at you?"

I faltered, sinking into the pillows of the divan.

"Do you love your daughter less or feel less responsible for her because she has a mind to think for herself?" Almah insisted. "Has the Mother ever demanded that you always love her, or that you blindly believe in her? She asks only that you care for her children. Could you ever do less?" She asked the last question severely, and then relented. "I think not," she answered herself, sitting down beside me, taking my hand. "No true God demands mindless belief and punishes the honesty of those who admit their doubt. The Mother knows you must doubt, to understand, to grow in wisdom. Do not be ashamed of your doubts, Mari. They prove your devotion to the Law."

"But the Law *is* the Mother," I said.

"Just so." She smiled.

I confess that I took her at her word because I wanted to believe her, to please her. The headaches eased after that, but they did not disappear.

Seth was still away at the time of the winter festival when I was made High Priestess of Isis-Ashera at Jerusalem. My parents beamed with pride and my heart was full, but becoming a Magdalene is a heady experience; I needed Seth's down-to-earth good sense to keep my feet on the ground. He had abandoned me when I needed him most. I nursed my anger, rehearsing the scoldings I would give him, but when he returned after Almah had departed for Alexandria, I knew his presence by my side was all I wanted in the world. I repeated my invitation to him to live as my consort, without marriage, and he accepted willingly, but he reminded me of the conditions he had outlined before.

I did not quibble about terms. He gave me such happiness I could deny him nothing. He was so young; it was hardly strange he did not wish to be tied in strings. Let him go as much as he liked, I thought. He would come back to me.

Like his namesake, the creator of this material round, the grand artificer who enticed spirit into matter and trapped it there, Seth enticed me into pleasure and delight—of the flesh, yes, but more than that. The everyday life of the Temple, the sunshine on a spring day, fresh shellfish in season, the mock battles of Misha's kittens, the children we cared for and instructed; every ordinary thing was to him extraordinary, a source of wonder, of joy. And it was with Seth that I became beautiful. I had been taught that my body was good, taught to reverence it as the temple of the Goddess. But Seth showed me it was beautiful. I was beautiful. I could give and enjoy pleasure beyond imagining, and it was meet and right to do so.

"Does it upset you that the stiff-necked Pharisees call you 'the Great Harlot' and the 'Whore of Babylon?'" he asked me some time after I had become Magdalene. We lay together in my bed.

"Does it upset *you*, my love?"

"Truly. I am sorry to be the cause of it."

"Would you wish instead for another to be the cause of it?" I turned my face to his as I lay on his arm.

"You know better."

"It pleases me to learn you have a conscience, though not so strong a one as would make you my husband."

"Your tongue has the sting of a serpent, my love."

"Forgive me, sweetheart; it was evil of me to speak so!" I stroked his face with my fingers. "I do not enjoy being called a harlot, nor do I think you to blame for it. Remember that Roman senator—Gallus, I think his name was—from the first night we met?" Seth nodded, as I traced my finger along the ridge of his eyebrow, his high cheekbone, the line of his jaw. "I remember he said something about the soul being imprisoned in the body, the evil of the body—all bodies."

"Breasts are evil?" Seth teased, "and pink bottoms?" catching a warm handful of each. We kissed, and I leaned my head on his shoulder. "Body and spirit are one thing, not two. But the enemies of the Mother set them apart, naming one good, the other evil, giving rise to shame," I thought aloud.

"They hate their own bodies, and they turn their shame on me." I leaned over him, pushing my hair off his face to see his expression. "That's it, isn't it?" I demanded.

"You are wonderful at doing philosophy in bed," he complimented pointedly.

"A woman," I insisted, "—any woman—by their thinking, is only flesh. She must be subject to spirit—a male—one man who makes her his possession; else she is a harlot. They have no other word for a free woman."

"If we were wed, you would not be free," he reminded me.

"Nay, love. I would yet be free, for I would choose you freely."

"Did you marry Philip freely then?" he wanted to know.

"Aye, and left him freely as well," I chuckled against his throat.

I recalled the day I was called into the presence of the Magdalene, Anna. Only fifteen, I had trembled when she told me Philip Herod wished to wed me in the spring rites.

"I was quite willing." I admitted.

"But he already had several wives!" Seth persisted.

"That is not so unusual, you know. I thought him rather attractive. He looked sullen—or bored."

"Jaded?"

"Maybe. He was about twenty-nine or thirty then—I suppose I saw him as some kind of romantic challenge." I marveled at my former innocence.

"Were you a virgin when you went to Philip's bed?"

"Why do you want to know?"

"So you were not! Wicked woman! I thought as much!" He nibbled at my ear. "Tell me, seductress, who ravished you, or I shall eat you up!"

"Eat me then!" I arched my body to his kisses. After some moments, he attempted a stern expression in the lamplight.

"Please tell me."

"Why?"

"I want to know who it was."

I smiled mysteriously. "It was the God," I said.

"The God?" Seth rolled his eyes heavenward. "All women say that!"

"But I am telling the truth," I insisted. "Do you want to know about it?"

"Were you really deflowered in a ceremony?" he asked delightedly. "Yes, tell me. I want to hear everything. Were you afraid?"

"Not as much as I was later of my marriage to Philip—leaving home and friends and everything familiar. We had always bathed naked together in groups and spoken freely of love. I was taught what to expect, though I had never known a man. But I was not virgin. That would have been against the custom."

"What custom, beloved?" His mouth was against my breast.

"The ancient taboo against the shedding of women's blood—"

He interrupted me. "The blood of women is sacred and has vengeful powers."

"Yes. The Great Mother fashioned the world and the bodies of the first humans from clay mixed with her menstrual blood. That magical force is also in the blood of the hymen—far too powerful a curse for a mortal man to bear. So the hymen of each virgin is offered to the Goddess in her coming-of-age ceremony, pierced on the stone phallus of the sacred statue of the god."

"And so it was with you? Were you frightened, beloved? Did it hurt you?"

His eyes glinted in the lamplight. How dear he was to ask it of me. I looked back to my girlhood.

"I was dressed in a white bridal gown, garlanded with wild asters and yellow thistle. We sang the hymn to Dumuzi at the ripening ceremony of each maiden on her fourteenth birthday, so everyone knew the words and music by heart:

> Inanna opened the door for her bridegroom.
> Inside the house she shone before him
> Like the light of the moon.
>
> Dumuzi looked at her joyously.
> He pressed his neck close against hers.
> He kissed her.

"The music had meanings for me that grew each year with new understanding. Many times I had sung it to myself in my bed, my hands between my thighs—so," I showed him.

"So," he whispered.

"Once, when I was only three or four years old, my mother saw me thus in my bed," I moved my hips rhythmically.

"What did she do?"

"She just smiled at me and said, 'The gift of the Goddess, my child.'"

Seth chuckled against my breast. The hymn of Inanna had been next in the ceremony, and I said the verses to him softly.

> My vulva, the horn,
> The Boat of Heaven,
> Is full of eagerness like the young moon.
> My untilled land lies fallow.

As for me, Inanna,
Who will plow my vulva?
Who will plow my high field?
Who will plow my wet ground?

"I will plow your wet ground," he whispered, in the very words of the song, "when you have told me all."

"Two priestesses, Iris and Naomi, who had gone through the ceremony themselves the year before, led me by the hands. They caressed my arms and my waist and comforted me with soft whispers, as we approached the statue of the god. It must have been carved by a god, too. It was of sand-colored stone with streaks of white and red like flesh and blood and bone—more alive than life. The eyes looked down at me, heavy lidded, like a lover's; the curving lips smiled as though we shared some secret—we alone. The phallus stood erect in his lap, like the pistil of a flower, curved upward to a rounded point."

"You are wonderfully poetic!" Seth interjected. "Was it huge?"

"It was blessedly small for the size of his body, but it looked fearfully large to me. The High Priestess anointed it with sweet-smelling oil."

"Thou anointest my head with oil," Seth marked.

"You are right again, my love! Then the hymn was sung. I felt lifted up by it, lifted and borne away." Reaching down and caressing him with my hands, I chanted softly:

He has sprouted; he has burgeoned;
He is lettuce planted by the water.
He is the one my womb loves best.

"Iris helped me raise my skirts. My heart beat in time with the music as I straddled the lap of the god. It hurt only a little, but the pain was sweet. The women's hands pushed me gently down, down, until I held all of him within me. The love song of Inanna and Dumuzi was sung in my honor, sung for me."

"Will you sing it?" he whispered, not wanting to break my reverie.

"I will sing it to you, my love."

My honey-man, my honey-man sweetens me always.
My lord, the honey-man of the gods.
He is the one my womb loves best.
His hand is honey, his foot is honey,
He sweetens me always.

We held each other in bliss. I felt closer to him than I had ever felt to anyone. My mind and body were one as on that day, sanctified and worthy to represent the Goddess in the sacred act of love. I was wed forever to my soul's beloved, the ever-dying, ever-resurrected Lord of Life and Death. My blood pounded against the hard stone within me, and an aching pleasure filled my loins, spreading upward to my tingling breasts and downward to my wriggling toes. The song coursed through my veins with my blood—my blood was the song, beating in resonance with the rhythm of life, of the Mother. I was a woman, and the sacred rite was a celebration of life, of spirit that manifests as flesh. Spirit as flesh, flesh as spirit. Seth was for me the incarnation of the god, and our ecstasy a shower of stars.

PART 3

The Descent into Hell

In the midway of this our mortal life,
I found me in a gloomy wood, astray
Gone from the path direct: and e'en to tell,
It were no easy task, how savage wild
That forest, how robust and rough its growth,
Which to remember only, my dismay
Renews, in bitterness not far from death.
Yet, to discourse of what good there befell,
All else will I relate discovered there.

Dante, The Inferno

16

Magdelene

Who is this that looks forth like the dawn,
fair as the moon, bright as the sun,
terrible as an army with banners?
Song of Solomon

The measured slap of leather sandals on the stone floor and a mighty whoosh of purple robes heralded Nina's arrival. She advanced into my accounting room, exploding the calm afternoon with the vitality of her presence, her billowing skirts stirring up little whirlwinds of clay dust on the floor.

I looked up from my work to see her large and excellent white teeth bared in a scowl of distaste. "His Eminence, Herod Antipas, awaits without. He prays you grant him audience."

"Let him wait!" I turned back to my accounting, seeking to quiet my suddenly racing thoughts with the tedium of my task.

Hay and grain, flax and wool, Tyrian purple and olive oil, were credited and debited in neat columns of marks pressed into the damp clay. The priestesses of Ashera had turned to Egyptian paper and lampblack generations ago for letters and messages, but tradition held us to the use of the nearly imperishable clay tablets for keeping records. Using a wet thumb to erase an error, I carefully smoothed the cool clay before making a correction with the stylus.

In my eleven years as High Priestess in Jerusalem, I had tried to stay out of Antipas's sight—not from fear but distaste. I shrugged at the impossibility of it, brushing back a wisp of hair that had escaped the coil at my nape. What business could Antipas, tetrarch of Galilee and Perea, have with the Magdalene? My belly knotted, and perspiration dampened my forehead. I recognized the familiar onset of a headache and realized I had not had one for a long time. Anything to do with the Herodians still upset me, still brought back my old fear of losing Salome. I had been divorced from her father for twelve years now and had two healthy sons by Seth. Could it be so long?

Philip had hated his brother Antipas. Years before, when he was given his puppetship by Augustus Caesar, Antipas had tried to wrest away Philip's territory north of the Sea of Galilee to add to his own.

But I did not fear and hate Antipas for the sake of Philip; Salome's father had given me abundant reason to love his enemies. No, Herod Antipas was my own enemy, and the Mother's. I had never forgotten his mockery of my wedding to Philip—his eyes and hands had been everywhere; he had been obsessed with despoiling his brother's bride. I would always feel ill at ease with him; I strained to gather my wits about me. Thank the Goddess I was no longer wed to a Herodian! I need only remember poor Deidre, murdered even as Mariamne.

I called on that earlier Magdalene for her blessing. "Holy Mother Mariamne, guard me now against your old enemy!" Yea, the robes of Isis-Ashera were no protection from death, nor from fear. Mariamne had worn them to her execution. She wore them even before she became wife to Herod; her hand had been the key to his legitimacy with the people, though Caesar had appointed him ruler of all these lands. As for Herod, he had languished near death himself for more than two years after her execution, tormented by ghosts and nightmares, eaten alive by remorse. People said Mariamne was the only woman he ever loved.

Holy Mother! That people could take such jealousy for love. Well, Goddess be praised, Antipas was not *that* Herod, but his son—one of the three he did not kill. Not even Herod could mock the Law and escape; he had paid dearly in the end.

My belly knotted as Lucius and Lysander silently took their guard stations behind me. I turned resignedly and shook the dust from my skirts in a motion of distaste. Better to get this unpleasantness over with.

I picked up the heavy pendant of gold and amethyst that proclaimed my office and put it on, centering it on my white surplice. Beneath this, I wore a single length of purple linen with a slit in the center just large enough for my head. It was the width of my shoulders where it lay over them, but flared to twice that at the hem, which almost brushed the floor behind me, but was raised enough that I would not trip over it in front. Beneath all this I wore the long, one-piece garment of white linen with flowing sleeves. Over it all was a coat of purple wool, identical to those of the other priestesses, open in the front and fitted beneath the white surplice, clean each day to protect the garments beneath it from soil. I arranged my robes about me, repeating silently the mantra that centered my thoughts.

"I am ready," I told Nina. Her eyes were fierce as she pressed a cup of willow tea into my hand. I drank it down gratefully, thankful that she always knew my needs before I could ask, that she could sense danger even when I myself did not.

I moved from the accounting room into the more formal and elegant study. The floor stones here were of many colors, polished mirror-bright and laid in the intricate patterns of those in Arabian palaces. The ornate shutters of white linen stretched behind carved grillwork admitted bright light even when they were closed. In winter, outer frames of waxed canvas were added for warmth except on the warmest afternoons, when we could open them and let in the welcome rays of the sun. The walls were hung with priceless tapestries, and there were art objects both ancient and in the latest fashion, for the priestesses of the Goddess held great wealth.

The light from the tall double doors was diminished and the quiet of the afternoon broken by the clatter of arms as Herod Antipas strode forward flanked by bodyguards. I regretted that I was not seated on the high dais in my formal chambers. From there I could have looked down upon him from a more comfortable distance. Only the delicate writing table with its fragile rolls of papyri was between us. It comforted me to know that the two eunuchs behind me wore breastplates and carried arms beneath their priests' robes.

But the tetrarch of Galilee and Perea bowed in perfect ease, and his dark face with its ringleted mustaches was all humility and friendliness.

"My dear sister, you are most gracious to receive me. I am deeply honored to see you again. To look upon your beauty refreshes my eyes as the sight of water to one lost in a desert!"

His effrontery at calling me his sister changed a half measure of my chill into heat. I saw that the years had turned him more to his father's looks than Philip's. Like old Herod's, Antipas's form was massive, powerful; his oversized head seemed small on its thick neck, hunched between heavy shoulders above a barrel chest. The black beard, oiled and curled, could not conceal his heavy jowls, which jiggled and vibrated with every word. Beneath black brows that met over a long hooked nose, his dark eyes glared. His thick lips, always wet, drooled insatiably. I had never seen Herod, father of Antipas and Philip, but I was certain this was how he had looked.

He bowed before me ingratiating as a puppy. Elegantly attired in the Greek manner, he wore only a few large gems on a band about his neck. I guessed he had underdressed, not to overwhelm me. I took refuge in my role as High Priestess and nodded coolly in acknowledgment of his greeting. I would have to give up the shelter of the writing table and offer him a seat. I crossed the Persian carpet with deliberate slowness, seated myself regally in an exquisite Greek chair before the courtyard terrace, and inclined my head toward another. The two soldiers backed off toward the door at some sign he gave them, but Lucius and Lysander moved nearer to me. Antipas scowled at them, but he could hardly ask me to send them away. He seated himself and leaned toward me, addressing me by my title of honor.

"Holy Mother," he began, dropping to one knee and kissing the hem of my gown, "I come in supplication. Grant me your favor." He remained bowed for some time, then raised his eyes, soft as his velvet voice. He launched into an oratory of flattery; never had my beauty been so lavishly praised, nor my generosity so amplified. Finally, he came round to his business.

"My people honor and love you, dear lady," he said. "Your recognition and support of me will give them great happiness. It will strengthen both our houses. Why should we not be allies and friends, since we both desire only the good of our people?"

Then I knew, and so incredible it was that Herod should require my endorsement, the right to rule that only the Goddess can bestow, that I almost laughed aloud with relief. Then, with a sick feeling, I saw that I could not easily refuse to do what he asked, and he knew it. He had ruled as the puppet of Rome for twenty-five years and never cared for the approval of the Goddess. Why now? If he desired the Sacred Marriage with a priestess of the Goddess to gain credentials with the people, it seemed a generous gesture on his part, almost an accommodation to the sentiments of his subjects, for he was ruler in any case.

Antipas was not content with the power he enjoyed, as was Philip. He was ambitious. He had never accepted the overturning of his father's last will, which would have deeded the whole kingdom to him. That Herod had come round to that will through a bloody process of elimination, accusing each of his sons of plotting against him and executing them one by one until only three remained, did not make it less binding in Antipas's eyes. But Caesar had held that only Herod's first will, the one registered in the courts of Rome and guarded by vestal virgins, was valid. And so he gave Samaria and Judea, with twice the land and twice the revenue of Antipas's kingdom, to Archelaus, who lost it in only a few years through foolishness and mismanagement. Antipas had raged like a wild ox when Caesar assigned the lands he believed rightfully his own to a Roman procurator. I suspected that he still nurtured some devious plan to win them for himself. The favor he might gain with the people of the Mother would be an asset to him, and I wanted anything but that. Still, I could think of no legal or customary grounds to refuse his request. I lowered my shoulders deliberately to ease the tension in my neck.

To match him unbeknownst to a false priestess, one known to have broken her vows, would be a sign the people could read. "I will think on the matter," I told him.

"There is little time for thinking, lady, the ceremonial day is but two Sabbaths away. I would have you represent the Goddess, yourself."

I struggled to keep my composure, groping for words that would be firm, yet not offend. The sheer presumption of his proposal was staggering, but I saw it at once for what it was—an attack on the people of the Mother. My voice sounded far away and surprisingly calm when I answered him.

"It is out of the question. I have no obligation to serve in the sacred rite except by my own choice."

"Ah, yes, you bed only the Scariot, so often seen with his friends of the Sicarii!" Saliva glistened on his thick lips as he smiled. He had executed many of the Sicarii and the Zealots for treason. It was true Seth had friends among them. Antipas was enjoying himself. He had reached the point of his visit.

I felt as if I were bleeding inside, and I fought to keep him from seeing it. I knew my unwed state was a source of dissention among my people that he would use against me. From ancient times, High Priestesses had remained unwed by tradition, taking a different consort each year, but memory was short, and I had been preceded in office by two Magdalenes who had maintained long and stable marriages. Antipas's sneer was but an echo of that of the priesthood of Jehovah. They had no place in their thinking, not even a name—except whore or harlot—for a woman without a husband, who bore her children outside the protection of marriage, as I had borne our two sons, Seth's and mine. I had long been outraged at the injustice of their judgment, but I could see well enough that my willfulness provided my enemies a weapon against me. I felt a familiar flash of anger at Seth. I would have wed him willingly, had begged him in the beginning, but he had continually put me off, and my pride had not let me bring up the matter for years.

Herod Antipas snorted in satisfaction. "Your concern for your traitorous lover will turn your choice in my favor," he jeered, his thick jowls shaking beneath their black curls. "We two shall make a noble pair of celebrants in honor of the Goddess, Mari Magdalene!" He dared to call me by the name he had once used to taunt me.

"Little Mari Magdalene!" he had wagged, when as his brother's wife I refused his advances repeatedly, "What is so sacred about whoring? Or a whore's marriage? Temple harlot! Abomination!"

Antipas had always flaunted his contempt of the Goddess and her ways. I knew the names of his several wives; he had divorced some of them. He kept a large harem as well, and took by force any maiden he saw to his liking. Yet he would pass judgment on me! Out of the red haze of my anger I heard my own voice, "Why is it you desire this thing?"

He dropped all pretense. I saw the naked hatred in his eyes, the deep fear and dread of the Mother, the desire to humiliate and possess her.

"I will have my way," he hissed, his black mustaches vibrating like locusts. "The Magdalene shall do my will before all the people! You shall serve me, lady! Everyone shall see who has power in Jerusalem! Look to it!" He turned and strode out, followed by his bodyguards.

17

Judas of Scarios

Your "self" is nonexistent, knowing one!
Dream not your actions by yourself are done . . .
Nuruddin Abdur Rahman Jami

Nina's face was flushed and her voice had a sharp edge, but the strength she exuded was comforting. She had heard everything, or knew without hearing. "Mari, what will you do? Seth will never stand for this, and Antipas will surely kill him!"

"We must keep him from knowing. How, I don't know. And he will find out sooner or later anyway. What then?"

"He is strong in the ways of the Mother," Nina weighed the possibilities. Sparks of colored light seemed to fall away from her as she shook her head. "But he has learned too much of 'pride' and 'honor' from his friends," she snorted. "He lives for the moment and worries about its fruits when they are ripe." She turned toward the door. "I'll get you something stronger for your headache."

"He would sacrifice his life?" I knew the answer as I spoke. "Could I make him understand why I must give Antipas what he asks?" Nina continued shaking her head as she went out.

It was done then. I watched the dying light of the afternoon slide away from the urns of fragrant jasmine in the courtyard and sensed my own life fading with it. Antipas had already gained what he wanted, and he knew it. He had destroyed my life with Seth, our happiness, and with one blow. If I refused him, not only Seth but others, his friends and mine, would die. They would die almost as certainly if I honored his request, and Seth would never forgive me for granting the favor of the Mother to his sworn enemy. I pressed my hands tight against my temples as if their coldness could draw the heat and pain from the blood pounding there.

The angry whoosh of Nina's robes announced her return. She handed me a stoneware cup—we never mixed our herbs in silver, for the metal could turn a safe remedy into a lethal poison. I drank the bitter draught to the dregs. Nina took back the empty cup, weeping in stoic silence, making no effort to wipe away the copious tears that coursed down her cheeks. I felt an overwhelming affection for her, and I laughed with the sudden pleasure it gave me.

"Darling Nina, your tears are as generous as the rest of you! Do leave off, or you will drown me." I knew she wept from sympathy, not fear, but my own heart turned in its need to Almah. If only Almah were here!

But Almah Mari was still on caravan from Egypt. If not for her love of Egypt and all things Egyptian, Almah would still be Magdalene and I wasting away in Philip's harem. I wondered what Almah would do in the face of Antipas's threat. But Antipas could never reach Almah's husband, the gentle carpenter, who had died in Nazareth nearly ten years ago.

Then I remembered Yeshua, Almah's son. The sweetest target of Herodian wrath was returning with his mother from Egypt. The little Hasmonian prince who had escaped old Herod's slaughter was now of age, returning to claim his kingdom. My thoughts flew back to this morning when Nina had first burst in upon the silence of the accounting room.

"*He* is coming with her," she had announced momentously, and stood beaming at me, her prayer beads swinging in a wide arc against her white surplice.

"Who, Nina? Who is coming?" I stared blankly, caught in the middle of adding a sum in my head, stylus poised in my hand over damp clay.

"Yeshua, of course!" she crowed, clasping me in her strong arms and lifting me off my feet, transmitting the vital force she radiated like light. "He is coming with Almah—ahead of her—Lysander says."

"Yeshua! When?" I had returned Nina's hug with a squeal of delight, unseemly for a High Priestess. I would have jumped for joy, but my feet were dangling above the stone floor. "Mother of Elephants," I scolded her, "put me down."

"Lysander says tomorrow; early."

Regaining my footing, I dropped the stylus into a jar of water and rinsed the clay from my hands in a ceramic basin. Drying them on a stained linen towel, I tried to command my racing thoughts. Yeshua was coming at last; Almah Mari's son, the Promised One of Israel—*Osiris*.

"Shall we receive him at breakfast, then?" I wondered aloud, "or is that too early?" Nina had sailed out in search of provisions, purple banners streaming. She would see that all the arrangements were made, complete with alternate plans in case the son of Almah Mari and his party should arrive late.

Sunshine still illuminated the great reception hall, livening the rich colors of the tapestries that drank up the echoes of my footsteps as I passed through. I entered the tall double doorway to my chambers and sank into an inviting pile of soft cushions whose faces were mosaics of colored silk set together and embroidered in geometric designs. The faint meadow smell of cattail down, the most prized stuffing for pillows, teased my nostrils, and I sniffed, evoking sunshine, bird calls, and flowing water. I laid my cheek against a square of scarlet silk and closed my eyes, facing the little courtyard garden I planted and tended myself. The early warmth had brought forth bees, buzzing among the narcissus and daffodils, and the sweet sound of pipes came faintly from the schoolroom, teasing my senses. It was Seth. No one played the pipes as he did, like a breathing, living voice that spoke without words. I made my own breath deep and slow. The fragrant breeze caressed my face as I waited for the soothing effect of the headache potion; I imagined my fear and anger flowing from my neck and shoulders, down my arms, and out my ten fingers into the all-forgiving earth.

I think I slept for a few moments, and the piping stopped. Ninshubur appeared almost silently, her slippered footsteps muffled, her garments barely whispering. "My lady, your consort seeks audience." The informal title was a nicety that honored the Magdalene's right to take lovers as she chose. I had never exercised that right except in Seth's case, but I had performed the role of the Great Mother in the Sacred Marriage more than once during his long absences from my side. It was my duty—not an unpleasant one—and it stated publicly that I, the Magdalene, was not the sexual property of my inconstant lover, nor of any man.

I arose, a little dizzily, and went to meet him. My dark imaginings had made him dearer. Eagerness sparkled like golden rays about him; he was bursting to share something momentous with me, but he accepted my fervent embrace as good fortune. Suntanned and clean-shaven, his curly chestnut hair cut short in the Greek manner, Seth was so comely it was no wonder all the young women in the College of Virgins were in love with him. But it was not only his appearance that drew attention. He had a power. A power I acknowledged but could not name. People listened to him, and followed him. Wherever he went, he led; whatever he said was taken for wisdom, whatever he praised was loved, what he denounced, hated. Yet he put his gifts to no great purpose. Had he been so minded, he could easily have ruled a kingdom of his own; but he was no king, and kings found him dangerous.

He did not appear so now, I thought, as Shaher and Shalem discovered him and came running from the next room where they were telling stories with Nina. He knelt to match their height, scooping them up and lifting one to each shoulder, then he whirled until they squealed with delight. He dropped them both, catching them just in time, flipping each in a somersault. Gasping with joy, they turned to beg for more, but he silenced them with a look. "Go and get ready for music lessons," he commanded.

Shaher went willingly, but Shalem held his short arms up to me, and I took him and kissed him, fondling his curls. Seth gave the boys their lessons himself. He was skilled with both the pipes and the strings. He taught them their letters, and mathematics, and to write poems and songs. Small wonder they moped and misbehaved whenever he was away. Now he seemed eager to speak to me alone, so I nudged our youngest son and sent him after his brother.

"Mari, I have met Yeshua!" Seth exclaimed. "There was something so amazing . . . so strange in the way he looked at me; in his face I thought I saw myself." His eyes still glowed with the astonishment of which he spoke. "But I cannot explain it to you; you must see it."

I smiled and nodded, hoping he would not see my growing despair. I had not seen Almah's son since the time she had brought him to the Temple when he was six. I remembered his merry laughter and golden eyes — eyes too great and too wise for his child's face — the fragrance of the rose he had placed in my hand, and his childish words, "I love you, Mari." I looked at the front of my gown, suddenly remembering the red stain.

Everyone said Yeshua had the legendary features of the Hasmoneans, but I often thought how like him my own Shaher looked with his red-brown curls, the narrow bridge of his fine nose, and especially his eyes. They were like Seth's, of course, big and wide open with long, thick lashes. Both Shaher's and Yeshua's had been blue in babyhood and slowly darkened to hazel. By the first birthday, they were brown sparked with gold. How strange that Seth, too, and now our sons, had the famous look of the Hasmonean princes.

"In the morning, he will breakfast with us," Seth was saying. "Whatever you have to do, it cannot be more important. Please, Mari!" He kissed me joyfully, never doubting I would be pleased, not seeing I was too distracted to think. For his own sake, I had to conceal Antipas's design from him. "Is something amiss?" he wanted to know. "I should have spoken to you! Dearest Mari, forgive me, I was too eager, sure you would wish it as much as I . . ." I stopped his lips with kisses.

"I do wish it, love; we have sent him invitation as well. I'm so pleased you persuaded him to come. There must be many demands on him." But Seth's questioning frown remained; his eyes searched into me. I smoothed the folds of his linen tunic where they fell away from the strong pillar of his neck, felt the comfort of his steady pulse throbbing there. "I am sorry, my love, to bring my cares with me," I told him truthfully. "I'm afraid I have let an afternoon audience upset me. You are right when you say I am too tenderhearted for my office."

"Not for your office, but for yourself," he corrected. "It is fitting the Magdalene should serve with compassion, as the Mother is compassionate. You serve her perfectly, as you well know." He marked the last with a gentle kiss, and I leaned into his strength, closing my eyes, resting my head on his shoulder.

Was Seth's destruction the real purpose of Antipas's plan? Or just a welcome consequence of my humiliation? It was so hard not to tell him my fears, most of all, not to warn him. I had never lied to him, never wished to. But I could not confide in him now and hope to save his life. Thank the Mother he did not, like Nina, read my mind! Still, he came near it at times.

Blaming my preoccupation on a petition to the Temple, I evaded further questions, since petitions were confidential. I feared my answer had not satisfied him, and I planned to distract him with lovemaking, but by bedtime my headache had progressed to a dizzying nausea, and I lay miserable by his side, sleepless, watching the white moonlight move across our bed, turning his sleeping face to sculptured marble.

The Dark Night

One prays for the life of tomorrow
Ephemeral life though it be.
This is the habit of mind
That passed away yesterday.
Master Ikkyu

Long after Seth slept, I lay awake — my head throbbing — searching for a solution to Antipas's threat against my life and happiness. Miriam was in Jerusalem to attend the confinement of the procurator's wife and had joined us for supper last night. If it had been difficult to deceive Seth, it was impossible to fool his mother.

"May we two spend some time together tomorrow afternoon?" she asked, seeing we had no chance to talk that evening. I would tell it all to her then. But what could she do? What could anyone do?

I slipped out of bed and went into my prayer room. The moonlight flooding through the high windows left no need to light the lamps. I knelt before the shrine and bent my head upon my knees, as I had done so often. "Blessed Mother, help me," I prayed, and waited for her peacefulness to ease the painful tension in my body.

Slowly, the image of the Goddess reappeared in my mind, as she had been when she had come to me so many years ago — fresh as morning, glorious, invincible. "You shall be of special help to me," she said. To serve her was surely the grandest of all destinies. But why had the Mother chosen to favor me? I, who still struggled against doubt even as I wore the robes of High Priestess? The power of her presence reassured me. Against her Antipas seemed impotent, insignificant, as nothing. Still, a small voice questioned, warned: It is all in my own mind—what I want to believe. But I pushed it away.

I willed myself to be comforted and calmed as I returned to my lover, who reached out and gathered me close even as he slept. I breathed the clean smell of his body, drawing his warmth into my chilled limbs. The powers that had brought us together in such joy could only be benevolent, I reasoned against the stubborn little voice, and would never force upon us the pain of separation. So I lulled my soul, but the Mother had not finished with me.

When I slept at last, the Dream returned like a howling wind out of Hell, dragging me down, down, into that dank and gloomy world, assaulting my every sense, filling my nostrils with the stench of decay and my mouth with the taste of mold. Though darkness surrounded me, I felt mocking, unseen eyes witness to my grief. I strained to throw back my head and wail out my sorrow, but I could not move or speak.

This time, perhaps because my fears for my own love had helped me to realize it, I knew clearly that what I sought in the dream and so dreaded to find was the body of Osiris, or the dismembered pieces of it. I felt the Goddess's terrible determination to recover all the parts of her beloved, despite her horror and dread. I stopped struggling to awaken and escape the dream. Instead, I was able to feel beyond it—or within the depths of it—my own involvement in some truth I could, as yet, little understand. I saw that in being allowed to participate in the suffering of the Goddess, I was highly favored. I waited, deeply awed, in a state of deep suffering and exaltation, until the dream released me.

When I was able to move, I once more arose, and freed myself gently from Seth's embrace. The violence of my visitation had not awakened him; he slept untroubled as a child. Not stopping for slippers or robe, I padded barefoot into my sanctuary and prostrated myself before the shrine. I staggered with weariness, but the priestess in me knew that I had been chosen for some purpose beyond myself. Those concerns that had appeared monumental only hours ago now seemed trivial and empty, a vanity of vanities, a rushing after wind.

For a long time I lay, savoring the blessing thrust upon me. The little questioning voice was not stilled, but it watched, waiting and wondering. I did not even articulate my thankfulness, but waited, open, receptive to whatever thoughts the Goddess might send me.

I would tell Almah the dream when she arrived and ask her to explain the meaning of it. Why had I never done so? Nina's ease in reading my thoughts made me believe the same feat would be simple for Almah. Almah knew my questions and could answer them or not, as she chose.

If only I could see into Almah's mind as Almah did mine! The thought circled around and returned again and again, like a pestering fly, until it became a real possibility, as suddenly as if it had come to rest on the end of my nose. I closed my eyes and made a deliberate and conscious plea.

"Dearest Almah, share with me your thoughts, if you are willing."

The image of Almah's face in my mind was extraordinarily vivid, but I could not be sure anything more than my imagination was at work. Deep respect, even awe, made me hold back, but Almah's countenance remained in my imagination lighted with love, trusting and commanding. I became convinced that I had not only her permission, but her command, to enter into her mind and soul.

Tentatively as a child who fearfully lets go of her parent's hand in wonder that she can swim by herself, I, Mari Anath, let go of my self-awareness and felt myself *become* Almah Mari at that time when she had begun her preparation to serve the Goddess in the Sacred Marriage. Almah's thoughts and feelings became my own, and I saw the world through her eyes at the time when she began her initiation period in preparation for her marriage to Sharon. Thus, when Almah attained the realization that she was the incarnation of the Goddess herself, Queen Isis, I shared that earth-shaking knowledge.

Strangely enough, I was not astonished. It was the confirmation of what my soul had always known. When I had blurted it out that night of my first meeting with Seth, I was as amazed as anyone at the idea, but it had seemed right, somehow, even then. The longer I lived with it, the more right it seemed, but I had always believed it a product of my own fancy.

My mind remained locked in Almah's. I found no power that could release me from the experiences that soon followed in her life. Through her eyes and mind I lived with her the meeting with the Sacred King, Sharon, at his anointing, and I shared her thoughts and feelings through the ceremony of their marriage and—Goddess forgive me—the sweetness and agony of their wedding night.

Nearly drowning in Almah's despair at the fast-approaching sacrifice, I fought my own helplessness at realizing that I could not escape witnessing Sharon's death exactly as it had appeared to her. Horrified, I watched him mount the steps to the altar; Almah's agonized scream tore from my throat as he plunged the blade into his own heart and the executioner struck. Only when Almah fainted was I released.

I could not recall for several moments where I was. Too weak to speak or move my head, drenched in cold perspiration, I knew only that I had fainted. Presently, my powers returned enough to realize that someone was shaking me. My scream had brought Seth groggy with sleep, to my side. "Mari, what happened? Are you all right?" His anxious grip hurt my shoulders.

I knew him before I could speak his name, and managed to inform him feebly, " . . . just fainted . . ."

"Holy Mother! You are half frozen!" He swore half under his breath, scooped me up in his arms and carried me to our bed, bundling the bedclothes about me and rubbing my hands to warm them. "What are you doing up at this hour? It's nearly morning!"

But I could not answer him at once, for as I recovered myself, the memory of what I had experienced came flooding back. The weight of Almah's burden oppressed me so that my throat filled with a hard knot and I could only look dumbly at my lover, unable to speak. Even in the half darkness of predawn, he saw my tears and brushed my wet cheek with his fingers.

Seth was not an excitable man, and being reared by Miriam and then living so privy to the Magdalene had greatly dulled his capacity for surprise. He was used to all-night vigils, trances, messages from other realms, and out-of-body meandering. He accepted it all as a matter of course—he was adept himself in spiritual discipline—but he could not bear to see me grieved. He did not demand to know the cause of my pain, but he did his best to soothe it, rocking me in his arms, crooning his love, and kissing my face until I clung to him peacefully, my hurt fading into memory where it belonged. Only then did he ask softly, "What is it, little one? Can't you tell me?"

I shook my head, smiling, returning his kisses. "It is nothing that matters," I lied convincingly. "Oh, my dear, tell me you will hold me like this forever!" I stopped, afraid my very tenderness would reveal my fears. "Oh, Seth, how weary I am!"

"Sleep then, and I shall hold you until you waken, no matter how long," he promised, settling himself with my head on his shoulder.

"But Yeshua is coming to breakfast," I remembered.

"No matter. He will wait. Sleep," he commanded.

I slept.

19

Yeshua

Behold, he comes, leaping upon the mountains,
bounding over the hills.
My beloved is like a gazelle, or a young stag.
Behold, there he stands behind our wall,
Gazing in at the windows, looking through
the lattice.

Song of Solomon 2:8–9, RSV

I awakened refreshed at my usual time of rising, convinced that the Mother would show a way through my trouble. I greeted Seth with a joyful spirit, and we made love in a delicious rosy haze. My mood was so light that if he was concerned despite my assurances, I convinced him that I had probably overreacted emotionally—tender heart that he knew I was—to some troubled suppliant's story.

When Nina came to dress my hair, I watched her amazement at the new revelation in my mind, for she did not share my trance states as she did my waking thoughts. She knew all in much less time than I could have hold her. "Mari, are you certain?" she asked once, then was silent, taking all into her shrewd mind. "Then it is as the Mother said when she appeared to you in Caesarea Philippi," she said softly, nodding her head in affirmation. "It is as Almah Mari that she has come to be with us." It seemed too appropriate to be surprising.

"Not to be with us," I corrected her, "but to give birth to Osiris as her son, unless this is all in my own mind."

Nina stood frozen, her hand holding the comb poised on high. "Master Yeshua!" she gasped. "Master Yeshua is the Lord Osiris! Come to walk among us!"

"Not for that, either, but to die and rise again. That is her design. Oh, Nina, do you think I am possessed?" My words made what I knew into something I was unwilling to believe. "How could Almah . . . ? Oh, I know she could not!"

"There is something we do not yet know. I am certain of it," Nina agreed. "Of course she could not. And you are not possessed, but favored by the Mother. We will understand it all by and by," she said positively.

Yeshua arrived.

He was not alone, and this would always be true of him. He moved surrounded by people. Perhaps the strange melodies of far-off lands he played on his pipes charmed them, calling them forth from every window and doorway. Some he had chosen; others attached themselves to him out of their own need. Most waited apart, not intruding when he went into people's homes unless he asked them to accompany him. My old friend John of Capernaum and his brother James were with him, and I greeted them all as they came into the garden patio where breakfast had been set out.

A white-clad young woman with great dark eyes trailed shyly behind the men. Yeshua paid careful attention to her, seeing to it that she sat beside him.

I had brought our children, wanting them to see Yeshua, to obtain his blessing. I glowed with pride as he kissed Salome—she was now a young woman of seventeen—and lifted solemn Shaher, then wiggly Shalem, in his hands, pretending amazement at the robust health of our little sons. Shaher was quiet and studious, while Shalem—like Seth—was frolicsome and high-spirited.

I could hardly take my eyes from Yeshua. It must be some wild delusion of my own making that he was Osiris himself, Lord of the living and the dead. Here in the bright sunlight and familiar surroundings, my revelations of the night before seemed dreamlike and far away.

Yeshua did not affect a learned or pious attitude. He was smiling and at ease, unadorned but for his beautiful chestnut hair, falling evenly trimmed in waves to his shoulders. His long robe was plain like that of an ascetic, but his full beard was also trimmed, his skin and hair clean and cared for. His garments were seasoned and worn, but clean and skillfully wrought of the finest cloth, unlike those of the wandering teachers he resembled in appearance. He took my hand and smiled disarmingly into my face.

"You are Mari," he said in a warm, familiar voice, "beloved of my mother."

I was so charmed by him that at first I did not see that his eyes were like Seth's, light and golden, large and clear, with the curling lashes I had always envied my lover. Alike, and yet different, for Seth's eyes always held laughter in their depths, but Yeshua's burned with a deeper fire, like glowing coals. His smile was warm, easy, his expression mild, but some suffering had left its mark in the shadow beneath his eye, in the hollow of his cheek. Nevertheless, the eyes, the voice, the long hand that held mine — all were unbelievably like Seth's. I stared, and heard my lover's low laughter as his arm slid around my waist.

"I told you there was something remarkable you would notice," he laughed. I kept comparing them, as we began our meal. They might have been twins! My eyes were drawn to Yeshua's face. His presence was so compelling that even Seth seemed ordinary within his sphere. Whether Seth noticed or reacted to this, I was too enraptured to notice.

My curiosity soon made me attentive to the exquisite, white-robed woman Yeshua kept near him. He had introduced her as "my disciple, Sita." Sita seldom took her fawnlike gaze from Yeshua's face, yet she never spoke. Her manner was so modest it was difficult to imagine a carnal relationship between them, yet his attentiveness to her would have been judged unseemly by the Jews even if they had been betrothed.

John and the others referred to Yeshua as "the Master," in deference to his years of study with the great teachers of wisdom in the lands of India, Tibet, and Egypt. It was said of him that he could levitate at will, command the elements, heal with the touch of his hand, and change water into wine. None of this would be remarkable for Osiris, I thought. This morning Yeshua was high-spirited as a young colt, laughing and joking with Seth and the sons of Sebedeh, flashing glances as brilliant as sunlight reflecting off a mirror.

"Is it true, Master, that you have visited John, the son of Zacharias, in the desert?" Seth asked him.

Startled, I caught the warning look that Miriam sent her son and felt Nina stiffen beside me. John, called the Baptist, was an ascetic hermit considered by the Pharisees to be a prophet. He had denounced the adopted Greek and Roman customs of the Sadducees as well as the ancient worship of Isis-Ashera. He did not presume to call himself the Messiah, but said he had been sent to prepare the way for him. I remembered unwillingly a day nearly two years ago when I had journeyed south for a holiday to bathe in the salty waters of the Dead Sea.

Near Jericho the Magdalene's bright caravan of painted, silk-curtained carriages with our matched horses and priest-retainers had drawn to a halt to watch the wild-haired Baptist preaching to a group of nearly a hundred souls. Barefoot and swarthy, he wore animal skins for clothing, but he was a powerful presence. We recognized him as the son of Zacharias from tales we had heard, and I recalled his mother, Elizabeth, from before Almah's marriage. Her husband, the priest Zacharias, had been slain by enemies of the Pharisees on his own altar. I had just time to wonder how Elizabeth fared when the ragged prophet, his voice terrible as an avenging angel's, turned and pointed his lean finger directly at me.

"Babylonian bitch whore!" he shouted. The people turned to stare accusingly. "Harlot! Abomination! Go back to your husband Philip and beg his forgiveness! You dare to practice your harlotry in the house of the Lord! Repent or feel the wrath of God!"

It was the first time I had felt hostility from a crowd, anywhere. I winced as though he had slapped my face, tears starting to my eyes. Then Lucius swiftly took my arm and turned me about. "The carriage, Lady, into the carriage! Quickly!" He bustled me up into my seat beside Nina as speedily as my dignity permitted, and we sped away. Later, I made inquiries about Elizabeth to see if she had need of anything and was not surprised to find that Almah had provided a generous pension for her.

All this went through my mind as Seth spoke. His bluntness had always charmed me, but now it made me angry. I hoped Yeshua would have some disapproving word or sign for the Baptist, but he did not.

"I intend to accept baptism by him," he said with a look that seemed to read my thoughts, "as a sign to the people." He turned to Seth. "Come with us and hear the Baptist, Judas of Scarios." But he said nothing to sooth my anger and disappointment. Seth ignored my feelings as well, and since he knew about the incident, this seemed inexcusable. I sat with lowered eyes, thinking he would see and be sorry for displeasing me. Then reason rose past the haze of my anger, and I saw the answer to my prayers. Here was a way to get Seth out of Jerusalem until I could deal with Antipas!

I breathed a silent prayer of thanks and opened my mouth to persuade Seth. But he needed no encouragement to go with Yeshua. I had been blind to what was happening before my eyes. Understanding slowly dawned that Yeshua's invitation to my consort was not idly given. He was inviting Seth—Judas, as he preferred to call him—to join his band of followers. Pure envy arose in my breast, and as if he had seen it, Yeshua turned his luminous look on me. "I would invite you also, Lady Mari, but I know your duties here are many and important."

"Thank you. You are most kind," was all that I could say, then I remembered what I most needed to know. "When will you return?"

"I have been invited for the initiation rites of the Essene Fathers in the wilderness of the Dead Sea. We shall return to you weary and hungry when the forty days are past." His smile was dazzling.

"You must go," I said to Seth. He barely heard me, so intent was he on Yeshua's words.

"There is a favor I would ask of you, Lady Mari," Yeshua said, and I felt a thrill of delight that he should ask me for anything.

"Only tell me how I may serve you."

"Sita, my disciple, cannot accompany us to Qumran because of her sex." Yeshua was gently pulling the shy maiden forward. "If she might remain here with you until we return . . . ?"

I took her small brown hand from Yeshua's, feeling a strong desire to know this mysterious being, to encourage her to speak. "Sita, we should be honored to have you here with us. Please say that you will stay."

She bowed her head in assent, then raised her fawnlike eyes. "I am most grateful, Lady," she said with perfect grace.

20

Sita

We are all the more one because we are many.
For we have made ample room for love in the gap where we
    are sundered.
Our unlikeness reveals its breadth of beauty radiant with
    one common life,
Like mountain peaks in the morning sun.

Sir Rabindranath Tagore

When the men had gone and the household settled into its usual rhythms, I hastened to learn more about my guest. I discovered Sita in the open patio before her sleeping room, still in the white wrapping she had worn earlier, except she had let fall the covering over her black, curling hair. Apparently captivated by the pots of flowering herbs, she nibbled a nasturtium flower as she stood framed by a mass of brilliant rose-red thorn blossom that climbed the pillars of the porch and across the doorway. She had not heard me, and I waited, fearing to startle her, so shy and lovely among the flowers. Then she turned, and seeing me, bowed deeply, remaining with the top of her blue black head bent toward me. "Please rise," I said awkwardly and gestured to a stone bench in the shade of the doorway. She arose, but would not meet my eyes, and after more awkward moments, I understood that she would not sit until I did.

We sat, a body's width apart. "Please, madame" I said gently, preferring to err on the side of grace, "tell me how I should address you."

She rewarded me with a shrill giggle, raising her glorious eyes, hiding her smile with her hand. "Please excuse me. Yes, I am 'madame.' I am a widow for a long time. But 'madame' sounds so strange to me. I am Sita. Please call me Sita."

A widow! I could not comprehend it. "How long have you been Yeshua's disciple?" I asked her.

"It has been twelve years since I first met Master Yeshua." Such eyes she had—large and soft and wide open.

"You were only a child then!"

"I was a married woman, though in age but eleven years," she explained, relaxing a little. "My lord—" she hesitated, wishing to make sure of being understood, "my husband, Jaral, became Master Yeshua's disciple the year I was sent to live with his family." She looked away. "Bad people came. They wanted to kill Master Yeshua." Her face revealed such suffering I put my arm around her, finding her body slight and delicate as a child's.

"Why, Sita? Why would anyone want to kill Yeshua?" But I knew why.

"Master Yeshua was greatest of all the sadhus, but he was not like other holy men, so they hated him."

"They hated Yeshua?" Thinking of Antipas, I believed her.

"He played the pipes and led the dance. The people all followed him, dancing and singing. The bad men said he was evil, and they came to destroy him. Jaral tried to protect Master Yeshua, and they killed him. They killed my lord." Sita pulled her white mantle over her face, and began to keen like a widow in fresh mourning. I could do nothing but hold her until she ceased wailing, sat up, and composed herself. "That is when I came to Master Yeshua," she said in her soft, tremulous voice. "I had nowhere else to go."

"But you were only a child," I said, "your parents could have arranged another marriage for you."

"That is not our way, Lady. A woman can be married but once. A widow with no son is a useless mouth to feed." I held back my protest, not wanting to stop the flow of words that had been so difficult to start.

"I can no longer wear ornaments or colors." Sita showed her brown wrists and hands, devoid of jewelry, and indicated her plain, white dress, a single length of loosely woven sun-bleached cotton, artfully wound about her body and over one shoulder. "My people believe when a young man dies, his wife has made bad karma for him. So she is punished the rest of her life to assure him a more favorable rebirth."

I had thought the Pharisees insensitive toward women!

"My husband's family, when he died, wanted me to do suttee." The soft voice fell away as Sita hung her head. She raised tear-filled eyes. "You know suttee?" she asked.

I shook my head.

"Suttee—" Sita let forth her high-pitched little laugh, "suttee is our custom to help the widow to a better life, by joining her husband in the cremation fire."

I gasped. Rage I had not felt since Deidre's death rose in my breast. "Sita! O, Sita! No wonder Yeshua took you away!" We sat silent, then she seemed to force herself to go on.

"It was for speaking against suttee that they tried to kill Master Yeshua. My husband died trying to protect him. On the day of the funeral, Master Yeshua came out of hiding and stole me away from the cremation fire. He faced their battle spears and arrows for my sake." The love in her face was so transparent—I hesitated, but I had to know.

"Why have you not become his wife?"

Her dark eyes dropped, and a warm glow suffused her face. But when she raised her head, there was nothing hidden behind her gentle gaze.

"Master Yeshua is a holy man—a sadhu. He is above the desires of the body. And I honor the ways of my people. I shall never marry again, even if he should wish it."

"But he is in love with you. I saw it in his face today." I wanted only to give hope.

But Sita rose to her feet and seemed about to flee. "Please, Lady, please! It is evil to speak of such things!"

"Dear Sita, forgive me! I did not mean to offend you. Let us be friends, please. It is my fondest wish to know you better."

"The fault is mine. I have done nothing to deserve your great kindness."

"Rest now. It is late. We will speak some more tomorrow," I told her. "You must tell me if you have need of anything."

Almah did not arrive until the men had been gone two days, and I had time to confide my Antipas dilemma to Miriam. My friend, the famous midwife of Scarios, looked not a day older than when I had known her nearly twelve years ago. She listened intently as I told of Antipas's demand that I perform the rites of Heiros Gamos with him, and of his open threat against Seth's life.

"How wise you have been, my dear, not to let Seth suspect anything!" Miriam praised me. "This must be agonizing for you!" She embraced me with deep affection. "You have shown great courage and restraint," she continued in her warm, rich voice. "Let us think on the matter until Almah Mari arrives. Together we three will find a way to thwart Antipas."

I felt as if Miriam had shouldered half my burden. Once again, Miriam of Scarios was my ally, and alone that night on my bed, I had peace enough to indulge in romantic fantasies about Yeshua and the mysterious Sita. What shameful waste that their beliefs did not allow them the pleasure of love!

When I awoke after daylight, Almah's party had been sighted little more than an hour away. After the flurry of last-minute arrangements and emotional greetings, Almah, Miriam, and I were finally together in the same small audience room where I had received Antipas. Almah looked about with obvious pleasure.

"What memories this room holds for me. You have kept it carefully, Mari." The serenity and strength that radiated from her comforted me mightily. I wanted to warm myself in those powerful rays, absorb some measure of her calm. Settling herself on the Greek lounge, she looked expectantly toward me.

I recounted my interview with Antipas, his demand that I wed him in the Sacred Marriage. "He will arrest Seth and try him for sedition if I refuse, and I fear also for Yeshua," I finished, my eyes on her face.

"No bargain can be wise with Antipas," she said firmly, showing little surprise at my revelation. "He would arrest them now if he dared. But your consort's wrath could give him the excuse he wants."

"Herod has courted favor with the Pharisees of late," Miriam disagreed. "He may well feel powerful enough to carry out his threat."

"His real purpose is to extort the endorsement of the Magdalene. He wants the people of the Goddess in his power," Almah said. For a long time she sat in thought, then she got up and paced the gracious audience room as she must have done many times in the past. When she spoke, the puissance of her spirit flashed like heat lightning.

"The ways of the Goddess are everywhere debased by these seekers of power, lovers of violence and war. You must not give him what he wants, Mari. The Mother forbids it."

Then Miriam spoke, startling me, for her voice had the tone of an oracle. "They cannot defeat the Mother," she intoned. "She is terrible as she is benevolent. She will dance in the light of their funeral pyres and drink the blood of their children. They may run far from her, defame her, and deny her, but she will have them all back—every one."

I shuddered, speechless, as Almah nodded in agreement.

"You are right, sister, it is the Dark Mother who can aid us now." Almah turned toward me, and her look was so intense it would have frightened me had I not known and loved her. It took all my strength to meet her eyes, but her voice was carefully gentle.

"Mari, darling Mari," she murmured softly, taking me by the shoulders. "Are you very, very brave? Would you face the Dark Goddess herself to keep this terrible thing from happening?"

I could only nod wordlessly. Did Almah mean I must die? Were things then as bad as I had feared, and no other way could be found? Of course I was willing to die—I had thought about it and made up my mind—but was there no other solution? Then, Miriam protested, "No, it is too dangerous!"

Who were these two beings who weighed so casually the destinies of mortals like myself?

"She will be safe, for I will protect her." Almah insisted. "I will go after her and bring her back if need be."

"And Herod will have a funeral to celebrate in place of a wedding!" Miriam agreed slowly, apparently persuaded.

Almah's words made my heart leap, for they affirmed powers that could belong only to the Goddess. Then I understood, and sudden fear followed like thunder, lightning. The descent of the soul to the underworld could be accomplished through meditation and, if done successfully, could produce a profound trance that would simulate death. But I had never heard the practice described without grave warning that return might not be possible.

"Are you saying I could achieve such deep trance Antipas would think me dead?" I groped for a place to sit down. "What about afterward? Could I resume my life and office after my funeral? Antipas would know it for a trick!"

"We must time it so that he would lose face completely if he dared repeat his demand," Miriam reasoned. "You must agree to the marriage and go through all the preparations, so he will suspect nothing."

"But I am frightened of facing the Judges at the seven gates and the Dark Goddess! I would be terrified! I would lose my resolve and flee in fear."

"Dearest Mari," Almah comforted me, "fear is the worst demon. You are more courageous than you know. Face each threat directly and move through it, and you will not be harmed. I will be with you."

Miriam nodded encouragement.

I lowered my tense shoulders and nodded slowly. "I will do it," I managed to say firmly, "with the help of you both, I will do it!"

When I opened the doors of our meeting room, Nina was waiting, her face grave with what she already knew of our plans and with the news she brought.

"Herod Antipas has published the announcement that he will celebrate the Sacred Marriage with the Magdalene. His criers are abroad over all Judea as well as his own lands."

"It is all right, Nina. We have expected as much," I told her.

"That is not all, Mari," the urgency in her voice broke through. "He has arrested the Baptist and imprisoned him at Machaerus."

"He has dared to lay hands on John!" Almah exclaimed. John was her relative, as I have said, the son of her cousin Elizabeth. "On what grounds has he imprisoned him?"

"Oh, Mari," Nina turned her agonized look on me. "He says it is for your sake! The Baptist cursed Antipas as an adulterer when he heard the bans; he says you are his brother's wife! And Herod has put him in prison saying his offense was that of insulting the Magdalene."

"That viper!" My anger was a relief. Antipas was planning to turn the people against me with a show of false gallantry and then humiliate me by this forced marriage.

"Where were Yeshua and his party when this happened?" Almah wanted to know. What if they returned before we could carry out our plan?

"They are closeted with the holy Essene Fathers and know none of this," Nina told us. We shared a sigh of relief and looked around into each other's faces. I took a slow, deep breath.

"I am ready," I said.

Inanna, the Morning Star

The soul regarding itself as ego is overcome by fear, just like the man who regards a rope as a snake. The soul regains fearlessness by realizing that it is not an ego, but the Supreme Soul.

Shankara

By evening of the day before the spring festival and the Sacred Marriage were to be celebrated, I was barely present in my body. I had adhered so rigidly to the prescribed discipline and diet—or lack of it—that my bones displayed themselves as through a thin garment of flesh, and my eyes loomed large in the mirror when Nina dressed my hair. As often as Almah and Miriam allowed I had taken Nehushtan's venom into my veins, and like an elixir of wisdom, the serpent's gift opened unexplored worlds within my unknown self. I had turned so deeply within that I seldom spoke or reacted to anything outside me, absorbed as I was in my visions and dreams.

On this evening I was to have a recess from my meditations. A much-rehearsed pageant in honor of the Goddess was planned for the eve of the festival. Salome had earned the greatest honor that could come to a Temple dancer—she would dance the role of the goddess Inanna in the ancient pageant of her descent and return from the Netherworld.

As the time approached for the ceremony to begin, Almah, Miriam, and I, the ranking priestesses, with our attendants and guests, crossed the wide outer courtyard and entered the tall gates of the Women's Court. The court was not exclusively for women; it was called the Women's Court because women were not allowed to enter any of the inner courts behind it, each of which was closer to the Holy of Holies. No Gentile or unclean person might go beyond these gates.

We passed into a chamber with a stone stairway leading to the rooftop gallery where comfortable seats had been set up. The three other galleries above the corners of the court were filled with the highest ranking people of Jerusalem, dressed in their finest clothing, weighted with ornaments and heirlooms beneath warm robes against the evening chill. These seats offered a privileged view of the curved dais before the Nicanor Gate where the Magdalene Anna had received us into the service of the Mother and where every sacred bridal pair had sat enthroned. Tonight it would serve as a staging area for the evening's pageant.

Many people sat or stood on the paved courtyard of the Temple, and a far greater number were outside the gates, unable to see the dancers or understand the singers but participating in the ritual through prayerful attention. The ceremony was not an entertainment, but a holy offering to the Goddess, a reverent reenactment of her courageous descent to the depths and her triumphant return — her world-shaking victory over the forces of darkness and death.

Herod Antipas, flanked by his courtiers, was seated in the gallery across from us in the place of high honor, since his was the wedding to the Goddess that would take place at the height of the festival. Normal courtesy required that I be seated with my husband-to-be, and my absence there was a statement that would not go unnoticed.

The fabulous Nicanor Gate was two stories high, entirely overlaid with Corinthian bronze and flanked by a pair of shorter, yet still massive, single doors, overlaid with the same beaten metal. It gleamed in the torchlight, the color of dark honey. Looming beyond its wide lintel of white marble, the towering facade of the Temple reflected the ceremonial torches from its surface of polished marble and beaten gold. The full moon that heralded the time of the festival was less than an hour in ascendence but already illuminated the western walls of the court and mingled with the torchlight, casting overlapping shadows in changing patterns and shades of violet. Innumerable stars glittered in the still darkening blue of the sky, as if the heavenly bodies leaned close to witness this spectacle in their honor.

Nina tucked another shawl around my shoulders, and I gave my attention to the invocational hymn to the goddess Inanna. It rose in the clear air, sending the glorious Queen of Heaven forth on her journey to the Netherworld. Inanna, the ancient story said, chose to abandon Heaven and Earth for the Netherworld in search of wisdom, for she knew nothing of that secret place, nor of the dark, hidden world within herself.

From the great above she set her mind toward the great below,
The Goddess, from the great above, she set her mind toward the great
    below,
Inanna, from the great above, she set her mind to the great below.

The mighty sound of a ram's horn signaled the beginning of the rite. The court blazed with the orange light of a thousand torches. It illumined the graceful body of the young dancer through a gown as fine as spiderweb, as she arose from among the singers, swaying rhythmically to the slow throbbing of stringed instruments. It was Salome, representing the goddess Inanna. With reverent ceremony, her two attendants robed and crowned her in the sacred symbols of her earthly power in preparation for her dangerous journey, as the song continued:

My lady abandoned heaven, abandoned earth,
    To the nether world she descended,
Inanna abandoned heaven, abandoned earth,
    To the nether world she descended.
Abandoned lordship, abandoned ladyship,
    To the nether world she descended.

The seven decrees she fastened at her side,
The shugurra, the crown of the plain, she put upon her head,
Radiance she placed upon her countenance,
The rod of lapis lazuli she gripped in her hand.

Small lapis lazuli stones she fastened about her neck,
Sparkling stones she fastened to her breast,

A gold ring she gripped in her hand,
A breastplate she bound about her breast.

All the garments of ladyship she arranged about her body,
Ointment she put upon her face.
Inanna walked toward the nether world.

Her attendants bowed low saluting the goddess, as she paraded in a circle displaying her finery. Then she moved slowly forward to the plucking sounds of the strings, but a graceful eunuch in demonic garb arose at her feet to a trill of shepherd's pipes, barring her way.

Neti, the chief gatekeeper of the nether world, asks the pure Inanna:

"If thou art the queen of heaven, the place where the sun rises,
Why, pray, hast thou come to the land of no return?
How has thy heart led thee to the road whose traveller does not
    return?"

"Come, Inanna, enter."

Salome whirled slowly with the stringed music to the left side of the dais, turning to face her right hand. The seven keepers of the seven gates, black robed in demonic masks, arose in a line to face her, twisting grotesquely to the madly blowing pipes. The singers, narrating the story, dropped their voices into a lower, more measured tone at the gate of each level of the underworld.

Upon entering the first gate,
The shugurra, the "crown of the plain," of her head, was removed.
"What, pray, is this?"
"Extraordinarily, O Inanna, have the decrees of the nether world been
    perfected,
O Inanna, do not question the rites of the nether world."

At this passage, the first gatekeeper slithered toward Salome and, removing her crown, allowed her to pass. As the chanting narration continued, the second gatekeeper removed her rod of lapis lazuli; the third, her necklace of precious stones; and so it went on, until she reached the last gate.

Upon her entering the seventh gate,
All the garments of her body were removed.
  "What, pray, is this?"
"Extraordinarily, O Inanna, have the decrees of the nether world been
    perfected.
O Inanna, do not question the rites of the nether world."

The last gatekeeper, with lascivious pantomime, opened the
neckline of Salome's gown. It slipped to the floor, revealing the
Goddess personified in the perfectly formed body of Salome, to
stand naked before her sister and the seven judges of the
underworld—Ereshkigal and the Annanaki. The courtyard was
hushed, reverent.

The pure Ereshkigal seated herself upon her throne.
The Annanaki, the seven judges, pronounced judgment before her,
They fastened their eyes upon her, the eyes of death,
At their word, the word that tortures the spirit,
The sick woman was turned into a corpse,
And the corpse was hung from a stake.

A wooden timber with a single cross beam was moved forward,
and Salome was tied to it by a spiral of soft cloth lacing her out-
stretched arms to the beam. Her body sagged convincingly as the
seven devils arose in a taunting, tormenting dance about her,
shrieking and yelling to the music. The priestess representing her
dark sister, Ereshkigal, clad in robes like those that had been
stripped from Salome but all in black, watched unmoving from
her dark throne.

When the Annanaki had finished their dance around the naked
goddess, all the torches on the dais were extinguished one by one,
until only a small fire and the cold moonlight illuminated the
hanging corpse of Inanna. The singers paused also, and the
morning and evening bells were heard three times. Then a priestess wearing wings to represent Ninshubur, chief messenger of the
gods, Inanna's personal handmaid, lighted her torch and raised
the alarm at her mistress's absence, running from place to place
about the dais, asking each of the great gods to help her, igniting

more and more torches until the scene once more blazed with light. At last Ninshubur obtained help from the water god, and she led the beings he sent to aid her round about the dais, down the steps and up again, to simulate the far distance to the nether world. There, while Ninshubur waited outside the gates and the music hovered in a monotone of rising suspense, the messengers sprinkled the food of life and the water of life sent by the father of the gods upon the lifeless corpse, and the choir of priestesses and eunuchs caroled the thrilling hymn to the Goddess's return.

Upon the corpse hung upon the stake, they directed the fear of the
    rays of fire,
Sixty times the food of life, sixty times the water of life, they sprinkled
    upon it,
Inanna arose.

Inanna arose!

The last line was magnified by the choir over and over in a joyous round that filled the night sky.

Salome began to revive artfully as they untied her arms. Slowly coming alive and looking about in wonder, she stretched her graceful limbs and stepped away from the cross, which moved backward out of sight. Still naked, she pantomimed her pleasure and delight, admiring her hands, her arms, her legs and feet, and then her whole body, leaping and whirling in joyful celebration of her restored vitality and sexuality.

A note of sadness came into the singing, and both the dancer and the stringed music paused eloquently, Salome's attitude one of serene dignity. To the deepest, most solemn tones of the shepherds' pipes, the Seven Judges reappeared, no longer taunting, but imperious and demanding in their stance. The choir sang with resignation:

Inanna was about to ascend from the nether world,
When the Annanaki seized her.
   "No one ascends from the nether world unmarked.
   If Inanna wishes to return from the nether world.
   She must provide someone in her place."

Slowly, sadly, to the dolorous repetition of the demand by the singers, Salome closed her slender arms about her high young breasts. Her long, dark hair fell forward, covering her, and she bowed her proud head in sorrowful assent to the Annanaki, the dark judges of the underworld.

Each of the demon gatekeepers stepped forward in turn, the first placing the Goddess's gossamer gown once more upon her shoulders and binding the cord about her narrow waist. The next returned the gold ring to her hand, and each in turn returned her breastplate and rod—all the signs and symbols of worldly power she had shed at her descent. As each gatekeeper stepped back, a small demon-garbed fledgling priest or priestess crept forward in replacement, following close on Salome's heels as she walked forward, imitating her every movement; each passage of her stringed accompaniment was echoed by a shrill pipe. The Annanaki had been appeased, but the price they exacted would be heavy. The singers' voices, measured and sad, sang how in return for her freedom, Inanna had agreed to send a substitute to the Netherworld, to death.

> As Inanna ascended from the nether world,
> The galla, the demons of the nether world, clung to her side.
> The galla were demons who know no food, who know no drink,
> Who eat no offerings, who drink no libations,
> Who accept no gifts.
> They enjoy no lovemaking.
> They have no sweet children to kiss.
> They tear the wife from the husband's arms,
> They tear the child from the father's knees,
> They steal the bride from her marriage home.

Salome and her train of demons wound about the staging area, up and down the curved steps. The young dancers who represented the demons drew restrained merriment and doting comments from their relatives in the crowd, despite the seriousness of the occasion.

The demons clung to Inanna.
Like reeds the size of low picket fences,

The one who walked in front of Inanna was not a minister,
Yet he carried a scepter.
The one who walked behind her was not a warrior,
Yet he carried a mace.
Ninshubur, dressed in a soiled sackcloth,
Waited outside the palace gates.
When she saw Inanna
Surrounded by the galla,
She threw herself in the dust at Inanna's feet.

Watching the dancers dramatize the words of the hymn, my body turned cold as ice. Would a substitute be demanded for my own return? Someone I loved? How could I send a loved one to die in my place? Tears spilled from my eyes, and I clutched the hand of my own Ninshubur.

The galla said:
"Walk on, Inanna,
We will take Ninshubur in your place."
Inanna cried:
"No! Ninshubur is my constant support.
She is my succor who gives me wise advice.
She is my warrior who fights by my side.
She did not forget my words.
Because of her, my life was saved.
I will never give Ninshubur to you."

The galla said:
"Walk on, Inanna,
We will accompany you to Umma."

As Salome continued her journey, followed by the galla, the singers told how they met each of her two sons in turn, in sackcloth and mourning for her. Each threw himself in the dust at his mother's feet, and I thought of my darlings, Shaher and Shalem, my heart's delight. As the demons tried to take as their substitute each son, the Goddess cried out in refusal. And each time, the demons agreed, and marched on.

The galla said:
  "Walk on to your city, Inanna,
  We will go with you to the big apple tree in Uruk."

But Inanna had gained wisdom in the underworld. She had faced and accepted her "sister," her own hidden, unrecognized self. She could never again deny that other self, never really leave her behind again; thus she must send a part of herself back to the Netherworld. A passage must be kept open from the Great Above to the Great Below, for she must not forget the despised sister, Ereshkigal. And so it will be for me, I thought, watching and listening, hoping for some sign, some way out. If it should come to that I would remain myself in the Netherworld, I thought, my eyes streaming.

Salome and her writhing train turned again, and in their path a throne appeared. On it sat a young man, whose shining robe barely concealed his shepherd's garb, bearing the crook, cup, and churn of Dumuzi. His haughty, preoccupied attitude expressed his annoyance with his wife's adventuring, his self-important distraction with the everyday affairs of the kingdom.

Salome's manner, when she saw him, altered to one of annoyance. In quick, angry movements she expressed her feeling that he was ungrateful and forgetful of her, the Queen of Heaven and Earth, who had placed him in his position of power and authority. "While I have been engaged in matters affecting my deepest soul," her dance accused him, "you have used my powers to make yourself more important."

In Uruk, by the big apple tree,
Dumuzi, the husband of Inanna, was dressed in his shining garments,
He sat on his magnificent throne; (he did not move).

The galla seized him by his thighs.
They poured milk out of his seven churns.
They broke the reed pipe which the shepherd was playing.

Inanna fastened on Dumuzi the eye of death.
She spoke against him the word of wrath.
She uttered against him the cry of guilt:
  "Take him! Take Dumuzi away!"

Dumuzi aspired to be a truly great king, but he was too taken up with his kingship to notice what his wife had endured. No sackcloth on him! He wore only the shining garments of power she had given him. He was in need of, and must make, the same journey of self-knowledge she had undertaken.

The galla cried:
"Rise, Dumuzi!

Husband of Inanna, son of Sirtur, brother of Geshtinanna!
Rise from your false sleep!
Your ewes are seized! Your lambs are seized!
Your goats are seized! Your kids are seized!
Take off your holy crown from your head!
Take off your shining garment from your body!
Let your royal sceptre fall to the ground!
Take off your holy sandals from your feet!
Naked, you go with us!"

I could not stop thinking of Sharon, Almah's anointed bridegroom. He had been neither insensitive nor prideful, yet his death had followed his anointing by one day. No wonder Seth was uneasy about filling the throne of Dumuzi!

The galla seized Dumuzi.
They surrounded him.
They bound his hands. They bound his neck.

The churn was silent. No milk was poured.
The cup was shattered. Dumuzi was no more.
The sheepfold was given to the winds.

Inanna's attendants reappeared to hold her back when, relenting, she tried to go to her husband's aid, then to comfort and support her as the awful realization of his death came home to her. Bowed in grief, Salome discarded once more the rich emblems of her queenship, her grace and beauty obscured by a fumbling awkwardness. Wrapping a coarse sackcloth about her, she prostrated herself before the empty throne as the scene and music changed to one of ritual mourning.

"My lady weeps bitterly for her young husand.
Inanna weeps bitterly for her young husand.
Woe for her husband! Woe for her young love!
Woe for her house! Woe for her city!"

Slowly, Salome arose to dance eloquently Inanna's grief, her supple body contorted with pain, her movements halting and half-finished; she roamed lost in overwhelming sorrow, tripping over her cast-off crown, rod, and breastplate, but empty husks strewn about the floor. A pure female voice, husky with emotion, lamented:

Gone is my husband, my sweet husband.
Gone is my love, my sweet love.
My beloved has been taken from the city.
O, you flies of the steppe,
My beloved bridegroom has been taken from me
Before I could wrap him with a proper shroud.

Inanna in her dazed wandering now came upon the broken cup and churn, fallen emblems of the Shepherd King, lying where the galla had thrown them. She took them tenderly into her hands, brushed them clean with her hair, then cradling them close to her breast, knelt with her head over her knees in a closed, motionless ball as the soloist continued.

The wild bull lives no more.
The shepherd, the wild bull lives no more.
Dumuzi, the wild bull, lives no more.
The jackal lies down in his bed.
The raven dwells in his sheepfold.
You ask me about his reed pipe?
The wind must play it for him.
You ask me about his sweet songs?
The wind must sing them for him.

Another priestess danced the part of the bereaved mother of Dumuzi while a low voice chanted:

"My heart plays the reed pipe of mourning.
Once my boy wandered freely on the steppe.
Now he is captive.
Once Dumuzi wandered so freely on the steppe,
Now he is bound."

There is mourning in the house.
There is grief in the inner chambers.

To embrace and comfort her mother came another dancer, Geshtinanna, the sister of Dumuzi, whose selfless love would redeem her brother from eternal death. Salome's friend, Siduri, sprightly as a young doe, fulfilled the role perfectly, holding the eyes of everyone even in her rough sackcloth. A sweet, warm voice told of her sorrow:

"O my brother, who is your sister?
I am your sister.
The day that dawns for you will also dawn for me.
The day that you will see, I will also see.

I would find my brother! I would comfort him!
I would share his fate!"

As Siduri moved, she addressed the very gods with the electrifying announcement of her love, the audacity of a love that reaches beyond death and the terrors of the Netherworld. Her body expressed despair and hope, the agony of grief and a reaching beyond it, the acceptance of the decrees of fate—of the Annanaki—and a challenge, a gauntlet thrown down. She loved him enough to share his fate, to take his place!

The choir paused; the perfect silence was as if the divine powers themselves stopped and listened. The grieving goddess Inanna slowly lifted her head, uncurled her graceful spine, and turned, amazed, to the sister of her husband. Slowly she rose, leaving aside the broken cup and churn, and walked toward Geshtinanna, her every motion an expression of the struggle between disbelief and hope. The pure voice of the Goddess began slowly, as if lost in wonder:

When she saw the sister's grief,
When Inanna saw the grief of Geshtinanna,
She spoke to her gently:
  "Your brother's house is no more.
  Dumuzi has been carried away by the galla.
  I would take you to him,
  But I do not know the place."

Salome reached Siduri, and the two stood looking into each other's faces for a long moment. Then they drew together gently, embracing. Salome, as the Goddess, took her sister's hand and led her toward the right of the dais, where the players parted to reveal the figure of Dumuzi. The singing rose in tempo, lifted by hope. Inanna reached out with her free hand and, taking that of her husband, lifted him to his feet.

Inanna and Geshtinanna went to the edges of the steppe.
They found Dumuzi weeping.
Inanna took Dumuzi by the hand and said:
  "You will go to the underworld
  Half the year.
  Your sister, since she has asked,
  Will go the other half.
  On the day you are called,
  That day you will be taken.
  On the day Geshtinanna is called,
  That day you will be set free."

The choir chanted in a reverent whisper, the single line:

  Inanna placed Dumuzi in the hands of the eternal.

Then they began a swelling hymn of praise that resounded and echoed the words over and over in a complicated round of many parts:

  Holy Ereshkigal, Great is your renown!
  Holy Ereshkigal, I sing your praises!

Then a discordant note arose from the gallery throne of Herod Antipas. Dimly, I realized he was attempting to make himself heard. The hymn ended, and the people turned their eyes toward the sound of Antipas's voice. He was asking for the lead dancer. "Bring her to me," I heard him say.

Did he know Salome was my daughter? It was hardly possible he did not. Salome did not go to him, but she turned to face the gallery where he stood, and bowed respectfully. Herod decided to make himself heard from the gallery, for he had a powerful voice.

"You have captured my heart with your dancing, kadeesh," he boomed gallantly, without seeming to shout. "I beg you to ask of me anything in my power to grant, and it shall be yours!"

I gasped in concert with Almah and Miriam and the indrawn breath of the crowd. They knew the lovely kadeesh was the daughter of his intended bride, if he did not. And they knew I would make this marriage unwillingly; some had turned against me already for agreeing to grant the sanction and support of the Goddess to bloody Antipas. They waited in the pregnant silence, hardly breathing, for her answer.

Salome bowed her dark head graciously in acknowledgment of Herod's offer, then straightened her back and spoke directly to him, her young voice clear and vibrant as a bell. "Sir, you do me a great honor. There is a boon I would ask of you."

There was a sudden buzz of surprise and approval from the crowd. The maiden was a true daughter of her mother, they said. My pride in her swelled my breast.

"Whatever you ask, shall be yours! I swear it!" Antipas crowed, and I read his intent. He would win over the daughter, and the mother would have to follow.

Salome had the presence of mind to wait for silence. Then in her clear, girlish voice, choosing her words carefully, she demanded, "I charge you then, release my mother from this humiliation you bring upon her!"

The crowd erupted into a roar of approval and turned its jeers on Antipas. His own subjects in Galilee would not have dared to treat him so, but he had no real power in Judea. He would lose face altogether if he did not honor his promise, but he made no attempt to reply to Salome, and the people did not press him. Let him take some time to think about how his posturing had been turned against him.

I arose with the others to leave, my mind returning to the message of the pageant. Love is stronger than death, I repeated over and over. I would hold fast to that.

Descent to the Netherworld

All that we are is the result of what we have thought: it is founded on our thoughts, it is made up of our thoughts. If anyone speaks or acts with an evil thought, pain follows, as the wheel follows the foot of the ox that draws the carriage.

Dhammapada

Next day, the day of my promised marriage to Herod Antipas, I prepared for my own descent to the Netherworld. I ate little and drank only mild tea of raspberry leaves and chamomile. I was no longer afraid.

"Remember, Mari, what you experience may be nothing like the seven gatekeepers of Inanna's descent," Almah cautioned me. The enhanced vision of my near trance made the tiny lines around her eyes into the endless dunes of a desert landscape where I wandered lost and alone. "You will most certainly see some form of the clear, bright light of Truth," she reassured me. "It will be dazzling. Remember, it is the pure radiance of your true self." She grasped my shoulders and gazed into my eyes, as if she would read my courage or lack of it through them. "Fear nothing," she said, and to me it was the Goddess who spoke, "or you will be impelled to seek refuge in some small vision unworthy of you." Then she stepped back, and I was facing Miriam of Scarios.

"Not only the light, but everything you encounter—good or evil—is but a form of yourself, and there is nothing outside the Law," Miriam counseled. Her warm voice made me feel safe, protected, at home. "Fear nothing, even the Dark Goddess, for she is but the self you have not known. Do not fail to love and forgive her with your whole heart, and she will be able to set you free."

"Forgive her? For what must I forgive her?"

"For being the Goddess of life *and* death—creator and destroyer. For making you remember they are inseparable, the condition of each other." I accepted Miriam's embrace, taking greedily of the strength and courage that flowed into me from her touch.

"Please," I hesitated, then voiced my deepest fear, "what of my substitute? Must another stand good for my return? Will the demons come back with me as with Inanna, to take someone else in my place?" Almah put her arms around me.

"No! Darling, no! You are not going to die, remember? You will only be in such deep trance you will appear to have died. You have learned to hold yourself back. There is nothing to fear." She picked up Nehushtan's basket, and held it toward me like an offering.

I unfastened the familiar lacings and removed the lid as absently as I would take off a sandal. The three of us caught the irony together, our quick laughter aware of the tension it shattered. "Come, little one," I coaxed, as the smooth coils wound about my arm. "Give me thy wisdom." I closed my eyes but did not wince as I took the serpent's sting. "Holy Mother, be with me." I was barely aware of Almah gently loosening the snake from my arm, replacing it in its basket.

Reassured by my powerful mentors, yet shaking within my soul, I left the world of my senses and entered the dark realm of my own mind in search of my hidden self. Years of practice and preparation made the first stages easy, and the relaxed state of light trance was reassuringly familiar. I felt my consciousness enter the realm where the thoughts of other minds were clear as spoken words. The memories of everyone living, dead, or yet unborn lay open like books in a vast library. I passed by until I stood on the cusp of time, where the past stretched away at my left hand with the clarity and detail of a summer landscape, and the future led away to my right, brilliant and clear, like a stage on which I could call up characters or events the instant a thought crossed my mind.

Even while I thus moved toward such deep trance I would seem to have died, a clear part of my mind remained present in the quiet room where we sat, but not within my body, for I saw my own motionless figure with the same detachment as those of the others who waited and watched. Nina moved about restlessly, fetching tea, ministering to everyone, while Miriam sat patiently embroidering to pass the time while the light lasted. In the deepening shadows of the waning afternoon, she put her work away, stretched herself, and resumed her vigil.

Almah was still as my own motionless form. I was certain she followed my every thought, as if she made the journey with me. As I descended into a deeper level of trance, the lucidity of the images diminished. Sensations of every kind assaulted me, unrelated in space or time. Colors I could not name blinded me; exotic odors gave rise to images and memories long forgotten. I was not alone. Surrounding me on every hand were beings — beings of ethereal substance and fantastic form — milling, wheeling, turning, brushing against me, massive and heavy as stones to crush me; rough and jagged to snag my flesh or so soft they threatened to envelop me; ceaselessly whispering and murmuring in languages I did not know. Their thoughts were accessible to me, but so disorganized and incoherent were they I could not fathom them with my deepest intuition.

A dazzling light came toward me, and the intruding whispers gathered themselves into one mighty force that was its sound. Dizzy and out of control, spinning and falling with nothing to grasp except my ghostly accusers, I fell into panic. Panic fear, as I felt it then, is the most unbearable of all sensations. In desperation, I recalled Miriam's instructions.

It is all a part of myself, I remembered; it is within me, Mari Anath, that all this appears.

The speed and the screaming noise of my spinning and falling diminished, and I felt more at ease. Yielding to the suggestion (from Almah I hoped) that I must provide some structure, I guessed that only chaos could result from my passivity. Inanna had given up something precious at each of the seven gates. I deliberately visualized myself giving up the crown of the High Priestess to the Annanaki.

"Yes," I affirmed to myself and to the myriad whispering beings who swam around and under and over me in that void, "I surrender it. It is gone." Soft sighs and moans came from the darkness on all sides as I thought how much courage my special role as the spiritual head of my people had given me. I contemplated my lost status.

The next gate had cost Inanna her rod of lapis lazuli, the sign of her earthly queenship. "I surrender my rank as head of the priestesses of Ashera," I resolved, waiting as the full weight of my words came home to me. Again, the sighs and whispers livened the darkness all around, and I longed for solid earth to rest my feet.

Now my mind whirled with a heady mixture of fear and elation. I saw—really saw—the glowing eyes of the third gatekeeper appear before me, and it seemed that I walked upright, though I felt nothing solid beneath my feet. Whether or not my imagination provided the image, the dark presence blocking my path demanded my necklace of lapis lazuli, and I understood that with it I was surrendering the power and privilege, however fleeting, that female grace and beauty had bought me. It could mean less than nothing in the underworld. Feeling increasingly vulnerable, yet encouraged, I warily checked the presence of myself and the others in the room, clinging to the familiar landmark lest my vision run too quickly away with me.

The demon keeper of the fourth gate loomed before me, more visible than the one before, altogether terrifying. I clearly felt his clawlike hand against my shrinking flesh as he ripped from my neck the sparkling stones, talisman of my family. I thought of the love my family lavished upon me, unquestioning and unquestioned, the safety and protection of that love. The invisible chorus moaned and wailed a loss that penetrated to the deepest level of childhood fears. I had never felt so alone. No mother or father could help me here. My own cries joined those from the darkness, and I struggled for some measure of courage before the next encounter.

But the fifth gatekeeper sprang at me with an unearthly howl and tore away the breastplate of the Goddess, the protection of my personal guards and attendants. The nameless voices were screaming now, like abandoned children being devoured by wild beasts. I could see my devoted Nina sitting reassuringly nearby, but I knew she could not help me. I thought longingly of Lucius and Lysander and their dedicated protection. I sent them a blessing of deep gratitude, and my fear fell away.

At that same moment an intrusion was taking place in the outer world. Loud knocking sent Nina flying to the door, anxious to quiet the disturbance, that her lady not be interrupted.

"My Lord Herod demands the presence of his bride in the Temple court," announced the largest of two guards in the Roman armor of Antipas's personal guard.

"She is in prayer and cannot be disturbed," Nina said firmly, shoulder to shoulder and eye to eye with the big bodyguard who had spoken. She made to close the door. Visibly threatened by so tall and formidable a woman, his hesitation almost allowed her to succeed, but he recovered himself in time, and the two pushed their way inside.

"The tetrarch will hear no more excuses," he threatened, his hand on his sword, his shrewd eyes weighing my fragile body, which looked as though a draught of air might waft it away. "If she is too weak to walk, we will carry her. Prepare her!"

In rising panic, I realized I had lost count of the gatekeepers. The next already loomed over me, reaching for my hand. I instinctively withdrew it, but fiery fingers grasped me, and the heavy gold ring of the office I would pass on to Salome was ripped from my finger. The wailing that surrounded me was broken by howls of rage, and I knew my tears of anger would be taken by those who saw them as fear of Herod. Trembling, I waited in the strange split consciousness that kept me also aware of events in my bodily world.

Almah Mari leaped up to face the two intruders, eyes blazing, her presence so formidable the soldiers would have bowed to her will, but she commanded instead, "Dress her, Nina! She is ready!"

I watched Nina and Almah lift my body from its sitting position on the floor, carefully and gently, so I would not be startled. I stood with open, unseeing eyes, as they adorned me in my bridal garments, my jewels, my crown, and placed the rod of my lady-ship in my hand. Then Almah spoke softly to me, and watching from that other place, I heard her words, though the doll-like figure gave no sign. "Go with them, Mari. Do not waken. Do not return. Do not be afraid."

The soldiers, mute with awe, watched Nina lead the High Priestess forth gently as if I were a fragile pillar of salt crystal, grown in a single day on the shore of the Dead Sea. A terrible look from the giant, Lucius, reminded them that the Magdalene's rules still held in my own domain. Antipas's guards stumbled back-ward and, trying to look in command, fell into step after the two eunuchs close behind me.

And in that other reality where my spirit journeyed, I felt the ghostly hands of the seventh gatekeeper before I saw his dreadful glance. Not roughly, yet with no gentleness or care, my robes were stripped away, and I was left with no protection, even of womanly modesty or human dignity. The chorus of voices moaned and sighed as naked, exposed, I watched the last gate swing open. At the same moment the eastern gate of the Temple opened to admit the High Priestess of Isis-Ashera. I trembled in my soul before the throne of the Dark Goddess while I stood in my frail flesh before the judgment of my people, from whom I had hidden myself since Herod Antipas had made public the announcement of our marriage.

I watched myself enter the side door of the Temple court and approach the dais. No loud cheers of welcome and shouts of affec-tion greeted me; instead, I was met by stunned silence, then a loud buzzing of disbelief and anger. They had never believed I would do it! They had loved and trusted me, and the bitterness of their disappointment enveloped me like a shroud. I burned to explain that I had not betrayed them, that I was willing to die—yes, would die—before I would make alliance with their enemy.

Those seated on the floor of the Temple court rose to greet me; angered as they were with me, the priestess, they reverenced the Goddess I represented. Herod, with his attendants, also arose to meet his bride. Nina led me to my seat, then stepped unobtrusively away. I watched the fragile figure in the bridal robes of the High Priestess take my seat. In that other place, which seemed ever closer to this one, teetering on the edge of panic, a thousand demons swarming round me, I felt a familiar stickiness between my thighs and realized I had my moontime. But the stickiness turned slippery, and the blood gushed down as I pressed my legs together trying to staunch the flow with my hands. The aching pull of the bleeding in my hips and back and belly, the familiar ache that every woman knows, grew into a monstrous thing, possessing me utterly. There seemed to be blood all around me, and I saw through a red mist the throne of the Dark Mother looming before me.

The Queen of the Netherworld lolled obscenely on her couch, naked as I was, her swollen breasts engorged with milk, her gaping vulva exposed beneath a monstrously pregnant, filth-encrusted belly. Her staring eyes were hateful, defiant, and she was like me, smeared and befouled with blood. Her hair was wild and matted, human finger bones dangled from her ears, and she wore a child's skull like a pendant about her neck. Her courtiers were beyond description—leering demons and creatures of darkness, gnawing on grisly pieces of human flesh and bone. Around them smoldered charnel fires where heaps of discarded body parts scorched and sizzled. The she-monster fondled a half-year-old infant with her bird-claw hands. She kissed it, and it giggled as babies do, and as she held it close, for a moment she seemed almost benign—even beautiful—then as I watched, unable to look away, she sank her fanglike teeth into its throat and drank deeply of its blood. The voices turned to shrieks and moans of terror, and hideous, mocking laughter echoed and rolled. Something was pulling at my hands, and I looked down to see horrid grinning creatures lapping and sucking at the blood that gushed from me in a growing stream. I screamed and screamed, as the hideous hag finished her meal and tossed the lifeless child upon a charnel heap, where near-starved jackals, eyes glowing, tore it to pieces. A host of batlike demons licked and kissed, pinched and scratched at me, drinking away the life that ebbed from my body. My senses were so altered that I heard the songs of my wedding ceremony to Antipas as from a great distance. I watched as through shimmering heat, from far away. I knew I was dying. I accepted my death and my fear fell away. What else could happen to me?

The myriad demons fondled and caressed me, danced and leapt around me. They bowed, mocking me, making hideous faces, gesturing obscenely. I waited for death.

The next hours were like a dream, with no sense of time passing. The beloved songs of the Sacred Marriage, satirized in vicious pantomime by prancing demons, the unearthly celebration of my union with the enemy of my people and of my soul, became a vicious parody casting the Goddess as a foul harlot in incestuous intercourse with her son. I, who reverenced the spiritual meaning of the ceremony, was a forced witness to its desecration, a victim of exquisite torture. A thousand precious memories were called up, each mocked and twisted, made repulsive or bizarre.

"All this is within my mind." The realization came at last. "It is of my own making." How had I lost control? In my imagination, I closed my eyes tight, straightened my spine, clenched my fists, and shouted with all my might to the dancing, yammering demons, "Silence!"

Large and small, they shrank back almost comically, falling over one another, clawing at each other in their flight. Stunned, I dared not savor my triumph. The flow of my blood had slowed. Perhaps I had already bled to death. How could I know? Slowly the Seven Judges, the terrible Annanaki, marched with measured decorum into their places on my left and right. They bowed their hooded heads with the glowing, empty eyes in a chilling obeisance to me and took their seats.

I took no comfort in their acceptance. What could it mean? My mind raced desperately. The light! I had not recognized the light and had turned away from it! Was it possible I had not made the descent to the Netherworld at all but was trapped in some horrible reality of my own creation?

The ceremony of marriage was finished. My heart raced, though the impassive bride beside Antipas gave no sign. If our plan was to succeed, I must achieve my deathlike trance quickly, but I had no idea how to accomplish it. Had I failed in my purpose altogether? The people rose to advance toward the bride and groom to bear them to their chambers.

But Herod Antipas bowed to his bride and gestured for silence. The rustling and moving about subsided. He wished to address the assembly. Antipas had a flair for the dramatic. He waited until not a sound could be heard, then announced with all the trained eloquence of the practiced orator he was, "People of Judea and Samaria, people of Galilee and Perea, people of our God and of the Mother, I salute you! I thank you for honoring me by your presence here tonight at my sacred marriage to the Goddess, which I have chosen on your behalf."

He went on in this vein for some time, and my private vision of the demons who mimicked and made fun of him was almost amusing. At last he got to the point. "Last evening, you all witnessed my sacred oath to grant whatever the beautiful kadeesh Salome asked of me."

"Yea, Herod! What of your oath?" "You owe a boon!" A loud expression of interest arose from the assembled people. In spite of their desire to see Antipas disgrace himself by breaking a vow, they would allow him fair opportunity to redeem himself. But their murmured questions were of how he could do so now, when the ceremony Salome had asked him to forgo had been accomplished. Would he magnanimously renounce the Magdalene to keep his promise? He held up his hand for silence.

"I swore before you to redress your High Priestess for the humiliation she had endured. Let those who would dare to slander her name beware! Behold my wedding gift to my bride!" he shouted.

A fanfare of trumpets at the eastern gate of the Temple court heralded a procession of Antipas's honor guard through the crowd to the base of the dais. The two guards at the rear bore in their hands a single draped battle shield from which, when they reached Antipas, he himself flung aside the linen cloth. The bearers righted the shield, holding it high so it could be seen by everyone, turning it from left to right and back again. Then they placed it with a flourish at the feet of the Magdalene.

The people suspended their breathing in unison at the grisly sight, for affixed to the charger, unseeing eyes glaring forth in fierce judgment, was the head of the man who had called me, the Magdalene, a harlot, and denounced Herod for his incestuous marriage with his brother's wife, the head of John the Baptizer, son of Zacharias.

I had no warning, even from my ghostly vantage point, before I saw the severed head of the prophet who had humiliated me. Any distinction I still held between this world and the realm of the Goddess of Death disappeared in horror. The shock snapped me back into my body with such a jolt that I fell backward in my seat. What I could not bear to witness with the eye of my soul, I stared at with my bodily eyes, transfixed and unable to move, as the people began to regain their senses and their voices.

A thousand things rushed through my mind at that moment. If the people believed I had desired the death of the prophet, they would never accept me again. Herod Antipas had destroyed both the Baptist and myself at one blow. He had obliterated every vestige of respect my people had ever had for me.

And Yeshua. He would never want to see me again, for I had caused the death of his beloved cousin. Seth and Yeshua were now in greater danger than ever because Herod had turned the people against me. I sat riveted to the sight of the bloody head of the Baptizer, its lips parted as if denouncing me, the dead eyes staring into the dust and ashes of my hope. Even the terrible realm of the dancing demons was more bearable than this, and thither, as down a screaming spiral of blackness, I fled.

When I returned to the Netherworld, I found its hideous queen in the throes of excruciating labor. She arched her back in her agony, and the screams that tore from her throat touched me more than those of the child I had watched her destroy. "You must forgive her," Miriam had said, "and she will be able to set you free. She is your own rejected self." Through the red haze—like a mist of warm blood, I saw her engorged breasts rolling against her swollen belly. Slavering demons crowded and pushed to devour her child.

I was moved to compassion. I tried to tell her how to breathe as Miriam had taught me, but another wrenching contraction possessed her.

It possessed me, as well. I was the one in travail in that black and dreadful place, and I could not remember anything Miriam had taught me. I screamed with agony and terror for an endless time that was longer than my life. I tried to escape down the long corridors of the past or the future, but they were all, all, filled with suffering and blood. I willed my death to escape the pain, but it continued unabated. Then, after a thousand years, over the sound of my screaming, I heard my flesh rip as my body tore open with a rush of blood and water. I could not raise my head. What manner of monster had I brought forth? I could see only darkness. I struggled for the consciousness I had tried to escape. Who would protect my infant, my little one, the child of my pain and travail, from the demons, from the Annanaki? Grief descended like a leaden weight, crushing my breath, and I slipped into deepening blackness.

How long I remained insensible, in a state where not even dreams were present, I had no way of knowing. Awareness returned slowly, but the blackness remained. The screaming seemed farther away. There was unpleasant, painful pressure about my head, then light thrust upon me. The light. I would not let it go again, though it dazzle or blind me, lead where it might.

I imagined that I floated up like a mist, following the light, and when I looked downward, expecting to see the Dark Goddess — my sister, Ereshkegal — and the Seven Judges with their glaring eyes, I saw instead my own body, not naked and bleeding, but lying fully clothed in the bridal robes of the High Priestess beside the battle shield that bore the severed head of John the Baptizer.

I wanted to shout and tell my people that I had never desired the death of the Baptist. In my frustration, I was slow to see that the disturbance on the dais was not due only to Herod's unspeakable deed. There was a frantic and anguished struggle going on over the senseless body of the woman who lay on the floor beside the shield and its grisly burden. An angry whisper began to rise around the fallen Magdalene, and it rushed from mouth to mouth like a groundfire, until it rose to a menacing roar. "She is dead. Dead. Our Lady is dead! She is dead of grief and shame, and Herod Antipas has killed her!"

23

The Return

Unless a grain of wheat falls into the earth and dies, it remains alone;
but if it dies, it bears much fruit. He who loves his life loses it, but he who
hates his life in this world will keep it for eternal life.

Gospel of John 12:24–25, RSV

A High Priestess is always a High Priestess; she does not step down from her rank, though she may see a successor installed in her place. So when Almah Mari appeared suddenly on the dais before her people – she had been present unnoticed in the plain robes of a lesser priestess for some time – they welcomed her as frightened children reach out to their mother in deep trouble. At her gesture, the crowd parted and made way for Miriam of Scarios, escorted by Temple guards to the side of their fallen Magdalene. Everyone waited expectantly while Miriam knelt over my body, carrying on a whispered conversation with Almah. In the meantime, Antipas, obviously suspecting some trick, insisted repeatedly that his bride had only fainted and would be fine.

Watching from my detached place that was no place and yet everyplace, I was as puzzled as everyone else seemed to be. The murmuring of the people grew louder. "Our Lady has died," and "Herod has killed her," were repeated over and over. "Herod has shamed our Magdalene," someone added. "She has died rather than bed with Herod!" a woman said with clear insight. "Antipas has killed the prophet of God and tried to blame our Lady," shouted a group of angry voices, and Herod's bodyguards moved closer to him, brandishing their weapons.

Lysander and Lucius brought a litter and laid me carefully upon it, but before they could bear me away, Antipas held up his hand.

"I command you to stop!" he shouted. "The lady is my wife! I shall decide what is to be done for her!"

"You have no wife!" Almah's clear voice startled the buzzing courtyard into silence. "Her spirit has fled for shame at what you have done!" A loud murmur rose from the crowd.

Herod demanded, disbelieving, "What? Is she dead then? What manner of woman can die so easily?" And my mind echoed his words. What manner of woman? Is she dead, then?

"You must let me take her to her rooms." Almah commanded. "She may yet be brought back to us, if we treat her with care." The people nearest her picked up her words, passing them on to others; they moved across and around the court like a breeze through tall grass, and I myself was like that breeze, rustling about with no place save Almah's words to rest my hope upon.

Antipas ordered his own physician to come forward, swearing he would not accept anything "that black witch" said about the Magdalene's condition. The people passed this message on, too.

His physician proved difficult to find. He had not expected to be called for on his master's wedding night and had made plans of his own. For nearly an hour the people milled about awaiting the outcome, while every word spoken on the dais made its way over and through the crowd on rushing wings. No one left, though the hour was late. The rumor of the Magdalene's death blew like a cold wind beyond the walls of the Temple court and through the streets of Jerusalem. I wondered if my mother and father and Grandmother Lili would hear it, and I felt grieved that I would be unable to comfort them. I wanted to enter the still body now shrouded in blankets, but I dared not. Our plan had worked after all. Miriam called for more blankets, chafing my hands and arms, trying to get me to drink warm herbs, or so it appeared. She was not really trying to revive me, I thought smugly. Not yet.

When at last the wayward physician made his sheepish appearance, he clearly feared for his life, but he was a dedicated doctor. He made haste to the side of my still form without taking time to excuse his tardiness. He took a long time examining his patient. "How long has she been thus?" he wanted to know.

"Sire, for nearly an hour," replied Miriam.

The physician was obviously puzzled. My body showed no signs of life. No breath nor pulse. And yet, it had not begun to stiffen. It seemed to sleep. Perhaps he had seen people before from whom the spirit had fled, but they had breathed. The pressure on him to make a firm diagnosis was strong, and I guessed he was handicapped by his honesty. He turned at last toward Antipas, who waited impatiently. The people all leaned forward and held their breaths to hear.

"Well?" demanded the aggrieved husband. "Does she live?"

"Sire, I—I, I am not certain," admitted the poor doctor.

Antipas exploded "Not certain!" he shouted. "What fool of a doctor is not certain whether one is dead or alive? Explain yourself, man, if you are able. Tell me, does she live." His fury forced the physician to make a difficult choice.

"If she is not dead, Excellency, she is too near it for any recovery to be possible. My suggestion is that she be taken to her bed and waited upon until it can be seen for certain she is indeed dead."

Herod Antipas, to the great good fortune of the little physician, forgot all about him in his fury. "Babylonian bitch whore!" he screamed. "She has cheated me by willing her own death! I shall grieve little for that, I promise you! Hear this, all ye people! I repudiate her! Do you hear me? I renounce and denounce the great harlot of Jerusalem! Our marriage I pronounce void! Take her!" he shouted. "Back to her whore's bed!"

It was more than we had hoped for. Antipas would not dare threaten Seth or Yeshua outside his own territory. His murder of the Baptist would have aroused even greater hatred against him in any case, but his attempt to implicate me in his rash design was so despicable it had incited the Judeans to near riot. He was forced to retire in haste to his fortress-palace, from which he departed for his own kingdom before sunrise.

Lucius and Lysander bore me swiftly to my rooms, where Miriam skillfully tended by body, and Almah, my soul. The rumors that flew about the waiting city in and out of every window and door said that I was dead, and that I still lived, that I had died, and that I would rise. And I was a ghostly presence dreaming about my rooms, as uncertain of the outcome as they. Lonely and weary, I longed to talk to someone, but no one noticed me. At last I settled myself at the foot of the bed where my still body lay, its splendid robes replaced by a gown of softest linen, my long brown hair combed out, shimmering upon the pillow. How small and strange my body appeared, lying there. The pale face appeared serene, untroubled, yet with none of the authority of a High Priestess. The forehead was unlined, the curved eyelids innocent, and the mouth had neither the firmness of a priestess nor the voluptuousness of the "great harlot" Herod had called me—only a gentle softness. I noticed the slender hands—I had surely looked at them often enough—but even they seemed different, little larger than a child's, seemingly incapable of all I knew they had done. Had these hands delivered children into the world, lovingly held my own little ones, mixed and administered the herbs that prevented more? Could these still hands have caressed my beloved, held Nehushtan and induced his sting? What a mound of wool their spinning would make! I was overcome with a great love for the frail body that had been my home. I loved the woman I had been, the life I had lived. I wanted to weep once more, to feel hot tears against my fevered cheeks, the solid heaviness of sorrow in my throat. But I was lost, lost.

In yearning love, I lay down over my body and tried to reenter it, but I could not. I could not recall ever returning voluntarily; it had always seemed to come about of itself. A terrible weariness pressed upon me; the pull toward unconsciousness, toward peace, was so powerful it outweighed everything. Not knowing whether I might waken ever again—or where—I slept.

The learned Masters teach that deep, dreamless sleep—in which no distinctions are drawn, in which the soul is at one in perfect unity with the All, is the highest form of Being, Consciousness, and Bliss. I felt no sense of time or space or self; moments or eons might have passed, when a gentle light began

to glow. I resisted the light. The bliss of oneness, of perfect whole-
ness, I could not surrender without struggle and regret. Even as
Mother Eve and Father Adam were cast unwillingly from Eden,
so, grudgingly, I returned from dreamless sleep. And with the
dawning of the light, the return of self-awareness gave rise again
to fear. What I should fear, I did not know, but my loneliness was
suddenly overwhelming; I was so tired of being alone!

"Mari. Mari, can you hear me?" The tenderness of the human
voice melted my heart. My joy and relief were so great that tears
ran from beneath my still closed eyelids, lids so heavy I had not
the strength to open them. "Mari, darling." A hot tear that could
not have been my own splashed on my hand. I tried to lift the
hand, but could not. Cold, I was so very cold. I tried to shape the
words with my lips; my mouth was parched, dry. A gentle hand
raised my head and a cup of clear water was pressed to my mouth.

"Rest, dearest. Do not try to speak." Almah's voice was buoyant,
joyous. Helpless and weak as I was, I knew with deep gratitude
that I was back. I had returned.

24

The Mirror Image

Since it has been said that you are my twin and true companion, examine yourself so that you may understand who you are . . . I am the knowledge of the Truth. So . . . you will be called "the one who knows himself."

Book of Thomas the Contender

Like the crescent moon, which appears reborn each month after she has disappeared for three days, and like the goddess Inanna, who hung on a stake in the Netherworld for three days and arose, so I, Mari Anath, High Priestess of Isis-Ashera, remained three days in the Netherworld before Almah Mari won me back to this life. But the green springtime was fast browning into early summer before I recovered sufficiently from my ordeal to resume the duties of my office. I knew I must satisfy the anxious curiosity of my people about me, so I chose to appear at the Festival of Naming, when all the infants born during the year were presented at the Temple. Only then could I lay to rest the rumors of my death—or my death and resurrection.

"I say 'Hail' to the Holy One who appears in the heavens," I intoned shakily, but my voice carried clearly throughout the Women's Court from where I stood before the Nicanor Gate with Nehushtan's coils laced through my fingers.

"We say 'Hail' to the Great Lady of Heaven," the people answered. Relief and joy rang in their one voice.

But I knew they marked my pale face, my eyes sunk back in their sockets like a hunted animal's. The shadow was upon me for any and all to see of some deep and terrible trouble.

What I most feared had come to pass. The greedy demons of the Annanaki had followed me from the Netherworld. They clung to me and tormented me night and day. Their fiery eyes flashed behind my eyelids whenever I closed them. Their accusing whispers filled every silence, whispers that they would never leave me until I surrendered a substitute to them to take my place in the Netherworld. I was haunted and possessed by darkness, driven to distraction by pounding headaches; I slept only when too exhausted to dream. Worst of all, I dreaded to meet any one I loved lest the demons take them before I could speak.

But for Almah's encouragement, I believe I would have surrendered to the demons and taken my own life. I knew the herbs that would bring me a friendly death, and I had hidden enough in my sewing basket, forgetting that Nina would know my intent before I could act.

"Be at peace, beloved," Almah's voice repeated over and over in my mind, "a substitute has been provided for you. You will know him when the time is ripe. Have no fear. The Mother will provide."

So I existed, each day a struggle against the darkness. When I repeated Almah's words to myself, the demonic voices quieted, the glowing eyes dimmed, and I tried to live as before. Every distraction was a blessing, but word of Yeshua and Seth's return filled me with such hope that the demons seemed temporarily banished.

The young women who dwelt in the cloisters of Isis-Ashera also awaited with rosy imaginings the return of my handsome consort. They watered their pots of scarlet anemones in honor of the sacrificed god and dreamed of the Sacred Marriage for themselves. Seth excited their romantic passions and was the object of their secret fantasies. I dreamed with them of his boyish smile and his fine figure. It was I who had slept in his arms and borne his sons, and the memory of that sent the warm blood through my veins, loosing the hold of death upon me. The days of that remembered bliss seemed from a lifetime past, though he had been gone but forty days. All my suffering had happened in his absence; I must have believed it would end with his return.

"Herod Antipas knows by now that you live, my lady," Lysander said to me as we waited for the message of their arrival. "But do not be afraid. He would never dare to act against your consort—or the son of Almah Mari—while the people are so outraged against him."

"His vile temper is a boon to me," I agreed, "since in his anger he denounced me and repudiated our marriage before all the people. They will hold him to his words."

"Aye." Lysander's black eyes smiled beneath his gorgeous lashes. "If he yet entertains hope of adding Judea and Samaria to his kingdom, he will have to wait for a better time to petition Caesar with his claim." We stood on the top of the massive western wall of the Mount where it rose from the deepest part of the valley. The city lay almost entirely on the other side of the enclosure, and looking west, the eye took in the unbroken beauty of the rolling hills stretching away toward the sea in shades of green and brown, adorned with bands of trees in the low areas where there was water. The hills comforted me. I had often come up here through the years for the sense of calmness and insignificance it gave me, but Nina was afraid if I came alone, the demons would tempt me now with that sheer drop to the rocky hillside far below.

"Meanwhile," I said, inventing conversation to fill the time, "Pilate is in many ways as corrupt and overbearing as Antipas, yet with the people he has one asset: he is not a Herodian."

"The evil men do is remembered more than the good," Lysander agreed. "King Herod gave the people good reason to hate him, and they love to nourish it in their hearts. They feed and water it like a tender plant, and it grows so large it hides the truth."

"Do not defend Herod to me." I had not intended the sharpness in my voice. "Mad as he was in his last illness—he intended to kill all the nobles of Israel to assure mourning at his death!"

"This and greater evils he did." Lysander assented agreeably. He often counseled me like a wise uncle and was never shy to press his advantage, but he had been gentler with me of late. "In their hate," he continued, "people forget that Herod did more than any of their kings to unite and strengthen Israel. It was Herod who set them in a place of honor among the nations."

"And it is Antipas's legacy to draw upon his head this hatred for all things Herodian," I realized aloud. "Why not Philip?" I wondered, then answered my own question. "Philip rules a mixed people, mostly non-Jewish. There are so many Greeks and Arabs, his problems are not Jewish problems."

"Just so, my lady," he encouraged me, "and he is not, like Antipas, militarily ambitious."

"What word have you of Yeshua's party?" I asked him again, impatient with the conversation. Messages had been arriving all morning, for Lysander was a master at news gathering. His network of messengers could deliver news or rumor with unheard-of swiftness. Thus word finally came that Yeshua's party was approaching the northernmost part of the city. They were crossing over the Mount of Olives. They were coming up the broad paved street bounding the western wall of the Temple Mount. At last they were at the gate.

By this time, Sita, Miriam, and I were enjoying the excitement and suspense with the other women, leaning over the marble railing above the cloisters as Yeshua and Seth came with the others into the Temple environs. Almah did not enjoy the crowds and preferred to wait in her rooms. Finally, after all these years, she and Seth would meet, as I had wanted them to for so long. It was beyond belief that he had always happened to be away whenever she visited me.

Gooseflesh ran down my arms as the crowds below us surrounded Yeshua's white-robed figure. His companions formed a protective circle about him. Sita and I hugged each other in excitement. At last I spotted Seth; he had eluded me by wearing a burnoose that concealed his bright hair.

"He has grown a beard!" I exclaimed momentously.

"Indeed!" Miriam chuckled. "He has threatened to long enough."

Yeshua signaled he would speak, and the clamor subsided. We could not hear his words, but his message must have satisfied the crowd, for presently they began to disperse, talking among themselves. My unaccustomed liveliness pleased Miriam; I could see she was relieved at my good spirits. "No wonder my son adores you, Mari," she encouraged me in her rich voice. "You fulfill your office with the grace of a great lady and yet remain exuberant as a child."

"You are too gracious, dear Miriam," I replied with a warm blush. I knew she had declined an important invitation to be near me until I recovered my health, and I loved her like my own mother. "I am in love with him, too," I told her, mindful of the happiness it gave me to say so and the ease with which I could always share my feelings with her. At that moment, my dark tormentors seemed far away, and I believed in light and love and hope.

Miriam hugged me in her warm, spontaneous way. "Enjoy your happiness while you may, dearest child," she said. "Destiny does not often enough allow it."

We hurried to the open patio where I received visitors during good weather and found that Seth had hastened ahead of the others to meet us as we appeared. He dutifully greeted his mother first, but Miriam, with only a quick kiss, pushed him toward me. "I can wait, my dear," she laughed. "Your lady is dying to see you."

Seth pulled me inside the doorway of the sitting room, and his kiss was all I had dreamed. Dusty from the road, flushed and warm, he smelled of fresh air and sunshine. I would never have enough of his arms. His emotions were at a higher pitch than I had ever seen them. "Mari," he whispered, "sweet Mari, how thin and frail you are!" His breath caught in a hoarse sob. "They said you had died!"

"Oh my dear, I was so afraid you would hear that. But see! I live and breathe." I covered his face with kisses, only then remembering his beard. "You look just like Yeshua," I said, feeling pleased. Anything he did would have pleased me at that moment.

"Mari, there is a reason for that, which you will soon know. I must talk to you when there is time." His voice held an urgency I took for desire to hear all that had happened in his absence.

"My darling, we shall talk all night if you wish."

"I cannot come home yet tonight, Mari." His words struck me like cold water. "I will explain when we can talk." And he swept me out onto the now filled patio before I could protest or make sense of what he had said.

Seth moved to Yeshua's side, and I stared in amazement. They appeared identical. With his hair and beard grown out, Seth could be distinguished from Yeshua only by the difference of his clothing. "I thought I saw my own face," he had said of their first meeting. Either of them would have drawn attention by his appearance alone; two such were unbelievable.

While everyone marveled at their likeness, Almah came into the portico and stopped, startled, the blood draining from her face. I caught her look and moved toward her, alarmed, turning to seek the souce of her unease. She was staring at Seth with an expression I had never seen before. Her face turned from white to red, and fire seemed to flash all around her. The room turned deathly silent at the dreadful aspect she presented.

Yeshua and Seth turned resolutely to face her as though they had long expected this moment, an identical mild expression on their tanned faces. Yeshua placed his right hand on Seth's shoulder, and opened his mouth to speak. "Mother," was all he got out before Almah, the outrage of her glance aimed all at Seth, shrieked in an unearthly voice, "Imposter! Get away from my son!"

"Dearest lady, do not upset yourself. Please, let us go together and speak of this." Miriam came swiftly to Almah's side and tried to lead her into the sitting room.

But Almah turned her awful fury on Miriam and hissed, "You traitor! You have betrayed me! You knew all along where he was!" She began to wail in the greatest despair, while Miriam, refusing to be put off, continued to speak softly to her, at last leading her into the privacy of the little parlor.

Torn between my desire to clear up the puzzle of Seth's statement to me and my wish to greet Yeshua, I followed the two women and closed the door.

Almah, through outraged tears, accused Miriam. "Why did you not tell me you had saved him?" she demanded.

"Dear sister, you did not ask what I had done with him."

"But you reared him yourself! And you knew the danger!" The shrill note crept back into Almah's voice. "And you have kept him from my sight until now!"

I groped behind me for a seat, suddenly dizzy with the crowding implications of what was now as crystal clear as it had been hidden only moments before. How could I, I of all people, not have noticed, not have known? Seth was Yeshua's twin! Of course. But why had they concealed it? My mind searched desperately for a reason—a reason to excuse Almah. Even now, I could not believe evil of her.

Superstition held that a twin was bad luck, an enemy. Some people said twins had only one soul between them. In royal families it was not unusual when twins were born for the weakest, less perfect, or simply last born to be destroyed. Everyone knew tales of such children being rescued by midwives or servants and reared in secret, then appearing later to claim their inheritance. But surely Almah did not believe such nonsense or, worse still, had abandoned or wished the death of her own child!

Her anger seemed to leave her as swiftly as it had come. She looked sadly at me, then at Miriam. "We must explain all this to Mari," she said. "She has a right to know."

"Are they twins, then? Seth is also your son?" I asked hesitantly, my breath rasping.

"It is true," Almah nodded unhappily, her rage now but smoldering embers.

"I understand," I said slowly, feeling impelled to explain or defend her behavior. "The prophecy of the holy child says nothing of his being a twin." Almah had had to give up one of her sons in order for the prophecy to be realized. "But how did you know which one?" I asked. "They are so alike, how do you know which is really the Messiah?"

The flames of her anger blazed up again; she looked at me, and I trembled. "It is impossible"—she bit off each word with her teeth—"not to know."

My face felt hot. "But Seth is not . . . I mean, he cannot be . . . he is not Yeshua's enemy," I stammered miserably. Why did it all seem so terrible? I had never seen Almah like this.

She was instantly contrite. "Oh, my poor Mari. How can I bear to have hurt you? Forgive me, dearest one." She rushed to put her arms around me. "Of course Seth is not our enemy. He is also my son, and I must beg his forgiveness." I wanted to be appeased, but over Almah's shoulder I met Miriam's unguarded gaze, and the naked pity in her eyes jolted me like a blow.

When Seth and I were finally able to talk in the quiet sitting room, my mind teemed with questions, but closest to my heart was the one I asked, "Why can you not come to me tonight?"

His face, tanned dark by long days in the sun, was pained, and I studied it, taking in the difference of the trimmed beard and longer hair. My eyes lingered with desire on the curve of his lips beneath the soft mustache. He no longer seemed Greek, but Jewish, and all of Yeshua's group called him by his Jewish name, Judas, as their master did.

"Little one," he said tenderly, taking my face in his hands. "It is time for us to part for a while. Each of us must follow our own destiny."

The words struck me like a sharp blow; I smarted from the sting of it, not sensing at once how deep and mortal was my wound. Burning anger rose in my breast. I saw the flash of glowing eyes in the darkness behind my own. Who was he to talk to me about destiny? The words were so beneath him, like the lies of an adventurer who would prey on the feelings of women. I pushed him away. "How long have you known Almah is your mother?" I demanded.

He did not protest or evade. He seemed relieved that I was angry and would not beg him to stay. "I have always known," he answered steadily.

"And you did not see fit to tell me? Knowing how important it would be to me?" My fury rose higher. "You willingly lied to me!" I felt the demons crowding, dancing, leaping around me; the sound of their laughter rang in my ears. I stopped, warned, and caught my breath, then was struck with the knowledge that Almah and Miriam had also lied to me. They had all lied! All! My outrage was at all of them, but I vented it on only him.

"If I cannot trust you, I do not want to see you!" The hoarse voice did not seem like my own. "Leave me!"

The Shadow

For there is nothing hid, except to be made manifest,
Nor is anything secret, except to come to light.
Gospel of Mark 4:22, RSV

My anger soon turned to regret, but Seth was beyond reach, gone with Yeshua, Sita, and the others. I had never pursued him with messages, and would not now. Perhaps he had meant to be away only for a while, but I had sent him away forever. Still, if he cared for me, he would come to me, my pride told me. I wanted him to wait as longingly, as achingly, for me as I had waited for him.

Alone in my bed, my fury abated by exhaustion, I wondered if Yeshua had asked Seth to take leave of me. Many of his closest disciples had no families or had perhaps even abandoned them. Still, Yeshua had given me no warning when he sought me out that afternoon before my quarrel with Seth.

"You are unwell, Lady Mari." His face was concerned, and he looked into my very soul; surely he saw the demons that tormented me.

"I am much better, thank you." I longed to unburden my soul to him, certain he would understand.

"Nay, Mari, you have borne much, and for me. I will not forget what you have done." His clear gaze was all-knowing. Almah was right. It was impossible, despite their identical appearance, not to know him from his twin. The tranquility I felt in his presence made my demonic tormentors seem unreal. My mind sifted a thousand possibilities, searching for a way to be near him, and he responded as if I had spoken, "Later, when you are stronger, perhaps you will join us."

"O, Master," I was as one drowning, shamelessly reaching out. "If I go with you, I will gain my strength more quickly." Then, fearing I had been overbold, "I should like to be with both you and Judas." When he smiled as if at some secret joke, I felt easy enough to ask, "Do you mistrust your brother as your mother holds you should?"

Yeshua looked long into my face, reading the unspoken questions I dared not ask. Are you truly the Lord Osiris? And is my lover Seth your mortal enemy by that name? Why then do you, who know all things, treat him as your brother and friend?

The corners of his eyes crinkled in a radiant smile. "Like all younger brothers, he bears watching, so I shall keep him close," he leaned over me, so only I could hear, "lest he steal my birthright, as he has stolen my bride."

The memory of that conversation was imprinted brightly in my mind; it softened a little my grief about Seth's leaving. Seth's remark about destiny still filled me with rage, but I could not drive it from my mind. Did he know about my destiny? Was Yeshua my true destiny, or had he merely joked with me? And had Seth knowingly usurped and perverted that destiny through intervening in his brother's place? I knotted and unknotted the blanket fringes with restless fingers; my need for him was stronger than my desire to know the truth. If Seth wished to go with his brother, it need not come between us any more than his other periods away from Jerusalem had done, my heart reasoned. Then the light behind my eyelids glowed red, and I heard the demon whispers rising. Destiny, indeed! Seth had stolen my destiny along with my love. I snorted in frustration and tossed in my bed.

The failure of all my attempts to arrange a meeting between Almah and Seth made sense at last. That first year while I was in training for my office, I had indulged him in his desire to keep our nighttime trysts secret. "You have enough to worry about, right now," he had argued, with tender looks from beneath his thick lashes, an irresistible pucker of his adorable mouth. "This is not the best time for you to introduce a lover to your High Priestess, and I would not be a drawback to you for the world." In all the years that followed, he always had some commitment that took him away just at the time of Almah's visits.

Miriam's deception was more understandable. She and Almah had almost certainly sworn each other to secrecy, and even their affection for me would not have been reason enough to break such a vow. But Seth could not have known his identity, had Miriam not told him. Still, I could not deny the justice of her telling him; he had more right to know than anyone. I recalled word for word Almah's fury at Miriam for her breach of faith. But on that day long ago in Caesarea Philippi when Miriam told me the story of Yeshua's birth, she had said nothing of a twin.

It came back to me that I had felt dissatisfied, as though Miriam had stopped her story short of its end. It was of Seth's birth she had avoided telling! Perhaps Miriam would tell me the whole story now, if I asked her; but no, that would betray my faith with Almah. I could never bring myself to question Almah. Besides, there were things that only Miriam knew. I punched the down pillow to make a deeper place for my head, sleepless as ever. If only I could know what had really happened!

But I could know, and it would be easy. I opened my eyes wide in the darkness. My skills in traveling through the seven levels of the soul had been sharply honed these past months. But would such use of the Goddess's gifts be for selfish ends? As Magdalene, it was surely my duty to learn what deeply concerned those I loved, especially when it carried importance for all my people. Besides, Almah would be certain to know I sought the answers to my questions in the past and could prevent me if she wished.

I had already climbed from my bed. My attempts to justify what I was about to do made me smile as I wrapped a warm shawl about me. Better not to get cold; Seth would not be here to warm me again.

I padded in lambs' wool slippers to my sanctuary and lit the twin oil lamps on the small altar. I settled into the familiar hollow in the sheepskin rug and composed my thoughts.

"Blessed Mother, forgive me if my intent is selfish, or hide the truth from me if I am unworthy." My breathing slowed by long habit into the measured cadence that integrated body and mind. I would not need Nehushtan for so simple a task as this.

Slipping into trance, I recognized the place where time became unreal, and the past, present, and future were equally accessible. I thought of that day when Almah Mari, heavily pregnant, circles of weariness beneath her eyes, had arrived with Joseph at the Temple from their home in Nazareth. I felt again my heartbreak when the Magdalene Anna bundled her daughter into bed with orders she not be disturbed. "But I would not disturb her!" the child Mari protested, and my cheeks were wet again with those tears.

"Please, Almah," I pleaded, "who is my beloved Seth? Tell me he is not your enemy."

The time moved forward to the day of the birth, and the events of that day in Bethlehem unfolded as Miriam had related them. Then I felt my consciousness combine with Almah's in assurance of her help and blessing. She had just arrived at the comfortable quarters in the refurbished stable that Miriam and the lady Anna had prepared.

The women bustled about, preparing her bath and settling her in her spotless, sweet-smelling chamber, bringing her broth and cool water. As Almah gave herself into their loving hands, I was drawn more and more into her consciousness. I sensed that she felt so protected, so loved and cared for, that the tension of the last few days eased a little, and she fell into a fitful sleep.

After a time, she began to dream, and in her dream she knew herself as Isis, and reached toward the comfort of her love for Osiris. The fresh horror of his death—Sharon's death—had made her memory of him so painful she was only now able to over-shadow it with the anticipation of his coming rebirth. Now that the pains were upon her, hope had driven out her grief, and in her heart she called to him eagerly.

She saw him before her. He had Sharon's face. His steadfast love was in his eyes, and warning. "Take heed, and do not fear, beloved. Our enemy is not vanquished; he will have his part in our plans."

I felt her terror as she gasped, "Seth? Here? How?"

"Do not be afraid," he insisted, "I am warned this time. And we have many allies. Our sister is with us and even now has come to your aid."

"Nephthys?" Suddenly Almah, and I with her, knew. The realization shook her body like an earthquake. Miriam! Miriam of Scarios, midwife to queens; witch, seeress, sorceress. Nephthys. Dear wise, faithful Nephthys. Then she whispered, "But what of Seth?" She spoke not of my Seth, but of the evil brother of Osiris—but they were one!

"Alas, beloved. My brother and I shall enter the world as twins."

Hateful rage against her old enemy arose in Almah, obscuring all else. The unborn in her womb leaped so violently she envisioned the holy child and his evil brother locked in mortal combat that would rip her to pieces. After all they had suffered to accomplish her plan, it seemed certain now to be thwarted. She sprang upright in her bed, startling the women and waking from her dream. "Seth!" she cried out in despair. "He has tricked me again! Oh, no, no, no, no! Not again!"

Unable to bear the burden of her tortured psyche, I was able to separate myself from it. Miriam was at her side in an instant.

Almah gasped in recognition and relief, throwing her arms around Miriam's neck, every muscle and nerve in alarm. Her womb convulsed in an excruciating contraction so she could not cry out or breathe. She began to lose consciousness before it released her, gasping, drenched with perspiration. When she could speak, her voice came in a croaking whisper, "Oh, sister, you must help me!"

Miriam motioned fiercely to the other women to leave them, and they scurried away like field mice before the scythe of the harvester, all except me, the invisible watcher, and Anna, too wise to be intimidated and too concerned to be brushed aside. Miriam glared at her with a look that had withered many a weaker soul, but Anna did not move. Miriam softened her threatening gaze into a nod of respect and complicity that motioned Anna to draw nearer.

"Osiris and Seth are together in my womb, and I shall bear them both!" Almah cried in a loud whisper. "I am bound to choose but one, but will I know which one?" She looked pleadingly first at Miriam, then at her mother, her face twisted in a grimace, for the time between the contractions was short, and she felt the next one tightening its grip upon her. Anna had been present during Almah's revelation that she was Isis, so she said nothing, and of the matter of Seth and Osiris Miriam also held her peace. Perhaps she did it out of concern for secrecy, or perhaps she merely humored a young woman in pain.

"The first thing you must do is lie back, breathe deeply, and will yourself to take ease," Miriam commanded. "Now, as for the Messiah, little sister, we shall know him, without any doubt. Have no fear." So, soothing and cajoling, serving yet commanding, the midwife took the situation into her capable hands. And Anna, the High Priestess of Jerusalem, and I, Mari Anath, who would serve in that same office twenty-eight years later and see these things once again just as they now happened, watched and marvelled to ourselves.

The birth was unbelievably easy. Almah made a valiant effort to calm herself, and her years of practice in meditative discipline soon diminished her pain to mild discomfort. At last, with a cry more of wonder than of pain, Almah Mari brought forth her twins: the holy child, with his brother's head fast on his heels.

Miriam picked up the firstborn—I took careful note of this—and he cried lustily, filling his lungs with the breath of life. Then he opened his great eyes and looked into Miriam's face with such directness and recognition that she started in amazement, as if expecting him to speak her name. That lucid gaze could belong only to a god! It could be none other than Osiris. She placed the child in Anna's arms and turned to the other.

The twin lay on his back between his mother's thighs, his eyes wide and untroubled, as comely as his brother, seemingly identical. He had filled his lungs without a cry, and he looked about him as a king surveys his domain. Miriam surely hesitated. Could she be sure? She cut and began to tie off the cord, watching all the while for some sign.

She looked up into the concerned face of the Magdalene, Anna. There must be no doubt. And she must make the choice. I watched Miriam meet Anna's gaze without pretense; to deceive her would be impossible. A long look of silent agreement and perfect understanding passed between them. Moving deliberately, Miriam wrapped the child in a soft blanket, then concealing him in the folds of her shawl, she let herself silently out the door of the chamber away from the room where the women waited and was gone. Almah, cradling her son, watched in silence. Neither she nor her mother spoke. Then they turned their attention to the marvelous child in her arms. But the unblinking eye of my mind followed Miriam. I saw her hand the child to a young woman when she had reached her own lodgings. I knew instantly the woman was a wet-nurse and that Miriam had procured her for just such an eventuality. Had she known? I watched as Miriam returned alone to the birth room and expertly addressed herself to Almah's needs and comfort. They did not question her. An unspoken pact had been made among them.

Slowly, I returned to my own time and place and opened my eyes. One of the lamps on the altar was sputtering, nearly out of oil. I arose stiffly and blew it out, then, carrying the other, I returned to my empty bed, my mind in turmoil. Could he who had warmed that bed, he who was so sorely missed by me now, be Almah and Yeshua's mortal enemy? And if he was that Grand Artificer who had deliberately entrapped pure spirit in this endless round of death and rebirth, why had Miriam not destroyed him? Yet this same creator of the material world was worshipped by my people as Jehovah, the Lord God. Seth, the Trickster. I shivered. The cold had penetrated my woolen wrapper. If Yeshua was Osiris, Lord of the Spirit, why did he not fear and distrust the diabolical twin who had nailed him into that coffin of mortal flesh? A dry sob of confusion, exhaustion, and grief escaped me. If Seth were only here, I would welcome his arms, let him be the very prince of devils himself!

26

The Demons

For whosoever has not known himself, has known nothing, but whomever has known himself has simultaneously achieved knowledge about the depth of all things.

Book of Thomas the Contender

"Promise me that you will rest and enjoy yourself," Almah commanded and kissed my cheek, trying not to look anxious. My wretched face and thin body worried her, but I was too preoccupied to care.

"I will be careful, I promise." It was pleasant enough to be sent off to Bethany—but I found enthusiasm for anything impossible to summon.

That had been two days ago. Now, I plucked the few weeds I could find among the lavender and rosemary in my mother's herb garden—except for the purslane. Mother liked to leave a little purslane, a tonic for the blood. I straightened, my back protesting. My whole body seemed out of joint, out of sorts. I frowned into the morning sunlight that shone over the distant roofs of Jerusalem. The Temple Mount rose beyond the rest, its massive walls secure, impregnable. Turning, I faced the large, comfortable house set in the hollow of the hill. I had been born in that house, and it had sheltered many generations before mine. It was good that Martha was mistress here. The touch of envy I had once felt for my sister was gone with all my other feelings.

"We have had precious little time in our lives to get to know each other," Martha had observed the day before, skillfully moving her shuttle across the great loom while I absently spun a smooth thread and kept an ear in the direction of the children. Martha's talkative, sunny spirit contrasted with her husband's solemn shyness; she was as warm and generous as our mother, and she had long ago outgrown her awe of my office, treating me as a sister not as a High Priestess.

"The two years I once thought placed you so beyond me seems now but a single day," she had confided.

"Aye, so it seems also to me," I had agreed, but I was dismayed by my inability to feel the affection of which I spoke.

Martha left her loom and planted a warm kiss on my cheek. Her look had been puzzled, but her love unquestioning. Remembering the worried lines above her black brows returned me now to my grief. I sighed heavily and pinched off sage and chamomile for the basket I carried, turning my thoughts to Yeshua. Lysander brought regular news of Yeshua and the excitement that surrounded him, but he had not returned to the Temple. I continued to dispatch funds through the messengers Judas sent—he was in charge of the moneys that supported Yeshua's wandering ministry, which came mostly from the coffers of the priestesses of Ashera in Jerusalem. Almah desired that her son's material needs should not interfere with his work among the people. Almah would care for the whole world if she could, I thought, just as she cared for me. The Goddess was in her. Sometimes I saw Her in Aethel, my mother; in Lili, the wise old crone; in the Magdalene Anna; in Miriam of Scarios; in Ninshubur and even Salome. Was She also in me? Once I had believed I served her, and felt her blessing, but that seemed long ago.

Almah Mari was the Goddess-on-Earth. The Goddess was not just *in* her, as She was in others. True, I had only my visions to confirm that Almah was Queen Isis incarnate, but everything I had ever known about Almah confirmed the truth of those visions. Why had I alone been so visited? But then, who was I to question the purposes of the Mother? In all the years we had known each other, Almah had never claimed to be the Goddess— but she had never denied it. And why ask for confirmation of what I was certain about? Until that day she had first seen and denounced Seth, I had never questioned my image of her. But her livid face, its beauty distorted by hideous wrath, had been a revelation of doubt to me. I could not forbid the memory of it that played over and over in my mind. Nor could I forbid the realization that she had appeared as one possessed by demonic, as well as divine, powers.

If Almah sensed my new misgivings about her, she expressed no reproach, only an excess of tender patience. I brooded about the bitter reality that the two people I loved most saw each other as mortal enemies. How was I to live with that? Almah's cruel words to Seth had planted a seed that had taken root when Seth betrayed me. He had betrayed me, I was now sure; he had deliberately played the trickster with me by stealing the love that had been meant for another, and he had destroyed my only hope of happiness. But since he had taken himself out of my life I could not pass one hour without longing for him. I rehearsed the scene when he would admit it all to me, beg for my forgiveness. But if Almah had wanted me to choose between them, Seth had made the choice for me. Would he come back if I renounced Almah's friendship? But even the thought, despite my doubts, was unbearable. I had chosen Almah, though my heart was choked with anger and rebellion against her.

But Almah Mari made it difficult to remain angry with her. Her tenderness and patience seemed inexhaustible. Yet it was she who had encouraged, almost commanded, me to undertake the most terrible risk to my body, mind, and soul. She had surely known it might change me forever.

Nevertheless, her concerned attention should have moved me. I wanted to love and trust her again. I tied the basil, sage, and rosemary into tidy bundles and sorted them neatly in the basket. Unable to summon any responsive emotion to conceal my shameful lack of feeling, I complied without resistance to Almah's attempts to look after me. She kept me as much as possible in the company of Shaher and Shalem and sent us all to Bethany for days at a time, hoping I would recover my spirits within the warm confusion of the child-filled household.

I pinched the lemon thyme and sniffed its fragrance. For a moment, from the corner of my eye, I thought I saw a tall figure in the sunlight near the stable. I did not turn around, for I knew Grandfather Claudius would disappear if I tried to look straight at him; I breathed deeply and sent a silent message of love into the void, grateful for the sharp pain I still felt at his loss. Was it only the dead I could love? Had my heart remained in the Netherworld?

I picked up my basket and went toward the house. I entered the center hall and went into Grandmother Lili's sitting room.

"Ah, Mari, come in." The old lady's voice crackled like dry leaves. Wizened as a fabled *jinn* after centuries in an earthenware jar, she sat facing away from the door in the tiny chair Lazarus had carved for her. How did Grandmother know it was I? She could neither have seen nor heard me.

"I have just picked fresh herbs to dry, Grandmother. Would you like some tea?" I kissed her shrivelled cheek.

"Leave them on the table, and the young ones will hang them to dry for me this afternoon," she instructed. "I'll have blackberry tea, from the jar on the shelf." Her black eyes looked searchingly at me, missing nothing. "Are you feeling better, my child?" She asked so gently I thought I had not really heard her.

"Yes, Grandmother."

"Mari, come here." I went and knelt before the ancient crone— my little grandmother. She was so small. She placed her gnarled hand on my cheek. "It will pass, my child," she said.

I dropped my head into her lap and let the blessed tears overflow the well of grief within me. I felt I would die of sorrow, of emptiness. My life had been returned to me, and for what? For the yet-to-be-paid price of another's. The guilty knowledge of it consumed me, and the accusing stares of the Annanaki glared from every shadow, every darkened corner, together with the sightless eyes of the slain Baptist accusing me with his death. "Harlot! Abomination!" The curse repeated itself in my mind over and over, like a song once learned that refuses to be forgotten.

I drew some comfort in considering the outcome, as Grand-mother Lili's hands, knotted with age, stroked my hair. I had escaped marriage with Antipas and given him the opportunity to discredit himself with the people. His threat to Seth and Yeshua had been turned aside, though at grave cost to myself. Yeshua, if not Seth, had thanked me so sincerely I was certain he understood why I had undertaken so perilous a journey.

Yeshua. He seemed my only haven against despair. The image of his face drove away the angry eyes that flashed through my darkness and the accusing voices that destroyed my solitude. It was not romantic longing I felt for Yeshua, no delicious and rosy imaginings as my thoughts of Seth had been—still were, had I had the heart to indulge in them. The thought of Yeshua was not so much a longing for his presence as a sense *of* his presence. It made me feel peaceful—peaceful and safe.

When I rose stiffly, Grandmother Lili opened her eyes, for she had drifted off into her dreams.

"Blessings to you, child," she said.

"Blessings to you, Grandmother." I kissed her. "And thank you."

After I returned to the temple, Yeshua was more and more in my thoughts and Almah and Seth less and less. I believed the Mother would see me through my troubles; she always had.

But the Mother, Queen Isis, incarnate in Almah Mari, had some plan to sacrifice Yeshua. There must be something I did not understand. My headaches grew more intolerable.

All my life, I had been certain that my headaches had to do with the Goddess—a doubtful blessing, from which Nina and I (because she shared my thoughts) drew rueful humor. "She wants to come out," Nina told me once.

"Out?" I queried, unamused.

"She is in you, too, Mari. If you let her out, perhaps it would stop your pain."

I knew she was right, of course. But I could not bring the truth of what she said to the level of real conviction. It is possible to believe many things one cannot know, but it is also possible to know what one cannot believe. Almah was the Goddess to me, and I was the Goddess to Nina, I thought. It was as simple as that. So I pushed away the truth.

Then one morning after a night walking the floor of my chambers in agony until Nina mixed me a second powerful draught of Miriam's headache potion, only an hour before my usual time of arising, I was visited once more by the Dream in which I became Isis. The world again seemed an endless swamp as I peered through tear-blind eyes into stagnant pools, clawed with mud-defiled hands through green and gritty slime, laboring to discover some decaying, worm-infested part of the once fair body of my love.

Again I felt the holy tears on the divine face of the Mother. She would bring her beloved to Paradise to be with her forever. She had borne him, as she had promised; she would anoint him and sacrifice him, also as she had promised.

"You shall be of special help to me." The words of the Goddess called up in my mind my solemn promise to serve Her in any way She might ask.

As I awakened from that dream, the grief it engendered so familiar I never shed it, I stumbled by habit out of bed into my sanctuary. I fell to my knees, too numb for tears, before the shrine of the Goddess. When I could speak, I implored, "O, blessed Mother, spare him! Spare him yet awhile! Do not take him from us so soon, for all men die; he can yet be with you."

The presence of the Goddess flowed over me, blessing me. But I felt no answer to my prayer. "Please, Holy Mother," I prayed, "do not ask me to do anything to bring about his death."

Then my face turned hot with shame. She chided me gently as a rebellious child. In my heart I heard the words of the Star Goddess, words first taught me by Aethel and Lili, repeated all my life in the Temple, words I had taught my own daughter and the children who came each year into my care:

My children may serve me only with free and willing hearts, for I ask only the service of love. What you do for me you will do in joy, and all that you do in joy, you do for me.

More hopeful than for a long time, but stiff with cold, I crept back into my bed and huddled among the woolen robes, trying to warm myself. Presently, it came to me that the cold was my chief discomfort; the familiar pain had eased. I felt lighter; my courage began to return. I resolved to face the guilt I felt for returning from the dead owing a substitute. Almah had assured me over and over that a substitute was already chosen. I had been unwilling, not unable, to understand.

I shivered with emotion. Yeshua. Yeshua, called by his love for the Mother—whose service is perfect freedom—Yeshua would choose willingly, even joyfully, to follow the path of anointing and sacrifice she had prepared for him. Yeshua would harrow the halls of the Seven Judges and take away their judgment seats; the terrible Annanaki would bow down before him. He would set free the myriad souls they held in torment. He would turn his mild and gentle gaze on the hateful Queen of the Netherworld; he would make love with the Dark Goddess of death—take her as his bride—she, the dread and rejected sister, would bud and bloom with light and life. All would recognize her as her true self, the Mother, and sing praises to her evermore—Queen of Heaven, Earth, and Hell, one Kingdom, eternal.

I lay captured by the power of my revelation, staring at the heavy beams of carved cedar above my bed, my tears running down through my hair, wetting my pillow. Overwhelmed with blessing, I found permission to go on with my life.

I arose purposefully and rang the brass gong for Nina. "Find us clothing such as merchant's wives might wear," I told her. "We are going out, but I wish not to draw attention. Where is Lysander?"

He appeared at once. "Tell me of Yeshua's whereabouts, for I will go to him." I spoke to him as I had not spoken in months. He looked at me with delight, past my face still red-eyed from weeping.

"Madame, he left the shores of Galilee two days ago, and travels this way through Lydda and Emmaus."

"He is so near, then!" A good omen. The loving concern in his face warmed me. "We should meet him if we go as far as Emmaus."

The household ran smoothly even during my absence or illness, and the preparations I requested were made before I had finished breakfast—my first whole meal in weeks. We rented a comfortably shabby carriage with good horses from a wine merchant and stashed supplies of food and money in ample compartments smelling of leather and wine. I took leave of Shaher and Shalem with many hugs and kisses, my love and delight in them alive once more. Though my tears lay close to the surface, I felt as though a hard lump had melted away.

We departed an hour before noon with Lysander and me inside the coach and Lucius and Nina mounted in front. Lucius turned the horses about, and we left the Temple Mount by the western gate, heading out across the lower city southward toward Emmaus. Descending from the heights of the city slowly to the plain, we had a sweeping view of the Kidron Valley, and beyond it the rolling hills of Judea stretching westward to the sea.

The broad road to Emmaus had been paved with heavy stones by Herod the Great, for it was a major route to the sea. It carried a heavy commerce of horses, donkeys, mules, and camels drawing every kind of conveyance imaginable. Some people rode in the growing heat of the mid-morning, and many walked, leading animals laden with merchandise or possessions. They rode in carts, wagons, chariots, and carriages, or were carried in sedan chairs. There were merchants, farmers, artisans, soldiers, and sailors. There were entertainers and prostitutes, servants and tax collectors, people of every race and color. In this mass of moving humanity, each person intent on her own purpose, his own task, I savored the sense of insignificance I found. Nowhere, among those many souls, could I see even one who might share, or even understand, my anguish. Surely my concerns could not be as ultimate as they seemed. Was it possible I was being foolish, or worse, possessed by my demons, out of my mind?

Two days later, in Jerusalem, at the house of Simon the Pharisee, we finally caught up with Yeshua and his roving band. My frustration had been lightened by the pleasure of being with Nina, Lucius, and Lysander, just the four of us. Like a return to childhood, a holiday in celebration of our friendship, we spent two days and nights in the freedom of being unrecognized. The last was in a comfortable inn at Emmaus, where we learned that Yeshua's party, traveling on foot by lightly traveled roads, had passed us and would reach Jerusalem that evening.

We made at once for the city, but I would not return to the Temple until I had fulfilled my quest, though I longed for a deep, hot bath. We washed ourselves in cold water from a stream and put on fresh clothing. Lysander had word Yeshua would take his evening meal at the house of Simon, so I timed my arrival an hour later, hoping I could reach him through the press of people.

Getting through the crowd was easy behind Lucius, who made way like a heavy plow. I was dumbfounded to see such numbers of the sick, the poor, the blind, and the lame, who followed Yeshua wherever he went, hoping for help from him, a healing word or touch of his hand. Even as I. The respite from my suffering of these last three days had been bought by that hope.

When we reached the doorway of the room where he sat, I leaned to peer through the iron gate barring my way, cradling an alabaster jar of myrrh I had purchased as an offering from the Temple store. Peter, one of Yeshua's companions, rumored to be a Zealot, was acting as doorkeeper, screening the petitions of those requesting audience. He had expressed grave displeasure with the Goddess and her priestesses when Yeshua had brought him to breakfast with us; I did not suppose he would act favorably toward me now. He was turning away the sick, blind, and infirm with some promise the Master would minister to them on the morrow. I pressed my face hopefully against the iron bars. "Please, I must speak with him," I pleaded.

The rugged fisherman looked down at me without recognition. "He is at supper now," he said gruffly. "Leave him in peace."

As quickly as I thought it, I said, "If you please, sir, let me speak to Judas, for I have business with him."

The big fisherman studied my face for a long moment. "Wait," he grunted at last, and disappeared from the doorway. My heart was leaping, and I resisted an impulse to run away. It had been so difficult to get this far.

"Mari! Is it you?" I heard a loud clang as the bolt was thrown and the gate opened, but stood rooted, unable to move. Seth's arms reached out to me, led me out of the darkness into the lighted room. He stood looking down at me, sincerely surprised and concerned, as the iron gate was closed and locked behind me. I steeled my heart, trying to see him as my enemy.

But he made no move to touch me when he had drawn me into the room, and I saw he did not repent his decision. Seeing him thus stilled my anger; I could accept his leaving in peace. More than that, I could move past him and remember why I had come.

"I came to see Yeshua." I watched my words strike him a blow I had not intended but could not regret. "I would speak with him," I said firmly. My voice sounded clear and strong.

Judas of Scarios took my hand with polished propriety and led me forward. We stopped a few feet from Yeshua, where he sat engrossed in conversation with his host. He looked up at me.

Yeshua's glance was like a blinding light that penetrated to my bones, warming my very marrow. Then, the unbearable knowledge of his impending death washed over me in a great wave and cast my soul at his feet like bleached and battered driftwood—beautiful in its nakedness. On my knees before him, I felt his hand caress my unbound hair. My mantle dropped from my shoulders as I groped for the lacings at his feet.

The stubborn knot of my pride slowly unraveled within me. I, who was able to be generous in giving of myself, had not had the grace to accept another's sacrifice. I dared to recall my fearful descent past the Seven Judges of the Netherworld. Then I had been stripped of every quality, every distinction. Could I have forgotten so soon that there is no rank, no privilege, in the house of death? The flesh of the coward is as sweet as the hero's to the worms, and the moldering bones of the wise make no finer dust than a fool's. Not only I, but everyone, must be redeemed from the house of death, and he who would pay that price had been chosen long ago. My face contorted, my chest heaving, I faced the awful truth.

Yeshua would die for me. Yeshua, so much more worthy than I, would die, and I would be free of the grinning, yammering demons that dogged my every moment. Like Inanna, who had pointed her finger at Dumuzi and screamed at the galla, "Take him! Take Dumuzi away!" I had chosen him—chosen *him*—an acceptable sacrifice in exchange for my soul.

Gently he suffered me to remove his dusty and road-worn sandals, and the room was silent, all eyes upon us. I took the alabaster jar from the pouch in my robe and opened it. The heavy scent of myrrh filled the room. I lavished it all upon his calloused, sunbrowned feet, massaging the fragrance into his skin. My tears fell down and mingled with the myrrh, and I wiped them with my hair, so they would not dilute my gift.

Yeshua's hand was so light on my hair I sensed more than felt its presence there. Overcome and transported by blessing, I could not, would not, move.

"What wasteful foolishness is this?" The scornful voice of Simon the Pharisee slashed the silence. "Such expensive ointment had been better sold to help the poor!" Then he got nearer to what troubled him. "This woman is not welcome in my house!"

Anguished and affronted, unable to move or speak, I clasped Yeshua's knees, shaking with sobs. His touch was liquid fire as he lifted my face to look at him. It was to Simon he spoke.

"Simon, you gave me no water to wash my feet, but this woman has washed them with her tears. You gave me no kiss, but she has not ceased to kiss my feet. Do not reproach her, Simon, for you did not anoint my head with oil, but she has anointed me for my burial."

Simon was subdued, but he protested. "Master, do you recognize this woman?" His face was all outraged propriety. "She is Magdalene, the great Whore of Jerusalem!"

His repetition of the Baptist's denunciation was less shocking to me than the prophet's words had been. Yeshua rose to his feet, meaning for me to stand also. He lifted me with his left hand, while he motioned firmly with the other to someone behind me. Gaining my feet, I saw Seth, his arms held fast by Peter and another man, his enraged gaze on Simon. He relaxed a little at Yeshua's look, but the men held him as Yeshua turned to his host.

"Mari is no harlot, but a great lady and a pure virgin," he announced to a collective gasp of disbelief. He continued in his words that caressed my spirit, "She has loved much, and love is of God. Because of her great love, Mari has died and been reborn, and all her sins are forgiven."

Forgetting everything except his face, I stood enraptured, wanting this moment to last forever. Gently, he led me to a bench, seating himself beside me, with a sign to his host he wished not to be interrupted. "Let Judas go," he said, and I caught Seth's glance for a moment, certain I saw a look of blessing.

"I hoped you would come, Mari," Yeshua said, and waited for me to speak. I could not find my voice, yet my heart spoke to him.

Oh, my shepherd Dumuzi, great Osiris, anointed Christos, you who have chosen to take my place in Hell, how can I accept your sacrifice? How can I live at the price of your death? Haltingly, stumblingly, I managed aloud, "I beg you, suffer me to remain with you awhile."

It was my unspoken question that he addressed. "No one can take my life from me," he said, looking into my eyes and heart, "unless I lay it down myself. You have suffered much for me already, and that is why you have understood what these others will not see though I preach it to them night and day." He continued with a look of deep tenderness, "Dearest, Mari, I shall ask you to suffer even more. Will you be able to bear it?"

I nodded dumbly; power and resolution flowed into me, hardening my very bones. My heart beat strongly beneath my expanding ribs; I would do, could do, anything.

From that day forward, I was freed from the seven demons of Annanaki.

PART 4

The Anointed One

When righteousness is weak and faints and unrighteousness exults in pride, then my spirit arises on earth. For the salvation of those who are good, for the destruction of evil, for the fulfillment of the kingdom of righteousness, I come to this world in the ages that pass.

Bhaghavad Gita

The Ministry

For love is victorious in attack,
And invulnerable in defense.
Heaven arms with love
Those it would not see destroyed.

Tao-te-ching

"**M**aster, this woman has no place in our inner circle! We are ashamed to be associated with her." Peter the fisherman, his voice dry and dust-caked as his clothing, spoke for others as well as himself. It was a late afternoon in the early summer, and we had walked until midday, followed and besieged by crowds of people. We had rested in a shady grove during the middle of the day and taken the road again until now. No village was nearby, so Yeshua accepted the hospitality of a shepherd who offered us the shelter of his tents for the night. I was so tired I barely realized Peter spoke of me before he went on, "Suffer her to live among the other women who follow you, and not with us. Women are not worthy of eternal life."

Yeshua clasped me by the waist and turned toward Peter. "Is it only males then, who shall see life?" he demanded mildly. Peter persisted, his face hot. "Lord, the Pharisees despise her as the Whore-goddess of Babylon. If you do not put her away from you, many will turn against you!"

"Peter, again I say to you, God is One: Father *and* Mother, Creator *and* Source. God's truth is manifest in Ashera, just as it is manifest in her spouse, Jehovah." He waited, inviting dissent, while the silence crackled. Then he charged, "He who has ears to hear, let him hear!"

It was only among strict interpreters of the Jewish Law that I was despised. I enjoyed great popularity with the common people, and those who recognized me welcomed and made much of me, for I was the High Priestess of Ashera, better known and honored among them in those early days than Yeshua himself. And it was meet to them that I should be with him, for he was known as a child of the Temple, born of a Magdalene. So I stood silent but unashamed as he defended my place in his inner circle. I had no doubt that I belonged there, nor did he. Let those who thought otherwise learn to live with it.

So the tension remained between factions of the group, though John and James went out of their way to make me welcome. Two influential Pharisees, Nicodemus, and Joseph of Arimathea, were also respectful and warm toward me. Peter saw my sickliness as the judgment of the Law, richly deserved for past sins, but my weakness brought out the protective gallantry in Joseph and Nicodemus.

"Know you, lady Magdalene, your blessed grandmother, Lili, is aunt to my mother, Althea?" Joseph asked me one day as we walked side by side.

"Why, I have heard her speak of Althea. Is she your mother?" I replied in pleased surprise. "But I cannot surmise how you and I are related. Does this make us third or fourth cousins, or are we uncle and niece, several times removed?"

Joseph shook his gray head good-naturedly. "Such questions are for those who understand these things—the women," he laughed, "but I shall be honored if you will call me uncle."

"It shall be my honor, Uncle," I told him, bowing.

"Why, then, kiss me, my niece!" he commanded graciously, bending to kiss me on each cheek. "We two shall be fast friends!"

Judas, as I was learning to call him, was solicitous and kind, but he acted as though we had never been lovers. As I grew accustomed to his Jewish name and accepted the thoughtful consideration of Judas, Seth became more and more a memory. Judas worried about my frail health, as did my brother, Lazarus, who was with us until the grain harvest called him home. The friendship between my brother and my former consort did not suffer from the change in our relationship; they cooperated but did not compete in looking after me. One of them always saw that I had a litter on long days of traveling. Still weak in my breath and limbs, I welcomed their help and was thankful for it, but I was hurt at Seth's coolness, outraged that he could act as if our sons had not been born. I pushed away my anger at him and filled my thoughts with Yeshua.

My strength was returning every day. We were out of doors most of the time, and my appetite increased. As I walked more and more, my tender feet grew tanned and hard with callouses, the henna faded from their nails, and the day came when they no longer ached unbearably after a long day on the road.

Nina was careful not to fuss over me, but she saw that a fresh change of clothing was always ready and was skillful at finding where a bath could be had. She kept my few necessities in order and carried them for me so my hands were free.

Yeshua did not disdain the Samaritans as did the religious Jews. We had been climbing slowly through Samaria, northward toward Galilee, for the hills were cooler than the rocky valley of the Jordan. Here the brown grasses were well cropped between scrubby areas of gray green foliage. Everywhere we were sought out by people who needed healing for themselves or for others.

"Honor to you, Lady." The stately leader of several gray-robed priestesses addressed me, rather than Yeshua. "I am Rhea," she continued, inclining her proud head ever so little, yet conveying the deepest respect. "We come to you as your sisters, for we also serve the Mother."

"Welcome, sisters," I replied. "May I know of your temple?"

The priestess placed a patrician, work-worn hand over her breast. "Our only temple is in our hearts, Lady, and our special work is to feed the poor lepers who are exiled to the caves near here. Because they are outcasts, they have lost family and friends, and their only help is from each other and our sisterhood. We beg daily for food and bring it here to them, but even we dare not touch them. They are the saddest and most miserable of all people."

"They have no nurses or medicine?" I could not comprehend such hopelessness.

"Some of our sisters have chosen to live among them, but once they go to the caves, they can never return. Two have recently died, and the only other is too ill now herself to be of help."

I looked at Yeshua, and his face was eager, compassionate.

"Bring to me any who will come," he said to the gray priestess, who bowed her head slightly and as respectfully as she had to me.

"You are the Son of the Mother and a great healer," she said, "but they are forbidden. You must go to them. Not to the caves," she added with a whithering look at the horrified faces of the disciples. "It will suffice if you will come as far as the place where we leave their food for them."

"I will come alone at daybreak tomorrow," Yeshua said. "There is no need for the rest of you to risk yourselves."

"I will come, for I can help," Sita said.

"And I," I agreed, knowing I spoke for Nina as well. "You will need help with the children."

The silence was heavy and thick as wool before John spoke. "Master, if you can heal lepers, you can heal us, too. We will all come." He looked around at the others to see if any were unwilling. "More can be helped if we are there." The men slapped each other's backs and gripped each other's hands like soldiers preparing for battle.

"You have all the courage of women," Yeshua said, not showing by his expression whether he praised or mocked them. I praised John in my heart, and we exchanged glances. He was right, for our combined belief always increased Yeshua's powers.

Next morning, guided by a single priestess—for the others were busy gathering that day's food for the lepers—our little band came to the place below the dreary caves where a shallow stream flowed among tall cedars. The sweet smell of yellow broom drifted down to us from the hills above the stream. All day the people came to Yeshua's hands, but it was a slow and painful business. Many needed to be carried, or led. The men worked to organize them into groups, and to record their names and places of birth in order to locate relatives or work after they were healed. The women guided, led, and carried them to him.

In the mid-afternoon, Nina and I, our clothing soiled from carrying unwashed and suffering children in our arms, moved among those still waiting. I took the leprous hands of a ragged boy and his smaller sister whose scaly faces showed the white marks of the disease. The little girl was already blind. Nina bore in her arms a boy whose legs were withered and useless, and Sita carried a filthy, ragged little girl.

As Sita moved forward to place her burden in Yeshua's arms, I took notice that her white dress was unstained, as always. Sita had welcomed me among Yeshua's intimates with generous affection, though I half expected and would have excused jealousy from her. Her heart proved spotless as her clothing, unstained through days of travel and jostling among the crowds.

"Take her and wash her," Yeshua said to Sita, when he had blessed the child, whose skin began to shed its dreadful scales. She accepted the little girl from his hands and moved toward the stream, her face radiant with the joy of her service.

Sita had lived many years the life of a homeless pilgrim, and no discomfort or inconvenience affected her serenity. She cared only for others, with no concern for her own needs, like the birds of the air and flowers of the field Yeshua spoke of. Once I had stopped to listen as she taught the Temple children. She had asked for salt and a bowl of water, and my own Shaher had brought them to her.

Sita stirred the salt into the water with a wooden paddle. "Where is the salt now?" she asked Shaher.

He pointed to the bowl, and the others watched, nodding in agreement.

"Can you see it?" Sita asked, passing the bowl of water among the children, who gazed into it, shaking their heads. "Taste it, then," she demanded, and they dipped their fingers into the bowl and licked them, nodding and murmuring assent. Sita waited until they all looked at her again expectantly, silent.

"That One, the spirit, is also unseen," she told them. "But it is there, hidden in all things and all beings. It is within you."

The children glanced sideways at one another, but they remained still, their attention on her face and voice. "It is your Self." She looked straight at Shaher again. "Where is that One then?" she demanded.

Shaher hesitated, then pointed to his breast, and the others followed, pointing to themselves and each other, giggling to deny the seriousness of what they felt. "No," Sita said clearly, and they stopped, puzzled. "Thou art salt, not water. That One is not *in* thee," she told them intently, "thou *art* that One."

I recognized in Sita a perfect spirit, and I longed for such serenity. She carried her possessions in a soft pouch of the same white cotton as her dress. She owned one extra length of white cloth, which was her clean gown, a blanket that doubled as a cloak against the cold, a comb of tortoiseshell for her long hair, and a flask or two of fragrant oil. She always took the last seat and waited until last to be served. She never asked for food or drink, taking only what was offered to her, yet she never suffered, for the others made up in concern for her what she lacked for herself. She was to me the living embodiment of the message Yeshua taught.

Now I stood before Yeshua with my two charges, and he knelt to look into their shy faces. "Ah, Mari, what have we here?" His warm voice and hands enveloped the children, as he stroked their faces and hair, their arms, legs, hands, and feet, healing as he touched. "Go with Mari and wash," he said, and I turned away with them, loving them as he loved them, and loving him more than I could bear.

I followed Sita to a sandy, open place between the layered rocks where we could reach the water, wiping my eyes with my soiled sleeve. "See, you are all new and clean!" I exclaimed, showing the children how the scales floated from their hands. But they pulled back from me, fearful. Lepers were not allowed to wash in any stream, for fear of infecting others. Neither of these little ones had ever been bathed by loving hands. "Where is your mother?" I asked, when I could command my voice.

"Dead, Lady," said the boy.

"And your father?"

"We have no father," he answered. Sita moved toward us with the child in her care.

"This poor babe is motherless, too," she said.

"You cannot adopt all the orphaned children we find," Nina warned, leading the prancing child she had carried to Yeshua. The anxious mother recognized her son and came running from the crowd to claim him.

"Oh, thank you! Bless you!" she stammered, as the boy wobbled awkwardly on legs that had never borne his weight before.

"I will have Lysander send for someone to take them to the Temple," I decided aloud. I stripped to my tunic and waded into the water, coaxing the brother and sister to follow me. "We will care for them ourselves in the meantime." I pulled off their ragged clothing and began washing them. "Tell me your name," I said to the boy.

"Lugal."

"Lugal! 'Big man.' I knew another Lugal long ago. And your sister?"

"Naomi."

"You are generous, Lady," Sita said shyly, "but it is possible some are here who have lost their own children and would gladly take to themselves these innocents."

"Sita, I bless you!" I whacked Naomi's garment against a rock. "I can think of two families already."

"This was your last clean gown," Nina said resignedly, picking up my soiled dress. "I know the people you mean, and another couple who would be delighted to take this little one." She indicated the pretty three-year-old who was emerging from the filth and scales under my hands, blinking her great brown eyes, blind but an hour before.

Lugal turned on me a startled and fearful look, and I took him in my arms. "These two must stay together," I promised. "We will see to that."

And it was as Sita had guessed. We found homes for five of the children among the people Yeshua had healed, and who had relatives and property that they would be able to claim. But Sita was so fond of little Celia, she had kept her until last, and Lugal and Naomi remained because I would not separate them.

Several days later, on a verdant hillside near the city of Nain, bright with flowers of white and yellow, a young husband brought his wife to Yeshua to be healed of her grief for their child, dead for more than a year. The poor woman had withdrawn so deeply into herself that she never spoke and would not eat unless her husband himself fed her each mouthful. When Yeshua took her face between his hands and looked deep into her eyes, she smiled, and began to bless those around her.

"Lady," Sita said in her soft voice, approaching the couple with Celia in her arms, "this child of God has been healed of leprosy, but has no mother or father. She will be well with you, I promise."

The new family went away praising God, but Sita turned her back so no one would see her tears.

It was not so hard for me. My own Shaher and Shalem would return from the seashore with Nana to be with me in a few short weeks. But Sita was mother to every suffering child. She had taken the harder path.

On that same day I chose a middle-aged merchant couple, Joshua and Dorcas, to endow with my treasures. Their dress spoke of comfortable means tempered by modest tastes, and their affection for each other showed through their every word and action. They had put themselves to endless trouble bringing the sick to be healed in their two stout carriages, and they had no children.

"Since you have shown yourselves to be so kind, I would beg a favor of you," I ventured carefully, bringing Lugal and Naomi forward to they could be seen.

The man and his wife bowed respectfully, for they knew me. "This is the greatest day of my life," the husband exclaimed, when he had kissed the frayed hem of my soiled gown. "I have seen the Master, and now you, our Lady Magdalene."

"Please, tell us how we may serve you," the woman said, her kind eyes on the two children. The little sister whimpered with weariness, and her brother took her on his back and carried her.

"The Master has healed these two orphans of leprosy, but they have no place to call home," I told them. "I will arrange for them to be reared at the Temple as foundlings, but it will take time to send for someone to fetch them. I hoped you might take them to Jerusalem for me, since you say your home is there."

"Why, that would be no trouble at all," Joshua answered at once. "Such a fine boy and girl. No family at all?" Dorcas plucked at her husband's sleeve.

"None at all," I said. "If you could just wait here with them for a few minutes, I will prepare a letter so they can be received at the Temple. Would you sign a declaration of responsibility to deliver them?"

I took my time about the letter and watched the four for nearly an hour. Dorcas took a comb from her pocket and began to plait the yellow flowers into Naomi's hair. Lugal was soon talking, apparently at ease. Joshua leaned over and whispered to his wife.

When I returned, he cleared his throat. "Lady," be began, with his eyes on Lugal, "a fine boy like this could learn my business and care for me in my old age."

"We had thought we would never have children," Dorcas put in, "but these two are so bright and so dear in their care for each other . . ."

"How easily I have snared you in my trap." I smiled my pleasure. The husband and his wife exchanged looks of understanding and laughed with me.

"We are caught for certain," Dorcas agreed, wiping her eyes. She looked seriously into the boy's face. "Lugal, we would be honored if you and Naomi would come and live with us and be our son and daughter. We promise to treat you fairly and love you as our own. Are you willing?"

Lugal was true to his name. Though hope and desire transformed his face, he turned to his little sister with a questioning look. "What do you say, Naomi?" he asked, and I could see he would respect her wish. Naomi's brown eyes moved from her brother's face to Dorcas's, and then to Joshua's, and back. She nodded slowly, and Dorcas burst into tears, holding out her arms. Naomi beamed shyly and went to her.

"I have written the letter," I told them. "You will have the length of the journey to think on it. Sign and deliver it to the Temple even if you decide to keep them. We shall want to keep in touch with you."

28

Capernaum

Why do you question thus in your hearts? Which is easier, to say . . . ,
"your sins are forgiven you," or to say "Rise . . . and walk?"

Mark 2:8–10, RSV

Wherever we went, we were surrounded by people who followed Yeshua to hear his stories and teachings and to witness his verbal contests with those who challenged him. Some followed believing him to be the Messiah promised in scripture, waiting for him to announce himself and deliver them from the Romans and Herodians. Many hoped to be healed; they pressed their sick on him unceasingly.

Others revealed in their haunted faces the guilt and self-hatred that held them back. I recognized their soul-sickness, the demon whispers that they were evil beyond all help, shrinking from hope when the prize was near. I sought these out and led them to Yeshua, and he took their trembling hands from mine and healed them.

Often, exhausted, he would have to withdraw with the help of his half-dozen self-appointed protectors—Lucius among them—who guarded his privacy when he wanted it. My trained bodyguards, who had learned to be unobtrusive and yet appear at the slightest danger, had much to teach the disciples with Yeshua's protection in charge.

Judas functioned as a double from the first. He wore a plain robe like his twin's beneath his striped long coat, with his hair bound up in a rolled turban, so the resemblance between them was less obvious. But when a large unruly crowd pressed upon Yeshua, Judas would slip to its outer edge and hand his coat and turban swiftly to Lysander, who would then kneel before him as if to ask his blessing.

"Here he is! The Master is here!" the others with them would exclaim, and the people not within sight of Yeshua would waver and draw away, attracted by the shouting. Moving swiftly, leading the mass of people, Judas and Lysander would pull the crowd away with them, then disappear.

Yeshua, in the heat of summer, often laid aside his long robe. He preferred the freedom of his short tunic to play the pipes and lead the round dance. When Judas sometimes appeared similarly clad and piping nearby, the people made no effort to choose between them, accepting Yeshua's appearance in two places at once as yet another of his miraculous abilities.

Here in Galilee, political unrest was high. Zealots and Sicarii persistently raided the holdings of the tetrarch, Herod Antipas, and bloody confrontations were commonplace between his soldiers and the agitators, who disappeared at will into the dry hills and caves away from the Sea of Galilee. Yeshua believed that the busier Antipas remained with rebel skirmishes the less likely he would be to trouble himself with the movements of a wandering teacher. But Peter and his brother Andrew spoke more and more to their Zealot friends of Yeshua as the Messiah, though he commanded them to keep silence until the time ripened.

In grassy Nazareth, where he had lived as a boy, the people refused to see him in a greater light, and his disappointment was visible on his face for days. We passed by Magdala, the "high place"—perched loftily among brown hills, looking north and east over the blue Sea of Galilee with its border of lush green. James and John had fished there since childhood, casting their nets in the clear, cold water. They knew all the families round about. Each day supper invitations were pressed upon us, and we split into half-dozens to make things easier for our hosts, but Yeshua kept me close to him, with James and John, Judas, Peter, and Andrew.

As we moved toward Capernaum, on the northern shore of the Sea of Galilee, Lysander learned that certain enemies of the Hasmoneans there had started rumors that Yeshua was a sorcerer whose powers were from Satan.

"Is this Satan the consort of the Dark Goddess of the Nether-world?" I inquired of Yeshua, as we took supper at the table of a tax collector who had welcomed the entire party. I was puzzled by talk of Satan, knowing the name only as that of a Persian prince of evil considered next in power to their creator, Ormazd.

"Why, well said, Mari, that he is, and more," Yeshua answered. "He is called the prince of demons, chief of the Annanaki, some say prince of this world as well."

I shuddered at the fresh memory of my own experience of the Annanaki, but the charge against Yeshua was so ridiculous I dis-missed it from my mind. "Will you avoid Capernaum, then," I asked him, "since it will be so dangerous?"

"I have promised to visit the home of Sebedeh and Priscilla." He said firmly. "I will cast out no demons in Capernaum, so we shall be safe. We can even play them a little game if need be." And he and his twin laughed together like boys.

The mood of Capernaum was ambivalent. Many did not believe that Yeshua consorted with demons; the most desperate cared little where the source of his powers lay if he could but help them, but he kept his word. After three days with the par-ents of James and John, we followed the road through the out-skirts of the city where it swung northward toward Caesarea-Philippi.

At this northern edge of Capernaum, above the town on the high limestone cliffs where the rushing Jordan emptied into the blue Lake of Galilee, was a Greek slaughterhouse and meat mar-ket with pens of sheep, goats, and swine. As we came near, a wed-ding feast was being celebrated at long tables on the dry grass around the merchant's stalls and spilling out into the road. Music and the delicious smells of Greek food tempted us as, dry with the dust of the road, we passed by reluctantly.

But the host recognized Yeshua and hurried forward, beaming with fellowship and good wine. "Learned Master, accept our poor hospitality," he invited. "Eat, drink! See, we have Jewish food too, for our many Jewish guests! Come join us! Welcome, welcome! You are all welcome!"

There were some thirty souls in our party, but the father of the bride made all welcome; we were soon lost among the three or four hundred wedding guests. There was food enough and more, and excellent wine, and we tarried until well past midday. As the heat rose in the early afternoon, Nina and Sita and I wandered through the colorful stalls of the market. Nothing threatening had happened despite Lysander's disturbing information, for Yeshua had been careful not to perform any healing before the crowds.

I paused to examine a necklace of hammered silver set with lapis. Looking up, I met the glance of a young woman, not unlike my sister-in-law, Delia, except for the sorrow in her dark eyes. Then I saw the child. He lay listlessly on a lambskin behind his mother, and even as I watched, he tensed himself and bent backward, emitting a piercing scream. His eyes rolled back; a strangling sound replaced the scream, and then I was on my knees helping the mother place a stick of wood across his tongue, which was rolling up into his throat.

When at last the little body relaxed and lay still, I wiped his chin and lips with my sleeve, and rose to my feet, carrying him. "Does this happen often?" I asked the mother.

"Many times," she nodded. "Many times in one day. I have sinned," she explained, her agony in her eyes, "it is the will of God."

He was about seven or eight, but light and frail. "God does not punish children," I retorted, and she recoiled as though struck. Ashamed that I had frightened her, I pleaded gently, "Come with me, please." The poor woman was in awe of me and would do anything I asked.

"He is over there, by the wine shed," Nina said, taking advantage of her height to spy Yeshua, eager as I to take him the child. We pushed through the throng and saw him; he looked up as we approached, followed by a half dozen women.

Then even as I held him, the small body stiffened, and the boy screamed in an unearthly voice, "No! No! I am afraid! I am afraid of him!" He struggled with such strength that I fell to my knees to keep from dropping him. Again, he doubled backward, rolled up his eyes, and lay senseless.

Yeshua was already beside me on the ground. He laid his hand over the boy's damp forehead.

"Come out of him!" he commanded, and the child shuddered and screamed again, so piercingly the imprisoned animals ran in circles in their pens. A gate broke or opened, and thirty or more squealing swine stampeded through the wedding party.

But the little boy sat up, the healthy color coming into his cheeks, and smiled at his mother, who fell to her knees before Yeshua and kissed his hand. The havoc that followed the pigs moved farther away, but a trader's tent collapsed, and a table of merchandise went flying. A large table of food spilled in the laps of startled, far from sober wedding guests, while gleeful children chased the pigs on purpose, screaming and laughing.

The wild procession swept across the road, and the men's voices rose in alarm as the pigs stampeded over the high cliff into the deep valley of the Jordan, some running down the steep incline, others falling or rolling. The whooping children scattered in sudden silence.

"Your wedding guest is the sorcerer we were warned of! See! He commands the evil spirits, and they obey him!" The speaker could not be seen, but his message was taken up by others. Judas, Lucius, and the others surrounded Yeshua, so he could no longer be seen. Nina was pulling me away toward the road.

About half our party reached the road and huddled together, not wanting to flee without the others. It was impossible to distinguish anyone in the swirling, yelling crowd. Shouts rose from a spreading knot of people near where Yeshua had healed the child. Then we heard the sickening thud of stones against flesh and bone. I screamed, but Nina held me fast.

"Fools! That is not the man!"

The voice had the timbre of an iron bell ringing over the spoiled wedding party—that amazing voice that could be heard and understood by five thousand at a time. It silenced the crowd like cold water on a fire, and they turned to see Yeshua, with Andrew and John, standing on the high embankment of the road where it turned back behind the cattle pens, beyond reach of the crowd.

The hands of some were raised with stones in them, but they stopped in midair, as people tried to decide what had happened. Muttering curses and protective spells, they moved away, their righteous rage displaced by uncertainty and alarm. Lucius was bending over someone on the ground. With chilling certainty, I realized it was Seth. His long body hung limp as the huge eunuch carried him toward us, flanked by the rest of our group.

"Is he dead?" The question rose audibly from worried remnants of the mob, but we feared to speak the words ourselves. We felt danger in remaining lest the crowd organize itself once more against us, so we straggled around a bend of the road in sight of the village, and some safety.

There we laid Judas on the grass, and I knelt at his bloodied head. The others stood back, out of respect for my knowledge of healing or for the sake of our former bond. He was barely breathing, his face gray as ashes, a dark bruise swelling above his eye. I moved my fingers over his face and head, and I could not but remember the happier times I had done so. My love for him blazed up, and I gasped with the pain of it. There was a massive lump above his ear, the source of blood that darkened his clothing and hair. The pulse at his throat fluttered, then stopped beneath my fingers. It fluttered again, weaker this time, and I realized I was holding my breath.

Nina hovered over us. "He is dying!" she cried, her voice hoarse, breaking. The faint pulse stopped.

"He is dead." I could not believe my own words, so I said them again, "He is dead. Oh, Nina, Seth is dead."

"He gave his life for the Master," James whispered reverently from behind me. "Would I might die as well."

"Amen, amen! That we all might!" the men agreed, in solemn unison, like the responses they offered when Yeshua read the scriptures. "Amen, amen."

I thought how Seth was even now embarking on the same dark journey I had taken, and I reasoned that since I had gone to the Netherworld and returned, Seth could also return. I would not give way to grief; I would hold fast to hope.

"We must find Yeshua and bring him here," I urged the others.

"Nay, better if he has returned to Capernaum," James said, "than this death were in vain. Safer to take Judas to him." A farmer stopped with his cart among the onlookers. "Pehaps this good man will let us use his wagon."

"Nay, do not move him. I am here." Yeshua seemed to materialize from nowhere. Still on my knees, I saw his anxious face through tears. "O, Master," I cried, "if you had been here, he had not died." "Nay, Mari," Yeshua's voice broke as he knelt beside me. He took the hand of his twin, and the arm bent backward, broken. Yeshua straightened it with his other hand, and commanded, "Judas, arise!"

No one breathed. But the pulse leaped under my fingers, and I felt a tingling shock where my hands touched him.

Slowly, the long lashes fluttered, and Judas the Scariot opened his eyes and squinted into the sunlight, puzzled to see us bending over him. I moved the shadow of my head to shield his eyes and pushed my fingers beneath the matted hair and blood above his ear. The lump was gone, the wound closed. My tears were falling on his face.

Joyfully, we helped him to stand, laughing and crying as he tested his limbs. He stood on one leg, then the other. The arm was not broken. Nothing was broken. Yeshua wept.

"I never thought it would go so far," he reproached himself. "My brother, I thank you for my life." He kissed Seth tearfully on either cheek, pressing him to his breast. We stood watching them, filled to bursting with love and joy.

They are as one, I thought. But one has journeyed to the Netherworld and returned. The other has yet to go.

Yeshua's twin raised a single eyebrow in the expression that was his distinguishing mark. "And I must thank you for mine," Judas said shakily, but his eyes were far away, lost in dark visions of the Netherworld.

29

Lazarus

As a lighted lamp does not need another lamp to manifest its light, so the Soul, being Consciousness itself, does not need another instrument of consciousness to illumine Itself.

Shankara

By late summer, when we returned to Jerusalem, my health was better than it had been for years, and I resumed my duties as High Priestess with greater energy and calm than I had ever commanded. Sita remained in the College of Virgins as our guest and teacher, Miriam sailed for her home on the Greek isle, and Almah once more turned longing eyes toward Egypt. She hated the rainy season in Jerusalem and made plans to spend the winter in sunny Alexandria. With Julia and Deborah, she departed overland with retainers and bodyguards, joining a caravan of wealthy merchants' families of the same mind and destination, only days before the first rainfall.

Yeshua, having some of his mother's aversion to wet weather, preferred the climate of the low desert around the Dead Sea to Jerusalem in the wintertime. His party left in early autumn to stay several months in the ascetic community of the Qumran fathers teaching and meditating. Many of his disciples went home to spend the winter with their families, but Judas and the sons of Sebedeh remained with him.

Geshtinanna had been married about eight years by this time to a Greek merchant, Jason, whose home and business lay in the port city of Caesarea, northwest of Jerusalem, on the sea—not Caesarea Philippi, which lay inland far to the north at the foot of Mount Hermon and the Jordan's source. Herod, father of Philip and Antipas, had built a great harbor at Caesarea, sinking massive stones in semicircular walls to break the waves. It was one of the wonders of the world—next to the Temple at Jerusalem. Shaher and Shalem had spent the summer with Nana and Jason at the seacoast and were escorted by them back to Jerusalem before the first storm. When the weather cleared, turning crisp and cold, I took my youngest children to Bethany for several days. They had missed the company of their cousins, and I was pleased at the prospect of some time with my family.

"You were with him longer than I, Mari; tell us, why does he ask those he heals to tell no one, when his power is already so well known that the sick flock to him?" Lazarus sat facing me across the great table where we had taken our family meal, his gray eyes crinkled at their corners, his pleasant mouth framing the half smile that was his customary expression. My brother was moderate of stature and slight like our father, but very like Grandfather Claudius in appearance, except for his size. He had a keen mind and a spirited tongue. Argument was meat and drink to him, and it pleased me that he found few adversaries more challenging than I, his sister. The family made a joke of keeping us apart for the sake of peace, but I loved our bouts as much as Lazarus did, and we sought each other out whenever we could.

"Many still count his miracles as tales and fables, and he wants the doubt about him to remain, for now. His hour is not yet come, he says," I answered.

"If he can heal the sick, then he is wrong to hide it," Father said reasonably. "The more who know, the more who can be helped."

"To heal the sick is good, but it is not his purpose," old Lili put in, with a piercing look at her son-in-law.

"You are right, Grandmother," I agreed. Even Lazarus would not argue with Grandmother; she seldom interjected an opinion and was treated like an oracle when she did. He nodded in his pleasing way. He was but two years older than Yeshua and Seth and had pleased our parents from his birth simply by being the son they had so much desired. He had pleased them also by preferring our father's vocation of farming and by making a good marriage with the daughter of a neighboring landowner. Delia was a pleasing young woman, and her children were handsome and well-mannered. Martha and I adored our brother, and approved of him as well. He was a good son, a good husband and husbandman, and a good brother.

Lili was growing a little deaf, but she was determined not to miss a word of any discussion. I was careful to sit close beside her so my voice came to her better ear, and she could see Lazarus's face clearly, as he spoke directly toward her.

"Then why does he not announce he is the Messiah" persisted Lazarus, "—beside that 'his hour is not yet come'?"

"I believe he is even more than the Messiah—much more," I started tentatively, not certain where my answer might lead.

"What? Are you not a good Pharisee? What could be more than that?" Lazarus spoke with light irony. But then, frowning, "What mean you, more than a Messiah?"

Now I was caught. What could I say? That he was Osiris? Lord of the living and of the dead? The Most High God? Son and Spouse of the Mother? Begetter of the worlds?

All this I knew in my heart but could not say before he himself had said it. "He has the powers of a god," I dissembled finally. "He is not as other mortals are."

"Yea, surely, he is a god," she-who-was-never-wrong intoned in her crone's voice, nodding her wise old head with grave certainty. "You will see."

"Could it be that our High Priestess has fallen in love again?" Lazarus teased. "Or do you mistake each for the other, since they are so alike?" My face turned hot. I hated myself for blushing so easily, especially before my brother.

"Did he not bring Seth back from the dead?" I reminded them, my voice and manner denying what my scarlet face confirmed.

"But are you sure he was really dead?" Martha, in sympathy with my embarrassment, ignored Lazarus's accusation and voiced the doubt everyone expressed when I told of Seth's restoration to life.

"I am certain, but I do not blame you if you do not believe me," I said resignedly. Let them think I had let the matter drop because of my brother's teasing. I wanted to tell them that I, too, had been dead and now lived, through the power of this man's mother. I wanted to tell them, but something made me hold back—did I think it would ask too much of them to believe that? All at once, I realized that I did not know whether my family had been told I had died, or only that I had lain ill for a number of days. I had thought it strange when they greeted me after my return from the Netherworld as though I had recovered from a particularly nasty cold. I supposed Almah had cautioned them about my delicate mental condition and warned them not to upset me. But why then had my family, the certain evidence of whose love had always surrounded me, on knowing me gravely ill or perhaps dead, not rushed to my bedside to learn the truth for themselves?

I waited until Martha and I were alone, and then I broached the subject as gently as I could. "Martha," I asked uneasily, "when Antipas threw the head of the prophet at my feet and I collapsed, heard you not rumors I had died?"

Martha's eyes were dark blue as the lapis lazuli broach on her full bosom and innocent as a newborn lamb's when she turned them to meet mine. "Why, yes . . . we did not attend the festival because Delia was in childbed, but we were warned of the rumor before it reached us by the grace of your lady Almah Mari. Her thoughtfulness saved us endless worry and grief. She reassured us you had only fainted and would be fine in a few days." Martha's forehead compressed into a thoughtful frown beneath the dark shadow of her hair, and I saw she had not troubled herself about the strangeness of my illness until now.

"But you were much sicker than we knew! Oh, Mari, why were we not there with you when you needed us!" Her black lashes glistened with tears, and tenderhearted Martha voiced the question I had been about to ask her, as though a veil had been drawn over the incident in her mind and torn aside only now. "Sister mine, you were near death! I know it, else you had not been so long in your recovery. And we could not guess or suspect it. How could we have been so careless of you! And you have reproached us not a word." Martha was crying in earnest now. I put my arms around her, kissing her repeatedly.

"Martha! Martha, you are blameless; all of you are blameless." I took hold of both her hands and made her look at me. "It was Almah. Only she could do this! Don't you see? She blinded you with some glamour, some power she has, so you would not even wonder about it until now." Martha stopped crying, looking puzzled as I went on, "She did it to me, too. Until a half hour ago, it never occurred to me you should have been concerned about me at that time."

"But why, Mari? Even if she could do that, why would she?" I felt helpless. How could I explain what had happened so that Martha would understand? Could I tell her that I had died and that Almah had deceived my family and everyone else for three days until she could bargain with the dark judges of the Netherworld and bring me back, for a price? A price she had planned in advance, that would redeem not only mine, but the souls of all beings, living, dead, or yet unborn? Could I tell her that Almah was herself the Goddess, Queen of Heaven, Earth, and Hell, and that her beloved son, who was his own father, would bear willingly by his death the price of all the evil done under the sun? I could not. It was not yet time. I caressed the long, black plait of my sister's hair and smiled.

"I cannot answer for her reasons. To spare you worry, as you say, most likely. Do not trouble yourself about it." At Martha's still-pained look, I teased gently, "Promise me you will not."

Winter passed. At the spring festival, the Sacred Marriage would be celebrated by Elizabeth, granddaughter of Joseph of Arimathea, and her bridegroom Ahasaurus, son of a noble family who were not, like the bride's, Pharisees. The alliance seemed to soften a little the harshness of the disagreements between the rival factions. The festival brought into the city everyone who could travel for many miles around, and Yeshua would soon reunite with his disciples here in the Temple cloisters, as my guests.

I behaved foolishly as a young girl in my anticipation, fussing for days over every detail of the preparation for his welcome. But I apologized for myself that since it was Yeshua, and Yeshua was who he was, no welcome could be overstated. I waited on the open gallery overlooking the courtyard, my pounding heart shamefully loud—baited by Lysander's announcement that they would arrive any moment by the eastern gate. Finally, I watched them enter, surrounded by masses of people, and agonized for the two hours it took for them to break away and come to my receiving rooms. Warned yet again that their appearance was imminent, I went to the open patio where we would gather, and when they did not appear, I hid in the small audience room lest I appear too eager and practiced breathing exercises to calm myself.

I stared, startled as the door opened, suddenly shy. He closed the door softly behind him and came without a word, his arms extended toward me. He kissed me, and I was in heaven.

"Mari, sweet Mari!" His voice betrayed him. It was Seth!

I jumped backward in surprise. He raised a single eyebrow and grinned down at me. "Seth!" I felt my face flame, but I could not summon my anger against him. Instead I hung upon his neck and kissed him again, laughing with happiness, forgiving him everything.

"He is here, just outside," Seth smiled—the charming thief! He had stolen Yeshua's kiss, but I was far calmer because of it. I ought to thank him, I thought, as he opened the door and followed me onto the patio.

Yeshua stood in the center of the portico surrounded by children, the sons and daughters of priestesses and the foundlings we cared for. Among them, the youngest priestesses blossomed in gowns of white linen, garlanded with flowers. He held a blushing six-year-old in his arms and talked to several of the smallest, kneeling to make himself of a size with them as he kissed and blessed each one. I watched, enthralled, remembering myself as they were now.

Then he looked up and saw me. He smiled—dazzlingly—and the stone floor shook beneath my feet. He stood, careful not to jostle the children, who fell away like flower petals, and came toward me.

Yeshua picked me up—me, the High Priestess—with his hands about my waist. He swung me around in a circle and set me down again. The littlest priestesses shrieked for joy and danced around us as he kissed me on each cheek. Too dizzy with delight to think of my dignity, I stood swaying and disoriented, weeping with happiness. A little hand slipped into each of my own, and we were all dancing in a ring, round and round. Across the circle I saw Seth hand in hand with Shaher and Shalem, and Yeshua was leading us all in song, piping a mellow refrain:

"Glory be to thee, Mother!" he sang.

"Amen!" the dancers responded.

"Glory be to thee, Father!"

"Amen!"

"Glory be to thee, Law!"

"Amen!"

Everyone joined in the dancing and responses, stepping leftward in a huge circle around the marble portico, with Yeshua in the center. Yeshua's eyes flashed, striking the dancers with a strange ecstasy. The magic of his piping led us forth, but his voice was the most beautiful of music as we danced with him.

"I will be saved, and I will save!" he chanted.

"Amen!"

"I will be freed, and I will free!"

"Amen!"

"I will be wounded, and I will wound!"

"Amen!"

"I will be consumed, and I will consume!"

"Amen!"

"Grace paces the round. I will blow the pipe. Dance the round, all!"

"Amen!"

"A mansion I have not, and mansions I have."

"Amen!"

"A torch I am to you who perceive me."

"Amen."

"A mirror I am to you who discern me."

"Amen."

"A door I am to you who knock."

"Amen."

"A way I am to you who pass."

Yeshua stopped us where we stood, our hands still linked together, and said softly but so clearly his words burned themselves into every heart:

"As you respond to my dancing, behold yourself in me, the dancer. You that dance, ponder what I do; your is this passion of humanity I am about to suffer. In your drive toward wisdom, you have me for a bed; rest upon me. What now I am seen to be, that I am not. You will know who I am when I depart. See through suffering, and you will have nonsuffering. What you know not, I myself will teach you." His voice fell to a near whisper, speaking to each individual heart, "If you would understand what I am, know this: all that I have said, I have uttered playfully, and I was not ashamed thereby. I danced, but as for you, consider the whole, and say: 'Glory be to thee, Father!'"

"Amen," whispered the dancers.

"Glory be to thee, Mother!"

"Amen."

"Glory be to thee, Law!"

"Amen!"

Almah Mari returned to Jerusalem soon after and surprised me by offering to take over my official duties for the summer months should I desire to travel again with Yeshua. I had not even entertained the hope I could go, since I had no illness as excuse this year. I was too happy to ponder Almah's purposes—if she had some hidden design in her mind, so be it. Salome begged to go with me, and I could not refuse her, so we two made our preparations, with Siduri, Salome's dearest friend, and Nina, Lucius, and Lysander, all of whom could scarcely contain their happiness at the prospect of another season in the company of Yeshua and his band.

We joined Yeshua before his group left Bethany. Lazarus would go with us as well, until the harvest. The little band that traveled with the son of Almah Mari had grown to twice the number of the year before. Past experience helped this year's group handle small problems more smoothly, and Yeshua's fame had spread to every part of the land. The men who followed him seemed more generous in their acceptance of me. Even Peter was guardedly friendly.

Many things happened that summer none of us would ever forget:

"Who touched me?" Yeshua stopped to ask in the midst of a jostling crowd.

"Master, many have touched you," James, who was nearest, replied curiously. "Why do you ask, 'Who touched me?'"

A well-dressed woman struggled forward and knelt before him. "Master, it was I. I have been unclean with an issue of blood for twelve years. No doctor has been able to help me." The poor woman looked so ashamed that Yeshua reached out his hand and made her rise to her feet.

"You have done no wrong," he told her kindly. "I felt the power go from me and did not know why."

"O, Master," she sobbed, "I did not want to bother you, since you were so busy, and so many needed you. I thought if I could but touch your garment, I would be healed."

Yeshua smiled gravely. "Your faith has healed you, sister, and has blessed me. I thank you for it. Go in peace."

The group of disciples who shared these experiences were drawn closer to each other. It was of these days we would dream when we were old, these tales we would tell to grandchildren and great-grandchildren should we live that long. If not—should death overtake us tomorrow—we could leave life without regret.

When we returned to the Temple in the late summer, I had a message from Bethany that my brother, who had returned three weeks before, was very ill. "Find out where Miriam of Scarios is," I told Lysander.

"Madam, she is yet in Alexandria, at the house of the king," he reported several hours later, as we sped to Bethany. When I arrived, I was alarmed to find Martha, Delia, and my mother, Aethel, all hollow-eyed from worry and loss of sleep.

"It was only a small wound, Mari," Martha mourned, "he but grazed his foot with the scythe. But it has gone bad." She began to weep from exhaustion and despair.

"Lazarus, can you hear me?" I pleaded, when I saw his swollen face dark with fever. "It is I, Mari."

"Even Miriam, if she were here, could not save him, now," I admitted to Martha and our mother when I was sure there was nothing I could do. I turned my attention to poor Delia, who sat silently rocking her youngest, her body heavy with the child she would bear in two months and a look of wordless horror on her face. I knelt beside her chair and tried to comfort her.

"Do not despair," I told her. "We will send for Yeshua."

No sign she had heard showed in Delia's blank eyes.

"He has gone to Jericho, but he will return. I know he will." I patted my sister-in-law's hand to rouse her, but she would only stare dully at the bed where her husband lay.

Lysander said he himself would take the message to Yeshua, if he could borrow our father's fastest horse. He clattered out of the courtyard as Mother and I put Delia to bed, having given her a sleeping draught. Then we joined Martha at Lazarus's bedside.

The poison had reached as far as his waist; both his feet were black and swollen, and the stench of his rotting flesh filled our nostrils while he yet breathed.

"I pray he dies soon," Martha caught her breath in a weary sob. "It is evil for him to suffer so. Oh, Mari, I am so glad you are here." She reached for my hand and clasped it, but there was no hope in her voice.

"Even then Yeshua can raise him, as he has done with Seth and with the centurion's daughter only ten days ago. I myself have seen it. Why will you not believe me?"

But Martha shook her head, and I looked at my mother, finding her eyes dark and dull with the grief of all mothers who surrender their children to death. "He will come, Mother. He will save him," I promised, but my mother protested wearily.

"His flesh is already corrupted," she said. "He rots while he yet lives. I could not wish him brought back to such a body." She turned away into her grief, and I saw that even hope seemed cruel to her now. I held my peace.

Lazarus had been dead three days, and placed in a tomb hollowed out of a rocky hillside behind the herb garden of the women of Bethany. The whole household, except for me—watching and waiting steadfastly for Yeshua—had collapsed in grief. Lazarus had been loved and honored by neighbors and kinsmen, so the household was deluged with offerings of sympathy and gifts, and stayers to meals. My mother retreated into a trancelike silence, and Father, who had survived the loss of his first little boy, found the death of this grown son who had given him so much cause for pride and happiness a greater grief than he could bear.

"It should have been I, not my son," he moaned. Grandmother Lili comforted them both. "Better to mourn a good son than a bad one," she said.

Martha took refuge in the work that heaped itself upon her. She moved like a wooden doll, her short, solid figure bent with the weight of her grief, preparing food, tending her children and Delia's, managing the servants, refusing to rest or think. I was afraid she was near collapse, but I could not make her rest.

I was glad I had sent for Miriam, though she would arrive too late to help my brother. I saw signs that Delia would deliver before her time. If anyone could help her tiny infant, it would be Miriam.

"He comes, Lady." I embraced my faithful bearer of messages, my throat too full for speech. "He will arrive by afternoon," Lysander said.

When he did come—he did come at last—he came with Judas and John, protected by an unseen escort of Zealots who faded into the hills. I ran to meet them, angry at my own weakness, for the tears I had held back until then came flooding. Yeshua took time to hold me and comfort me, and then I saw that he was weeping too, and I remembered his love for my brother.

"Mari, I am sorry," Judas said, and I went to his arms. In all our years together, we had never shared sorrow. "Have faith, little one," he admonished me gently, as if we had never been apart.

"Have no fear, Lady," John said to me, with a grim smile. "There is power, here."

"Lord, he is dead these three days," I stammered brokenly. "Oh, Master, if you had been here, he had not died." We wrung each other's hands, then walked together toward the house. They were all dusty and tired from days of walking, and my concern turned to their comfort. "There is food on the table," I said, leading the way toward the center dining hall, but Yeshua stopped me.

"Take me to him."

"Lord, his flesh rotted even before he died. Our spices could not mask the stench," I apologized.

Yeshua's tears continued as he approached the tomb, now followed by the whole household. He stopped to embrace Martha, then confronted the heavy slab of stone that was the door of the tomb. "Open it," he commanded, not even looking around to see who would obey him.

Judas and John thrust their shoulders against the stone and rolled it past the opening of the tomb. The evil smell of death engulfed us.

Yeshua threw back his head and called out with all the power of his wonderful voice, vibrating with emotion and thick with tears, echoing and reverberating back and forth from the hills about, so that the very stones cried out.

"Lazarus, come forth!"

It was a voice to wake the dead. It raised the hair on my neck and gooseflesh on my arms. No one breathed. The two dogs that had been my brother's raised their hackles and howled pitifully, trying to hide themselves. When I could no longer keep from drawing in my breath, the smell of death no longer scorched my nostrils. A sweet wind that bore the scent of grassy meadows and spring flowers rushed past our mourning, rattling the dry leaves on the gnarled and ancient olive trees.

Some of the household broke away and ran. Others fell to their knees. A cry of fear, disbelief, and joy arose as the figure of Lazarus was seen moving within the darkness of the tomb. He appeared suddenly in the sunlight, blinking in amazement to see the grave wrappings on his hands and the strange attitude of those who awaited him.

I recognized my brother's deep shock and went to him. "Do not be afraid, my dear," I crooned, holding him close, "you are with us once more. You are well." Then Yeshua was sharing our embrace, we were all laughing and crying together, and his kisses were on my face.

There was a great celebration in Bethany that lasted for several days. Lazarus recovered his composure swiftly and became once more his gracious and jovial self. Our father and mother sat beaming, barely able to believe their good fortune. Only Lili remained as calm as ever. When Lazarus greeted his grieving wife, I feared the excitement might go ill with her, but so much of the marvelous power that had raised him from death still clung to Lazarus that Delia emerged from her husband's embrace in joy and health. All would be well with her and her child.

On the eve of his departure for the retreat of the Qumran fathers, Yeshua stood in his place at the table and raised his cup. "I wish to petition the Magdalene," he announced, his smile so ravishing he possessed the hearts of all who looked on him. "When spring has come, I humbly ask her to bestow upon me the highest honor of the Mother, by consenting to be my bride in the sacred rite of the Heiros Gamos."

I could not speak. I had half expected—no, only dreamed—such a thing might come to pass, but I was unprepared, disarmed, in the presence of my whole family—here where I was daughter and sister, not High Priestess. In the silence that followed, I felt the eyes of the others turn to me in expectation. I looked around at all of them, and there was surprise, disapproval, goodwill, even joy, on various faces.

For a long moment I studied Seth. His gaze was softly tender, but he made no effort to hold my glance. I would still have gone back to him then, had he but given me some sign, but I could not guess his heart.

Slowly I allowed myself to be captured by the irresistible attraction of Yeshua's look. Held fast by the light of his eyes, basking in the radiance of his smile, I arose as in a dream and lifted my cup. I felt his warmth and light fill me and lift me, and beam forth from me; my face felt warm and glowing as the sun, shining with happiness.

"Master, you do me great honor." I answered him clearly and with all the dignity of my high office. I held forth the silver goblet, and Yeshua took it and drank. I accepted his cup and drank, a sweet draught. All the company then raised their cups and drank to us, the betrothed couple, and expressed their good wishes.

I caught Seth's glance once more that evening, and he seemed to smile at me, but I could not read his thoughts. If he had once interfered with my destiny, he would not do so again. So be it, I sighed to myself, so let it be.

30

The King of the Jews

For truly I say to you, til heaven and earth pass away, not an iota, not a dot, will pass from the Law until all is accomplished.

Matthew 5:18, RSV

"**M**ari, you must come out!" Lysander forgot all formality in his excitement, not hesitating to command me. "He will enter the city by the western gate. He has revealed himself as the Messiah!"

It was beginning. I could not move for a moment. All around me, flowers bloomed, birds and insects chirped and twittered. Little pots of blood-red windflowers crowded every window and doorway. I tried to shake off my sense of dread as I followed Lysander's instructions. We went forth from the Temple walls, Nina, Sita, Salome, and I, and Miriam of Scarios, with our women. Almah Mari, the Star of Jerusalem, came also. She had returned a full month earlier than usual to help with the wedding preparations, even breaking with her usual custom of avoiding crowds. We came forth to take advantage of the invitation Lysander had obtained from Nicodemus the Pharisee to watch the festival procession from his rooftop. Here, above the milling crowds, we had a full view of the Genneth Gate, midway in the north wall of the city between the Palace of Herod and the Temple Mount, through which Yeshua would pass. From there he would move eastward to the wall of the Mount, turning south on the broad thoroughfare that followed the deep valley separating the upper from the lower city. On each side, terraces of dwellings rose up behind each other like stair steps, their flat roofs bright with colored awnings and potted palms and the scarlet windflowers of the god. It was from one of these houses on the highest concourse that we watched. Nicodemus had pitched a spacious white tent with fringes of scarlet to shade us from the sun and covered the floor with a Persian carpet and bright colored pillows.

The sun shone from a cloudless sky, warning of the hot summer to come, but the breeze was still cool, the spring foliage lush and green. Every spring festival brought back to me that first one, when I had been dedicated to the Mother. Tears stung my eyelids, and my throat swelled painfully. But another part of my self watched dispassionately, wondering that such childish emotions still came when no innocence remained, only terrible, unwilling knowledge. I caught Miriam's sharp look and knew I was not alone in that sentiment. Thankful for her silent empathy, I meditated upon the insignificance of my own cares and concerns in the face of the earthshaking events that were beginning to unfold before me. "Vanity of vanities, all is vanity," I said in my heart.

I longed to see Yeshua with a necessity that was greater than any desire. My mouth was dry as ashes, as though my body had given up all its water except for my tears. I caught the salty drops that ran over my lips to wet my parched tongue. My last memory of him was fixed in my mind, when he had bid me good-bye and gone away with Judas and John from Bethany toward Jericho, escorted by an invisible host of Zealot protectors.

"I will come to you for the feast of the Sacred Marriage," he said as we parted, his intense gaze recalling other words spoken to me alone. "You have suffered much for me already, and I shall ask you to suffer even more. Will you be able to bear it?"

I was caught like a moth by the bright flame of my love. I knew Yeshua would die. I did not know how or when, but that he was moving steadily toward that end, I was certain. Even his marriage to me was part of that plan, the beginning of it. I struggled against thinking of anything except that we would soon be together, and while the burden of what I knew filled my whole breast, it could not crowd out the joy I felt in my coming marriage. The more I loved him, the more I hated myself for my guilty compliance in his sacrifice. If I refused him, his plan would be forestalled, perhaps long enough for him to change his mind, but I could not refuse him because of my own desire, my own weakness. His question burned in my mind. Would I be able to bear it? How does one bear the unbearable?

Lysander had brought news of Yeshua almost daily that winter. No minor event escaped his notice, from Galilee to the Dead Sea. He knew the contents of every letter that passed to or from Rome, official business or private, no matter how secret, and he gathered the winds of gossip near and far in his wide sails, letting slip forth from them whatever would best confuse the hired ears of the Roman procurator or Herod Antipas.

And the news was as exciting as it was alarming. Talk of Yeshua was on every tongue. It had grown louder and bolder each day of the long winter, and we could hear it now in excited phrases from our rooftop vantage point.

"He is born to the house of Hasmonias" was repeated most often. I heard it again now. "He is a healer, a miracle worker—proving his favor from God. Have you heard how he healed Simon the leper?"

"He straightened the legs of my cousin's child, deformed from birth, with a touch of his hand!" a cultured matron told her companions.

"Not all of his followers are happy with this marriage to the Magdalene," said a man's voice, "or you may call me a fool, truly."

"How can he rule as the Anointed One, if he does not make marriage with our Lady?" a woman demanded sharply. "Only she can anoint him."

"He is true king of Israel," another was saying, "and rightful High Priest as well. He will banish the line of puppet priests to the oblivion they deserve!"

"Do you hear them saying he will proclaim himself both High Priest and king?" Miriam exclaimed in her mellow voice, but her expression was guarded, unreadable.

"And that he will lead in the overthrow of the Roman rule!" I added ironically. Miriam rewarded me with a throaty chuckle. Better to laugh than weep—my mother's favorite rule applied more and more often for me.

"Hosanna! Blessed be He!" The voices of people beyond the city wall rose in praise and acclamation. Now his name was everywhere, but people had been slow to speak their hopes openly. The most hopeful had been the most concerned about Roman and Herodian spies, and they had craftily woven false stories and plans to cause whatever of their real hopes that might reach the wrong ears to sound just like the world-weary and constant carping of subject peoples everywhere. But the massing of the Zealots in the hills and the excitement of the farming and shepherd folk quietly arming themselves had increased until it surpassed that of any time since the death of old Herod. It would have been sheer folly to imagine it passed the eye of Rome unnoticed.

I turned and looked into the serene face of Almah Mari, who needed common robes to keep from being recognized even more than I, the Magdalene. Our people still adored and honored her as their unofficial queen and princess, swarming about her to see or to touch her if she deigned to go among them. In her plain blue mantle, without her ornaments, she appeared like any other matron—unless she looked at you with those startling blue eyes.

My devotion to Almah had been transferred to her son, but with the mother's blessing. That I knew this to be Almah's will did nothing to diminish my ardor. Sometimes even I was caught up in the messianic hopes of my people. Through the sacred rite he would become the Anointed King, the chosen of the Mother. He would lead his people through the apocalyptic battle that would cast off Roman might and establish a thousand years of blessedness. This was the dream in which I was invited to believe.

Almah smiled and took my hand, and I remembered that not only Nina read my thoughts. "Let us take one day at a time," she smiled.

I nodded and sighed. I was not foolish enough to suppose the passion that fired the Zealots came from any hope of victory. Death was to them infinitely preferable to tolerance of false rulers.

But not all the people were of a mind to be willing martyrs. Most were not so hot-blooded they preferred death to the accommodation of some evil, and like Grandmother Lili, they did not subscribe to the strong sentiments of the Zealots.

"Never was a time when most people didn't find themselves ruled by some power or other, good times or bad," she had observed one afternoon as the family sat together. "None of them are perfect, and some're worse'n others. But the worst of them in peaceful times is better'n the best of them when they make war. Killing and raiding and raping never makes things better for most folks." Lili grinned, showing the half-dozen worn-down teeth she still possessed. "I know I'd never met your grandfather, if Rome hadn't marched on Judea," she admitted, "but that can't change the truth. War is nothing but childish quarreling of powerful men and hurts everyone. Fighting and killing never leads to anything but more fighting and killing."

I had agreed absently at the time. Now I considered that many people, pehaps most, must agree with this wisdom. Rome was powerful, perhaps even invincible. I could not believe that Yeshua would foolishly lead his followers against Roman might. It would be to their death, and for nothing.

Just so. He intended to die. But others would die as well, due to their own foolishness or because they believed in him. If he made himself a traitor to Rome, all his friends and followers would be outlawed, including myself—perhaps the whole priesthood of the Goddess. Yeshua would never be so irresponsible. I took comfort in the faith of love. He could never be so careless of the welfare of those who believed in him.

Still, though reason told me that many besides Yeshua would be endangered by the events being set in motion before my eyes, I was capable of little concern except for the fate of my beloved. In the face of his death, how could anything else matter?

"Mother, he is coming! I can see Peter!" Salome spoke excitedly, her black hair bouncing as she jumped about. The buzzing of voices swelled to an ear-splitting roar, and Yeshua appeared through the eastern gate surrounded by people waving palm branches. Because of the prophecy, he was mounted upon the ridiculous, long-eared animal named by the prophet Isaiah, an ass's colt. Could they not have allowed him a horse? I was embarrassed for him; the white ass offered an endless source of hilarity for the Roman military.

But Yeshua was not ashamed. Clothed in a kingly mantle of purple, smiling and nodding, his every glance capturing all within range, his presence made the poor donkey a prince's stallion, affecting the crowd with such emotion it became monstrous—wild—singing and dancing its delight, out of control.

"Hosanna! All hail!" they shouted. "Behold! He comes! All hail!"

Almah's face was alight with very human love and pride. She is just like any mother, I thought, surprised. I reached out and pressed the hand of Yeshua's mother, and she returned the pressure wordlessly. The press of people swept him past Nicodemus's rooftop and up the broad street toward the Mount, leaving us, his waiting bride and mother, to struggle with our attendants through the crowds as best we could back to our Temple cloister.

When Yeshua and his procession did not enter the western gate of the Temple enclosure, I guessed they would use the southernmost gate, going directly into Herod's Basilica, where the commercial enterprises of the Temple were housed. When Yeshua and his high-spirited followers came streaming in, they carried everything before them like a tidal wave, overturning the tables of the merchants and moneychangers.

After Almah and I and our party entered the Temple environs by the western gate, it was closed and barricaded behind us by a boisterous group of well-armed men. Across the courtyard, the gates in the eastern wall of the Mount were being closed and barricaded also.

"Antonia has been taken by the rebels!" Lysander announced. The fortress of Antonia stood astride the northwest corner of the high wall that enclosed the Temple Mount and was customarily occupied by a garrison of Roman soldiers.

"They have closed all the approaches to the city," Lysander went on breathlessly, "Jerusalem has been taken in the name of the Messiah!"

Almah's face was triumphant. "You must prepare yourself for the ceremony, dearest Mari," she said. Urgency and tenderness were in her voice. Her view of this day's business was not concerned with the joys and sorrows of individual lives.

Salome embraced me, her face alight with happiness, asking to be allowed to help. I returned my daughter's kiss. Let her be happy a little longer, I thought.

As Sharon, his father, had come to Almah, his mother, so Yeshua came to me, dressed in the ritual garments of Dumuzi, the Shepherd King, escorted by attendants bearing his sacred cup and churn. The Ram Without Blemish—the sacrificial lamb.

I stood resplendent in the ceremonial robes of the High Priestess on the dais before the burnished doors of Nicanor Gate, and the Women's Court of the Temple was packed with the most curious and enthusiastic crowd I could remember.

"Hail, Lady! All hail to you, Blessed Lady! Hail to Magdalene!" the people shouted as I stepped forward to meet my bridegroom.

"Hosannah! Hail to the King! Blessed be He!" they shouted, as Yeshua stepped up to the level on which I stood and took the trembling hand I held toward him. I almost drowned in his eyes. If he had not dropped them to kneel before me, I could not have moved. The people became silent. Their awe and reverence hung in the air like the heavy smoke of the incense, as I motioned to my cupbearer. Slowly, as in a dream, I dipped my fingers in the holy oil and placed them on his hair where the sunlight made a halo of gold.

"In the name of the Mother, Inanna-Ishtar-Isis-Ashera, I anoint you," I announced to the hushed silence, "Sacred Son, Chosen King, Holy Bridegroom. You are found worthy of the Seat of Dominion."

For several moments he remained, kneeling reverently, then slowly he raised his head, and the voice of the people arose with him in acclamation. They were on their feet when he stood and turned to face them with the left hand of their High Priestess in his own.

"Hail, Christos! Anointed One! Hail the Messiah who will redeem Israel! Hail, our King! All hail!"

All that day Yeshua and I remained enthroned, side by side, as we accepted the acclaim, obeisance, and petitions of our people. We gave blessing to newly betrothed couples, fondled and named babies, and acknowledged new owners of lands or businesses. We were royally feasted for hours, though we could not eat. At last, we were briefly separated and ritually dressed in our bridal garments, then once more enthroned before the bronze doors under a billowing canopy of purple and gold for the rite of the Sacred Marriage.

One small disappointment clouded the perfect picture, like a slim finger of shadow pointing to that of which I dared not think. Shaher and Shalem would not see their mother wed to the anointed King. Yeshua had insisted that Nana and Jason, as soon as they arrived from Caesarea for the ceremony, leave at once with my little boys for their home in Caesarea. Judas, who adored our sons but seldom interfered with my choices in their behalf, urged me to agree. "Please, Mari," he insisted, "they must be safe, above all." I relented, though it broke my heart to see their tears of disappointment and rage when I sent them away. Nana, too, was tired and disappointed, but the children's safety was her greatest concern.

Slowly, all these things left my mind as the ceremony began, to be replaced by memories of the other times I had taken part in this same sacred rite as a bride. The first had been my marriage to Philip, but the others, as that service of my office—not lightly given, for it had been refused to Herod Antipas and others—to rulers or princes deemed worthy of the recognition of the Goddess. This gave me no cause for shame in my own mind, or in the eyes of my people, but I knew the more patriarchal of the Jews were compromising the high value they placed on female chastity to gain for their Messiah what they could obtain no other way. Only I, the High Priestess of Isis-Ashera, the representative of the Goddess on earth—she who was called the Seat of Dominion, the Throne of the Most High—could anoint their king, and only marriage to me could grant kingship.

I recalled listening with mixed feelings when Yeshua insisted to his Pharisaic supporters that I was a pure virgin because I had died and been reborn. I think they supposed he spoke in a spiritual sense only, though they recalled rumors of my death and resurrection, which they surely saw only as a reenactment ceremony in honor of the goddess Inanna's descent and return. Yeshua did not specify his meaning.

Despite my early years as the fifth wife of Philip Herod, I did not share the traditional view that allowed men of economic means multiple marriages and concubines while holding their wives to the strictest of chastity. I could never stop speaking against the belief that seduced maidens were no longer fit for proper marriage and must be sold into lifelong servitude. Still, I had listened without hope to Yeshua when he reasoned with those who objected to his choice of me as his bride.

My skepticism did not escape him, and he interrupted himself one day in the midst of glaring at Peter, who persistently questioned the propriety of his keeping me near him.

"Peter, you have allowed me to play the fool, certainly, for answering you in terms of your own judgment!" he exclaimed with a burst of laughter, slapping his thigh and looking about to see who shared his joke on himself. "Tell me this. What is the duty of the tanner of hides?"

"Why, to scrape the flesh from the hides, and make them into leather," Peter answered, a little warily.

"And do we think the tanner is defiled by handling dead flesh, though it would defile another man?"

"Any man who handles dead flesh is defiled," Peter answered more positively, "including the tanner. But there is a purification rite that takes away his uncleanness."

"Well said, Peter. Now, tell me, is it the same with a soldier? Is he made unclean by the exercise of his duty?"

"If you mean by killing in battle or executing the condemned," Peter answered, gaining confidence, "it is the same. The soldier is made unclean through killing, but is purified by the rite."

"By the rite alone?" Yeshua had persisted.

"Through sincere repentance, and the rite," Peter supplied, eager to show that he had not forgotten that lesson.

"Tell me then, what is the duty of the Temple priestess?"

Peter, his color heightening, saw he had taken the bait but was determined to swallow it all. He answered reluctantly, "To perform the part of the Goddess in the act of marriage." Then raising eyes dark with the discomfort it cost him, he admitted boldly, "She is no more defiled by the practice of her duty than these others, then, and no less easily made clean." He knitted heavy brows in an unhappy frown, and said at last, "Master, by this argument, even a common prostitute is made pure."

"You do well to see it, for I would have pointed out this very thing to you next," Yeshua praised him.

"But there is something wrong, then," Peter objected, "something I do not understand." He groped uncomfortably for the right words, his face hot with righteous anger, but Yeshua only waited, saying nothing. "Everyone knows a prostitute—or any woman—who has given up her virginity except through lawful marriage is defiled," he charged.

"Who has defiled her, Peter?" Yeshua pressed him; then seeing he was to receive no answer, he prodded gently, "What does everyone know, Peter?"

After a time, Peter raised his agonized countenance and pleaded, "Master, is no one undefiled?" At this, Yeshua, recognizing what he had sought in the grizzled face, leaped up and clasped Peter to his breast in deep affection, rousing a guffaw of fellowship from the big fisherman.

I smiled inwardly at the memory. Despite our differences, there was deep respect and affection between me and the disciple most responsible for the strong link between Yeshua and the Zealots.

> As a quince among all the trees of the wood,
>   So is my beloved in the company of other men.
> I sat down in the shade with great delight
>   And his fruit tasted sweet.
> He brought me to his banquet hall
>   And his banner over me was love.
> Revive me with grapes,
>   Refresh my mouth with quinces;
> I faint for love.

I turned to face my bridegroom, chanting the words of the bride from the Song of Solomon. That I sat here beside Yeshua, my hand clasped in his, was incredible, like a beautiful dream not expected to really happen. But his touch was warm and full of life, and his look of helpless love was all too human. He sang his responses only to me, holding back the power of his wonderful voice, which could have overcome all the others.

The people arose to bear us to the bed of the Goddess. Surrounded, protected, and lifted by love, our happiness was so complete we cared for nothing beyond the bliss of that moment. The many hands of the people bore us high over their own heads, passing us gently as on the crest of a wave to other hands, across the court, through the high, two-storied doors, and across the outer courtyard to the bridal chamber.

And through all this my own hand never left his; firmly, tenderly, he held me fast. He, too, was moved by the ceremony and the outpouring we had received. His eyes glistened with tears as he looked around him at the armed men on the walls who would guard our wedding night. It seemed he was blessing those who touched him. When he turned back to me, the glowing orange of the torchlight went out of his eyes, and I saw in them the cool light of the full moon.

When they had placed us on the high bridal bed, the people filed past us in endless procession, giving and asking blessing. It was for this purpose there were two sets of doors to the chamber. Whole families came, carrying and leading their young children, their elderly parents, their ancient grandparents. There were young men, and shy girls, and widows, all honoring us for the blessing our fertility symbolized. Because of our ritually blessed and perfect union, all would be well with our people.

Priestess of Love

You do not understand that it is expedient for you that one man should die for the people.

John 11:50, RSV

The last of the celebrants filed around our bed, and the eunuchs closed the tall doors of the bridal chamber. My bridegroom, Yeshua, and I, the consecrated bride, lay back on the scarlet and purple robes of the high bed of Ashera and let the peace of our solitude flow over us. We turned to each other when we had collected ourselves. A mischievous twinkle, like Seth's, lit his eyes.

"I must make a confession to you."

"Beloved?" I sent him a look of melting love, but it leaped into my mind that he would not consummate our marriage because of a vow.

"I am virgin," he admitted gravely, as if confessing a fault, but his face broke into a broad smile, as though he thought this a tremendous joke on himself. Then he turned serious. "I am afraid I will not know how to please you."

So that was all! I let go my breath with a relieved laugh. "I am no shy maiden who will not tell you how to please me," I promised. I lifted his long, sun-browned hand to my lips, then placed it gently over my breast. For the first time since I had known him, I saw that he wanted to speak, but could not. I waited while he found the words.

"Oh, Mari," he breathed in great gasps, "how I have wanted to do this!"

I voiced my last misgiving then, caressing his face, our lips an inch apart, breathing each other's breath. "Swear to me, dearest one, you transgress no vow for my sake."

My need for reassurance restored his speech. "Oh, no! Sweet Mari, my sister—my wife," his voice was husky and intense, "I do not break, but fulfill, a vow, when I come to your holy bed. More than that, it is my own will, the desire of my heart," he held me away from him, to look into my face, "as you, wise in the ways of love, well know."

"And did you choose me for my worldly wisdom, then?" I teased gently, undoing the fastenings of his garments.

"I would have chosen you, only you, no matter," he pleaded, "but I did not." That startled me, and he paused in helping me off with the Magdalene's heavy collar of gold. "We were chosen for each other from eternity, Mari. It could not be otherwise." He gathered me close.

I stifled a little sob of happiness and nestled against him, wanting our embrace to last forever. But at last we stirred, and climbed out of the bed to undress.

"Wait," I cautioned him, reaching into my bodice, withdrawing my hand with Nehushtan's coils spiraling up my arm. I turned toward the round basket beside the marriage bed.

"Let me." He reached for the snake.

I hesitated, questioning. "You do not fear him?"

"Since long ago, I have eaten of his fruit," Yeshua smiled, charming the little snake with his voice and touch. Nehushtan's gleaming body laced through his fingers and entered the open basket as if commanded.

I tied down the lid and put away the serpent, adoring Yeshua's face with my eyes. Trembling, as though we unveiled the Ark of the Covenant in the Holy of Holies, our motions weighted with feeling, amid sobbing indrawn breaths and little cries of delight, we uncovered the freshness and purity of each other's flesh—the smooth, childlike skin unblemished by wind or sun—to stand before each other naked, our life's blood throbbing in our eardrums.

Yeshua laid worshiping, sun-browned hands on my shoulders. "You are fair, my love," his practiced voice wavered unsteadily over the words of Solomon, "above all women."

"Your body is more beautiful than a wild deer's," I whispered truthfully. The words were my own, and from my heart. Then I could not help saying it, "You are a Ram Without Blemish."

"Our love will make this ram a fit sacrifice." Yeshua's voice was a groan of pain, and I saw the darkness in his eyes. Then it was forgotten as he appealed like an anxious boy, burying his face in my hair, "Will you show me how to please you?"

"In your deepest self, you know, my love. Thus the Mother blesses her children. Do not fear to follow where she leads you."

"O, Mari," he murmured thickly, "*you* are the Goddess to me. You are Isis, and Inanna, and Venus, and Eve—Eve, the mother of my heart's birth into love."

"And you are Dumuzi, my Tammuz, my Adonis. You are Osiris, Lord of all the gods, and of my heart."

We mounted the bed of the Goddess, and the sacred ritual we performed there was holier than a psalm, or hymn, or prayer; yet it was all that and more. I remembered his plea of innocence, his inexperience, for only moments. I would have forgiven awkwardness or haste in him—forgiven him anything—but there was no need. He cared only for my pleasure, my delight, matching my passion moment by moment, with exquisite sensitivity. I do not think that the gods envied our rapture, but took their own delight through ours, for we were their embodiment. Our flesh was consecrated, divine.

"Mari." Yeshua's voice called me from sweet slumber, where I had drifted, sated with love.

"My husband." The words were a song on my lips.

"There is much I must tell you, beloved, our time is short."

I wanted to protest the invasion of tomorrow's events on this most precious of all nights, but his urgency stopped me. I rolled off the gentle hollow beneath his shoulder, to see his face, grave but serene, in the yellow light of the perfumed lamps. "You are so fair, my Yeshua," I murmured, drunk with love.

"It delights me this body pleases you," he smiled.

"And what of yourself?" I asked gently. "Has your body not pleased you, this night?"

"It is you, my priestess, my wise one; who has shown me the sacredness of this flesh. You have made it a temple."

Then anguish darkened his face, his breath caught as though a dagger pierced him, "O, Mari, I love you so much!" And he began to weep great choking sobs. Weeping with him, I pulled him close so my naked breasts were bathed with his tears. Thus we shared our great sorrow as we had shared our great joy.

How can I tell of my tenderness for this gentlest of all men, who wept without apology in my arms and made no show of protecting me by bearing his burden alone? I cradled him like a little child, and I blessed the gods it was given to my arms to hold him. When he had spent his grief, he sighed a great sigh, and leaning back on one elbow, dried my breasts and face with the bed linen, kissing them profusely the while.

"My poor Mari," he mourned. "It grieves me I must bring you so much sorrow. But I have never deceived you, and you are braver than any man I know."

"You honor me above all women," I protested. "I have never known such happiness or believed it possible."

"Wise as you are, you must promise me you will keep the memory of our happiness and not grieve because of what must be."

"O, Yeshua, I know it must be, but not now!" I pleaded. "Let us have some time together before—" I broke off, unable to say the words.

"Tomorrow," he said, "tomorrow or the next day, they will take me."

"Jerusalem will fall?" I barely breathed.

"The garrisons from Caesarea will be here by late morning," he said. I must have looked stricken, for he added with finality, "There is no hope."

"Then many will die." I felt sorrow for the rebel Zealots.

"They will if they choose to resist," Yeshua said, "but most will not. Only their leader will be put to death." I gasped in unwilling understanding.

"They will crucify you!"

"It is better that one man should die for the people," he spoke the words with deliberate care.

"Then you will die as a Sacred King, as did your father, Sharon!" I was incredulous as it all came clear to me. "You will skirt the Roman law that forbids sacrifice of the King by getting them to do it for you!" My voice rose shrilly, as I sought the comfort of anger to ease my grief. "Oh, it is beautiful! Brilliant! What a joke on your enemies, and on your friends! The Messiah has come! He will reign for an eternity of one day!" I stopped and waited, sobbing, for his reproach, but he said nothing. Among silken, down-filled pillows, he held me close, stroking my hair patiently, until I could calm myself.

"What will happen to the Temple?" I quavered, after a time. "Lysander says you foretold its destruction. What will happen to all of us?"

"The Temple will be destroyed, but not now," Yeshua said, with the certainty of a prophet. "My death will buy time for another generation to rise in anger and outrage against Rome. Then, no quarter will be given. They will all die, and Jerusalem will lie a wasteland. That is why you must take yourself and your household away from here. Joseph of Arimathea will come to you with a plan. You must do as he tells you." I struggled with this new burden, but did not speak.

"Caiaphas is a wise High Priest, and with the help of old Annas, who served before him, he will convince the others the sacrifice of the King is the only way to satisfy the anger of Rome," Yeshua continued.

"But they will have to persuade the procurator," I said.

"Pilate will be quite happy to see me crucified, though he will not want it held to his account," Yeshua predicted. "He may send me to Antipas, if he discovers I am Galilean, in the hope Herod will condemn me as a traitor. One way or another, Pilate will cause the priests and the people to beg for my death and take my blood upon themselves. It will be held against them, unjustly for all time."

"Why unjustly," I demanded," when they will have cried out for it?"

"Because it is the only way they can save their homes and their children. My death is their only salvation."

I tried to nurse my rage, but it melted away, leaving me bereft of hope. Ashamed, I raised my face to his. "Forgive me, my husband. You have honored me above all women, and I have no better mind than to reproach you."

"You honor me by telling me your heart." He kissed my wet cheeks. "You are right to feel you have been robbed of what you richly deserve."

"I will never deserve such blessing as even one moment with you brings me," I said, letting my taut body sink into blissful repose against him. "Paradise must be like this," I sighed.

"It is within us," Yeshua said.

"So say the learned Masters of the East," I agreed, my scholar's soul aroused to interest, even in the midst of our trouble.

"That is where I learned it," he smiled, "from the followers of Gautama, the Enlightened One."

"Aye, we had teachings of his in the Temple."

"I am ever amazed your education has been so thorough," he praised me. "The teachings of Gautama have reached the heart of all peoples, but few recognize their source."

"But did not the Enlightened One take much of his wisdom from the Brahmins?" I asked.

"You are resourceful in philosophy as you are in love," he chuckled, and I saw that his passion had revived. With a cry of joy, I arose and leaned over him, covering his body with kisses, and he sank backward on the bed of the Goddess with a groan of ecstasy.

We were awakened at dawn by Lysander, his message so urgent it could not wait.

"We are surrounded," he told us. "You must flee at once." Nina appeared with shepherd's robes to make us as inconspicuous as possible, and we dressed quickly. The sun reached the beaten gold of the Temple facade in blinding glory as Yeshua strode to the center of the courtyard and held up his hands for silence. I was amazed to see so many people within the walls of the Mount. Most were armed—Zealots and their supporters, by the look of them. They ceased moving. Even the men on the walls listened attentively. Judas and Peter appeared from the direction of Antonia, followed by James and John and the rest of the disciples. They stopped where they were as he began to speak.

"Praise be to the Father!" he proclaimed in his matchless voice.

"Amen!" The response came from several thousand throats.

"Praise be to the Mother!"

"Amen!"

"Praise be to the Law!"

"Amen!"

"My brave and faithful friends, the news I have is not good. I have told you I am a man of peace, and no warrior, but even Joshua would be of little help to you now. The garrisons from Caesarea are here already, as we expected. What we did not expect are two legions under Varus, coming from Alexandria. They will reach Jerusalem in two days. If you choose to fight, it will be many days before you are all killed, but you will all die, and this holy place will be utterly destroyed."

The men's voices rose in angry protest over the weeping of women and children. The people milled about wailing and cursing in their distress, but soon they turned once more toward Yeshua and he quieted them.

"It is better that one man should die for the people." The words that had chilled my heart thirty years ago struck me like crashing surf.

"I have been anointed and proved in the bed of the Goddess!"

They cheered him lustily.

"I am your Anointed King."

They cheered again, unwilling to let go of hope.

"Make me your offering to Rome, and save yourselves!"

A stunned silence followed, broken by the whimpering of a child, then the wailing of the women began, as if in acceptance of his death. My flesh, still warm and flushed from our bed, turned icy cold.

All but a few of the Zealots melted into the hills, whence they had come, and the people hastened to their homes and went about their business. The Roman garrison imprisoned in their own jail in the fortress of Antonia found the keys mysteriously within reach, and when reinforcements from Caesarea arrived to liberate them, they insisted sheepishly they had been captured, though no captors could be found. The soldiers discovered the gates of the city and the Temple Mount closed, but not barred, and everyone going about as if nothing had happened. Three Zealots, one no more than a boy, attacked the rescuing garrisons, preferring death to the dishonor of enduring one more hour of Roman rule. They were taken prisoner and put to torture, in an attempt to discover the hiding place of the King of the Jews.

Yeshua and I, the royal bride and groom, fled with our disciples and attendants through a drainage tunnel beneath the massive wall, down the steep eastern descent of the Mount and from thence to the nearby estate of Joseph of Arimathea. Almah was with us and Miriam of Scarios and Salome.

It was a long and anxious day, relieved only by messages Lysander brought. Yeshua agonized over the fate of Matthias and Reuben, and Reuben's young son, Barabbas, the three captured Zealots. "None of them is so in love with death to have done this, except to convince the Romans the whole uprising was nothing more than the actions of a handful of malcontents," he told us with tears in his eyes. "They have bought the lives of many with their life's blood."

Even as you will do, I thought, but I did not say the words. It seemed to me I stood aside watching while another who looked like me moved and spoke. How can she bear to go on when such calamity is upon her, I wondered of the strange woman called the Magdalene, the tireless priestess who moved among the shocked and disheartened band spreading calmness and detachment.

The mother of Yeshua was as calm as I, his bride. Her face was white alabaster, set with the jewels of her eyes – more ethereal and otherworldly than ever – as if she might dissolve like a heavenly apparition. Truly, she was not of this world.

Solome was always by my side, unwilling to accept what was happening, hoping desperately for reassurance.

Nana, with Shaher and Shalem, would safely have reached the port of Caesarea by now. Thank the Goddess Yeshua and Judas had persuaded me to send them away! Yeshua had sent Sita with them. She went unwillingly, obedient to the last, but the hurt in her doelike eyes touched my heart. "Oh, Sita," I begged her tearfully, "please help Nana protect my little sons." It proved the best thing I could have said, for Sita's face brightened at the thought she could be of service. Perhaps she was not being sent away just for her own protection, or worst of all, to spare her the pain of seeing her beloved lord wed to another.

"They are looking everywhere for you, Master, but they seem to have no idea where you are," Lysander reported in the late afternoon.

"If they are so clumsy they have not come for me by nightfall, we shall have to help them, lest others be put to torture and death," Yeshua told him. At this, Salome lost all hope and collapsed in despair. Yeshua took her from my arms and held her against his breast. "You will be happy again, and sing for joy, I promise you," he told her.

When evening came, a simple meal was laid for us in a long upper room not part of Joseph's main house. Yeshua broke the bread and blessed it, then he performed a rite practiced in Egypt, where barley cakes baked in the shape of the dying god are eaten, and barley ale is drunk as his blood, making the celebrants like him, immortal.

When Yeshua had broken the bread so all could be served, he passed it to John, on his right, and as it moved from hand to hand around the table, his face took on such perfect peace and awful glory he seemed indeed the God.

"This is my body, broken for you. As oft as you eat it, remember me."

We ate, not from hunger, mingling our tears with our bread. Then he raised the cup, and drank, and passed it to his right around the table.

"This is my blood, shed for many," he said. "Drink it in remembrance of me."

No sound was heard until all had drunk, and I, on my husband's left, set down the cup with a shaking hand.

"One of you will betray me."

Stunned silence greeted Yeshua's remark, and his eyes flashed with impatience at the slowness of their understanding.

"If the Temple police cannot bring me before Caiaphas, it will go ill for all of them with the procurator. One of you must play the traitor and lead them to me for a price."

They began to talk all at once among themselves and to Yeshua, saying, "Not I, Lord," "Lord, not I." He held up his hand for silence.

"Mari and I will choose a sign," he told them. "Whoever first does what we agree on, is chosen. Say it is your will."

"Aye, aye," they all consented, grumbling a little, resuming their meal uneasily.

Yeshua turned to me. "Choose a sign, beloved, as you have done before." I had, of course; it was the way we often allotted tasks among ourselves—but never before a task like this. I leaned toward my husband and whispered in his ear. He nodded gravely and kissed me. "So be it," he said.

The meal proceeded in silence. Once, Yeshua looked up just as Andrew dipped his fingers into the salt jar. The big man started and asked, "Lord, is it I?"

"Peace be with you, Andrew, no." Andrew sighed in relief, and friendly laughter broke the tension for a time.

Then Judas reached out and dipped his bread in the meat juices at the same time as Yeshua, so their two hands were together in the dish. I gasped, and Judas blanched. "Lord, not I?" His words were pleading, unbelieving, and he dropped his face into his hands.

Yeshua's compassion was in his voice. "What you must do, do quickly," he said.

Judas pulled his long legs from beneath the table without another word and began to wind a colored cloth about his head, pushing his curling locks up beneath it. The sympathy of the others permeated the room, and their blessings followed him.

"Bless you, Judas!" "Go with God, Judas!"

Yeshua spoke above the others, "I will be in the garden," he said. Judas stopped briefly in the doorway for one long look into that face so like his own, and vanished.

I swallowed hard, but the lump in my throat remained. I thought my heart would break for Judas. His was the hardest task of all. He would be branded a traitor to his master, and a traitor has no home, anywhere. I recalled earlier overhearing Yeshua say to his brother, "It grieves me, Judas, you will never be safe in this land after this business is done. 'Twere better, I think, you are thought dead, if you take my meaning."

"I had thought as much, myself," Judas replied. "But do not be troubled for my sake." His voice was heavy with words unsaid.

"There is a charge I would ask of you, though I fear I am over-zealous to ask for what you already intend."

"If I read your meaning, you speak rightly," Seth nodded gravely.

"The holy vessel of my blood I place in your keeping," Yeshua said, and Seth nodded.

"I shall guard it with my life—willingly!" he swore emphatically.

I was mystified, unable to guess their meaning, a position annoying as it was unfamiliar. The puzzle kept coming back to haunt me, until Yeshua led us in the eucharistic rite, when we passed from hand to hand and lip to lip the silver cup of consecrated wine.

I was glad, even in my grief, to have solved the mystery. But Judas had not taken the cup, and Yeshua apparently had forgotten it. As we all rose to leave the room where we had taken our last meal together, it stood empty on the table where I, the last to drink, had set it. What if Judas had forgotten his promise under the weight of the new charge laid upon him? Feeling like a thief, looking round to be sure no one saw, I slipped the silver goblet into the folds of my robe. I would deliver it myself into Seth's hands, since both he and Yeshua attached such significance to it.

"It is time to say good-bye," Yeshua said when we stood in the spring twilight. "You must return to the Temple now. Everything will be as I have said. Be prepared to fly when Joseph comes for you. Do not grieve, beloved."

I could not speak. My voice had been taken away with my heart. I clung to him, and he clasped me fiercely for a long moment. Then he gently loosened my hands from him, and walked away toward the Garden of Gethsemane.

I sank to the ground, too mortally wounded to cry out. They left me there, out of respect and love, for a time, alone with my grief. Then Nina and Salome lifted me gently between them.

The Cross

Thy tears are for those beyond tears: and are thy words words of wisdom? The wise grieve not for those who live; and they grieve not for those who die—for life and death shall pass away.

Bhaghavad Gita

I have said that mine was a story that must be told, and I have trusted the Mother to reveal it to you in her own good time. Now that I sleep again in my beloved's arms with red-haired baby Anna at my breast—now that we have safety and laughter in our lives once more, I can try to speak of those last days to you. But you know most of the story already, and it is so painful to me. It comes back in broken images, not pictures only, but sounds and smells and bodily weakness and pain: Nina and I, led by Lysander, with Lucius behind, following the path blindly—the moon not yet risen, the darkness a solid wall around us. The deep shadow of the olive grove, the sudden flare of torches; Judas walking toward the ancient stones of the garden shrine where Yeshua prayed.

Lucius's strong hands pulling me back, Yeshua rising erect and graceful—a ripe stalk of grain before the reaper—turning to meet his twin. Two still figures against their own dancing shadows by torchlight. Judas kissing his brother on each cheek.

Everything came to pass just as Yeshua had said it would. I can never cease remembering Herod Antipas preening like a cat, savoring the gift that had fallen into his lap. Herod laughing, slapping his thigh; leering at Yeshua, baiting the crowd's impatience, relishing their discomfort. And the people, faces tense, holding back their rage, exposing to him their need; willing to suffer any abuse if he would give them this death they must have to save themselves.

And my hating them. Hating them as Antipas hated them; my temples throbbing, my gut retching to his laughter, the taste of gall in my mouth.

There was more, much more. The steepening incline of Golgotha, sparsely treed with straggling olives, a blaze of red windflowers, wide open, shiny as fresh blood. Trampled earth and clusters of red anemones. It seemed as though I stood outside myself, observing rather than feeling, with intense awareness. Afterward, when I was told that Yeshua died after only three hours, I could not believe it, for I lived half my life while he hung there; the whole time from my birth until our wedding night was not as long.

It was during the last hour that John of Capernaum came. He looked full on the figure of Yeshua, has face transfigured by some ecstatic inner joy. My own suffering made me eager, and I questioned him.

"John, you have seen a vision?"

"Yea, Mari. I came from the garden, from the same grotto where he prayed before they took him last night. And he came to me there, and spoke to me just now."

"But he could not—he is here. We have watched with him here."

"Mari. Is anything impossible with him? He came to me, I tell you, and he laughed at what is happening here." I watched Yeshua and saw he knew of John's presence. The faintest smile crossed his face. John never looked away from him as he spoke to me. "It is only a shadow here, dying before us. What he is—even what we are—never dies. He laughed when he told me this. 'They think they are putting me to death,' he said, 'but they are giving me life, for I will leap up stronger than ever.'"

Grief is a physical process. The body mourns as truly as the soul. *Viraha.* Sita told me her people's word for that special pain is *viraha*—the pain of separation from one's beloved. Nina sat by my bed wringing her strong hands helplessly. Salome sat on the bed beside me hour after hour, or lay down with me, holding me in her arms. She started in protest when I sat up and said I must go to Almah. I had to know the truth; only she could tell me. Yet I dissembled.

"She is suffering as much as I am." My words hung in the space between us, and Nina could not restrain herself.

"She has brought it on herself, then!" Her face contorted in hard lines. "Oh, Mari, she has sacrificed you as well as Yeshua to her plans, and she has not lost him as you have, but made certain she can keep him forever."

Salome looked puzzled but said nothing. Often more could be learned by listening than by asking questions.

Viraha had darkened my thoughts like the ornate shutters closed against the afternoon light, but I understood that Nina, who worshiped me as I had Almah, must have struggled all these years against jealousy. How natural for Nina to think Almah had used me for her own purposes. I put my arms around my dear, faithful Nina, so wilted and weary; she had been too busy caring for me to rest herself. "Nevertheless, I must go to her," I told her gently.

"Well, you cannot go barefoot," Nina sighed. "Fetch your mother's sandals, child," she said to Salome, ready to kneel and strap them on my feet. But Salome dropped to her knees and fastened the thongs herself.

I squinted in the afternoon light of the gallery outside my darkened chamber. The daylight hurt my head, but it cheered me to see that the sun still shone and life went on.

Almah's apartments were empty; she and her women must be about the preparations for Yeshua's burial. The thought of the embalming chamber returned us to our gloom. Muttering, Nina fetched a torch. We passed, three purple-robed priestesses, through the passageway to the long stairway, descending from the upper floors of the cloister past the ground level where the kitchens and herb gardens were. It grew dark as we moved beneath the level of the street, and the orange torchlight cast our violet shadows like monstrous gorgons with long, claw fingers on the uneven stone walls. We came into a winding passage where the vast granaries and storage houses of the Temple were hollowed out of rock beneath the thick walls of the Mount. Room after room held grain, dried beans, pulse, and herbs, enough for seven years of famine. There were barrels of salted fish and jars of olive and palm oil. I had tallied inventories of these supplies time after time; I knew where all were kept, how much was used in any year. We passed rooms stacked with bolts of wool woven by the holy hands of priestesses, dyed with finest purple from Tyre. Chill penetrated our clothing, and Salome shuddered. I put my arm around her trembling shoulders.

"You could wait in our rooms," I suggested.

"I watched him die," Salome said. "It can be no worse to look on him now."

The heavy door of the embalming chamber was open, and the smell of funeral spices, like death itself, enveloped us. Myrrh and frankincense permeated the very stones with their heaviness. I led the way hesitantly. Almah and Miriam looked up from their sorrowful task as we entered, and I saw the grief-ravaged countenance of Yeshua's mother. But her voice was calm and filled with compassion.

"Dearest Mari, Nina, Salome," she moved toward us. Then her woman, Julia, stepped aside.

I saw the bloodless form of Yeshua stretched on the long table before me. The women had washed him so that his many wounds shone bright as red anemones against the gray pallor of his skin. My eyes took in his still-damp hair and beard, washed and combed, darker than in life, the curl of long lashes against his cheek, his serene brow unmarked but for tiny wounds the thorns had made. His mouth was innocent, almost smiling. Why had I never noticed the perfect coil of his ear? A rising roar filled my head.

Haltingly, I reached out and placed my hand over the marks the thorns had made on his cold forehead, remembering the pain and humiliation that had been heaped upon him. The roar increased.

"Dearest Mari." Almah embraced me, and I accepted the comfort of her arms, trying to drown the roaring in my ears, letting my tears flow freely. Almah, too, wept, and for a moment I was once more caught up beyond myself in sympathy with the great sorrow and travail of the Goddess. Almah was mourning both a husband and a son, I thought. The grief I feel she has endured for thousands of years, and now she suffers his loss afresh. But the sound grew louder, and Nina's bitter words pushed into my thoughts like a raging flood, carrying everything before them: "She has brought in on herself, then; she has sacrificed you as well as Yeshua." Overwhelming anger arose in my breast, choking and strangling me, and I pushed Almah away, staring into her face as if I had never seen her before. I opened my mouth, but my words rushed over each other in such haste I could not speak them. And the roar burst forth from me, inarticulate, like a wounded animal in pain, not from my throat but from the depths of the burning agony in my breast.

Almah stepped backward, her mouth open in surprise. "My poor Mari," she started to say, but her voice was drowned in the roaring which seemed to have a will or power of itself. I could neither control nor stop the fury that tore from me, rasping my throat and lungs sore. Nina held me, Almah pleaded, Salome wept; I struggled to possess my monstrous rage.

Julia and Deborah moved to protect Almah, but she waved them away, and Miriam snapped, "Leave them alone!" Almah recognized herself as the object of my outrage; her puzzlement turned to compassion; she thought my grief had unbalanced me. She reached out to me, but I pushed her hands away.

"You had no right," I croaked hoarsely, "no right to hurt him . . . hurt me, too much . . . , too much." I stumbled on through tearing sobs, "You used us . . . , we loved you, trusted you, wanted to serve you; but you wanted too much . . ."

The uncharacteristic expression of alarm made Almah's face even stranger to me. "I do not understand, dearest Mari," she pleaded, "why do you think I have done you some injury? Please, let us meet later in our rooms, and unburden our hearts."

My rage rose again, and I tried to shout, but managed only a hoarse, broken, "No!" Lowering my voice to a level I could control, I demanded, "You must answer me. I must know."

"I will answer anything you ask," she promised.

I took a deep breath, resolved to ask what I had never dared ask before. "Are you . . ." I began, agony wringing the words from me, "Are you not the Mother, Queen Isis herself?" My words echoed back and forth off the stone walls of the funeral chamber, growing weaker each time, until they were only a whisper, waiting; and the women stood, waiting.

"The Mother is in us all, yourself as well, Mari; you know that." Almah spoke carefully.

"No, I mean," I choked, desperate, "are you not the very incarnation of Queen Isis herself?" Almah's expression did not change, and I plunged on. "Come to give birth to Osiris in this flesh, in order to sacrifice him . . ." my voice cracked as I inclined my head toward Yeshua's corpse, "so that you can be together for eternity?" My effort took my last bit of composure, and I collapsed into anguished weeping, hiding my face in my hands, in dread of Almah's reply. If the answer is yes, how can she forgive me, I thought; and if no, then how can I live?

"O, Mari, my poor Mari." I felt Almah's arms encircle me. "I thought you understood." I raised my eyes to her look of amazed understanding.

"Then it is not true?" I whimpered.

"You know it is true," Almah said; "you have known it since I shared my vision with you. It is the truth of your own vision you do not understand."

She grasped both my hands and shook them, so I would look into her face. "Have you forgotten your journey to the Netherworld, Mari? Yours was the dark vision. It was as the Devourer that She came to you; it was the Queen of Hell that you recognized in yourself, and through her gave birth to yourself anew. Your vision was as true as mine."

I had tried to erase the memory of that dreadful time; now the images came flooding back, and I saw that they were less terrifying than I remembered. Almah drew my hand toward her face and placed my palm against her wet cheek. "Dearest Mari," she controlled her voice with great effort, "in my body, She bore him, and nurtured him with my milk. But it is through you that She wed him. It was in your body that She united with him in the Holy Rite." Her voice broke, and she pressed my hand against her face, shedding her tears into my palm, and I made a cup of my fingers as though they held a gift.

"But you *are* Isis," I insisted, as from a trance.

"Yes," she whispered piteously, "but I am Almah, too, a mortal woman who has lost her son. And you yourself are Isis, as well as a bereaved bride."

"Then She has used you, too, for her own selfish purposes. Does that not anger you?" My rage was spent, but the reason for it remained clear in my mind.

"The union of the Goddess with her beloved is the source of all things; I cannot see it as selfish," Almah said thoughtfully. "Their love is the fount of ours."

I flushed with shamed understanding. The truth of her words washed over me, cleansing, renewing, reviving. "Oh, Almah," I begged, "forgive me! My selfishness blinded me to the truth."

"You? Selfish?" Almah remonstrated. "You are right to feel that you have been unjustly robbed of your happiness. And I . . ." She looked away, her voice breaking. "I so much wanted you to be the mother of my grandchildren."

I put my arms around my friend, she who was the Goddess to me, the grieving mother of my beloved.

"I am the mother of your grandchildren," I reminded her gently.

Understanding dawned suddenly, and intense joy transformed Almah's face.

"Oh, Mari," she whispered. "I have another son." She turned to Miriam. "If he will forgive me," she said. "I beg your forgiveness as well."

"There is nothing to forgive," Miriam said. "We have all done what we could, what we had to do. We have each served the Mother, and the Law."

Lovingly, together, we anointed and wrapped the body of the Sacred King and followed the disciples who carried him to the new tomb of Joseph of Aramathea.

33

The Third Day

I am the Father of this universe,
and even the source of the Father.
I am the Mother of this universe,
and the creator of all . . .

Bhaghavad Gita

Early on the morning of the first day of the week, while it was yet dark, I, Mari the Magdalene, came to the tomb in the Garden of Joseph of Arimathea. In the gray half-light before dawn, I stopped, startled, and stood still, for what had appeared as I approached to be the deep shadow of the olive tree was nothing else than the open mouth of the tomb. The stone had been rolled away. Prickles of fear raising the hair on my neck, I retreated back along the path. I glanced behind me, half expecting to see some visible, hulking shape.

"Quickly, Lysander, call Peter and John! Someone has taken him away!" I cried in a loud whisper. Nina, Lucius, and Lysander stood waiting, respecting my desire to go there alone. Most of the disciples were still guests of Joseph of Arimathea, who had obtained Yeshua's body from Pilate and allowed us to place it in a new tomb within the very garden from which he had been arrested only four days ago.

Peter and John came running in only a few moments, and I followed them back along the path. John reached the opening of the tomb first and peered within, but did not enter. He seemed to react strongly to the uncanny presence that had frightened me. It recalled my nightmarish descent into the Netherworld.

But Peter, when he reached the open tomb, stooped his big body and went inside. John took heart at this and followed him. They found the linen grave wrappings carefully rolled up and the napkin that had bound his head lying in another place, neatly folded.

"But why would anyone remove the bindings?" Peter wondered aloud.

"Who could have done this?" John echoed. He looked at me with compassion. "Go home, Mari," he urged. "You can do nothing here."

"Yes, I am going," I agreed, and walked back up the path with them. But when they turned toward the house of Joseph, and were out of sight, hardly knowing why I did so, I motioned to Nina and the others to remain where they were and went back to the tomb alone.

The air crackled with the aura of some powerful unseen presence, but I steeled myself to go on, driven by rising suspicion, pushed forward by hope. At the opening of the tomb the unearthly force was more pronounced. My clothing molded itself to my body, and my hair lifted off my shoulders and flew wildly about me, though I felt no wind. Trembling so I could scarcely stand, I forced one foot before the other and stooped at the entrance, dreading what I might see. A blinding light struck my eyes with such force I fell to the ground, just inside the tomb.

"Holy Mother, give me courage," I prayed, trying to accustom my eyes to the brilliant light. Then it softened, and the radiance before me felt warm, like the life-giving rays of the sun. Believing it might be my last earthly action, I raised my head.

The walls and ceiling of the tomb had become as vast as the dome of heaven, yet it was filled to overflowing with that blessed presence I had known so often in my dreams. Around her head was a crown of stars, and the moon was under her feet. Her mantle was the blue of space, and she was garlanded with all the flowers and fruits of the earth. It was She, Isis, more glorious and radiant than ever, and she was not alone. Her marvelous eyes, whose sorrowful tears had touched my heart, were alight with happiness, for embracing her, clothed in glory and majesty, shining like the sun, was her beloved Osiris. In his face I saw Yeshua, but Seth was there, too, and Sharon. His hands were clasped in hers, their fingers and bodies entwined; they gazed rapturously into each other's eyes, and a powerful, vital force flowed from them into the earth beneath.

Transfixed in awe, I basked in the warmth and light of that vision, and my soul dined on nectar and ambrosia. Then both the radiant beings before me pulled their eyes from each other and turned to gaze into my face, with looks of such love and tenderness that I thought my heart broke with rapture and poured forth like water at their feet.

Then they were gone, and the earth grew cold beneath me. How long I lay there, unwilling to leave that place where Heaven had touched the earth, I did not know; but at last my normal sense returned, and I remembered Nina would be worried about me.

I arose slowly and moved out into the daylight. The sun had risen and was pushing away the morning mists. Dew sparkled on every leaf and blade. I was so loath to leave the place that my eyes filled with tears. Then I saw Joseph's gardener on the path and called as I caught up to him. He turned, his head silhouetted against the morning sun, half-blinding me, making a rainbow of my tears.

"Mari."

My heart leaped so strongly I grasped at my breast with both hands.

"My husband!"

"Do not touch me, beloved, for I am no longer flesh and blood," he said gently, but my spirit soared as if he had caressed and kissed me tenderly. We spoke, in those moments, of many things, and without words, for they were not needed. And then he went away.

My feet were light on the flower-bordered path, as I passed the wondering eyes of my faithful friends who waited at the entrance to the garden. They followed me to the house of Joseph, and I burst into the room where his guests sat at their simple breakfast, too deep in despair to desire food. The eyes of the brethren widened at the intrusion of a female unannounced into their midst, but propriety was far from my mind.

"I have seen my Lord!" I announced.

"Mistress Mari," James said gently, breaking the stunned silence, "you are overwrought. You should be at home with your women."

"He came to me in the garden—just now," I insisted. "He spoke to me and sent me hither with his message for you. He is risen!"

"The woman speaks foolishness!" declared Peter. "I came early with you to the tomb—with John also, and saw no one. Why would he come to you and not us?"

"Why, indeed?" answered John. "You can never admit, Peter, that he loved her more than us!" He asked me eagerly, "Tell us his message."

"I am amazed how willingly you give in to false hopes! I will listen to none of this!" Peter rose to his feet and stalked about the room. "Can you not see the woman is out of her mind with her grief? Well, I, too, loved him, as you all know, but I have the courage to face the truth. We shall never see our Master again in this world."

"Perhaps it is you who lack the courage to hope, Peter," John spoke up. "The Master did say many times he would rise from the dead, and we have often discussed how he may have meant it." He turned to me. "You say that the Master lives?" he encouraged me.

I looked from one to another of these men with whom I had shared so much, and reminded myself I was not a mere woman intruding on men's prerogatives, but the chosen bearer of momentous truth. I straightened my back and lifted my chin, calling up all the dignity of my high office.

"I know that my redeemer lives." I spoke in my best trained priestess's voice. "He has descended into Hell, and taken for himself the dread judgment seat. He has balanced the scales of the Annanaki with the infinite weight of his love, and he has redeemed the Dark Goddess of death, and taken her as his bride. He has paid with his blood the ransom for every soul that is, or was or will be. He has abolished the boundaries between Heaven, Earth, and Hell, and made them One Kingdom, eternal." I paused, and waited, but no one spoke. "As for his message, it is this," I said: "he has fulfilled the Law."

Hesitantly, Andrew, the brother of Peter, spoke, for Peter would not. "By the Law, I take it you mean the Law of Moses?" he asked. One must be careful how one uses words with the Magdalene, his tone implied, since the tradition she represents is tainted with paganism.

I felt I no longer stood in the dappled sunlight of Joseph's dining hall. I seemed to have grown very tall, and looked down as from a great height. I was no longer Mari only, but the Mother of All Things, and I understood what Yeshua had meant with his patient insistence, "I and my Father are one." It was what Sita had taught the children with the parable of the salt.

"Thou art the salt, not the water—thou art that One." I was, I am that One. I stood once more on the cusp of time, but there was no past behind me, no future before, only this eternal moment, in which nothing that had been could ever be lost, and the long awaited fulfillment of hopes and dreams and sacrifices is realized and forever present. I looked at these faithful men who had loved and followed my husband, and my heart filled with a great tenderness. They will not understand now, I thought, but one day they shall, and so in the timeless present, we are all redeemed, we are One.

"Love is the Law," I said. "The Law is Love."

Rebirth

Whoever thus knows my birth as God, and who knows my sacrifice, when he leaves his mortal body, goes no more from death to death, for he in truth comes to me.

Bhaghavad Gita

Life loves life and hates death. As soon as Yeshua's child stirred in my womb, my thoughts, even my sorrow—*viraha*—turned slowly from my dead husband toward my living lover. Where had Seth gone? I paid no attention to the rumor that he had hanged himself in remorse for betraying his brother to the authorities. We feared Herod and others might try to kill him to prevent him from claiming he was Yeshua, risen from the dead. Indeed, that is what many believed when stories of Yeshua's resurrection began to be heard. The betrayal had been no betrayal, and Yeshua had advised Judas to let it out that he had died, so we did not believe the rumors, though we helped to pass them on.

We were kept busy with our secret arrangements to flee Jerusalem as I had sworn to Yeshua we would, but I had plenty of time to wonder about the strange way that Seth had moved out of my life as if to make room for his brother. It seemed preposterous, even with all his talk about destiny, that he could willingly have done so. Had he feared Yeshua? Or loved him that much? And what of myself? Why was I never able to prefer one over the other, but loved each with total and consuming passion? And why did neither of them ever reproach me for it?

I watched Nina's face, absorbed as my own. She looked up, smiled and shook her head. Then she called Lysander before I could ask her. When I told him I wanted news of Judas, he shook his head. Seeing my disappointment, he offered a straw of hope. "Perhaps at Scarios," he said, "– at Scarios perhaps we shall learn something."

The boat that took us away from our homeland was a swift Greek trader owned and captained by Jason, husband to Geshtinanna, who came along herself to enjoy the trip with us, bringing their two little girls. Jason, who looked like the very hero whose name he bore, did not fill his galleys with rowers as the Romans did but depended on his skill at sailing, the lightness of his craft, and the good winds that could be counted on this time of year before the winter storms. Joseph of Arimathea, the truest of all Yeshua's disciples, had sold or given away all his mighty estate in order to carry out Yeshua's wishes that he see us to a new life. He brought with him only two stewards and a few trunks – a small cargo compared to the barrels, boxes, and trunks of provisions he had urged that we bring with us to Gaul.

Salome was stoic in her sadness at leaving all her friends behind, and I grieved to go so far from my family, but even if I had not promised Yeshua, just knowing that he had wished me to go would have been reason enough. Our excitement distracted us from our sorrow at leaving our home. Shaher and Shalem barely realized that they might never see Jerusalem again. I tried to lose myself in their excitement to keep my mind from my grief at parting with my mother and father, knowing that I would not see them again in this world, and that when they died, it would be Martha and Lazarus, not I, who would lay them to rest. Nina and Geshtinanna fussed over me, bringing me ginger tea to control my seasickness, trying to keep the children from jostling or disturbing me.

But the children were a comfort and a distraction. In amazement I watched Nana's black-eyed little girls teaching my sons all about the ship and the sea. At five and seven, they were already experienced sailors, able to predict the weather for each coming day and to discover schools of dolphins before we came upon them. They could see Scarios, too, far off, long before we, their elders, could glimpse anything at all, and when the jewel-like island finally appeared, it was exactly where they had been pointing for nearly an hour.

White gulls dipped and swooped over the small, perfect harbor where our ship dropped anchor, and we climbed into the boat that would carry us ashore. My heart pumped madly at the sight of a tall, clean-shaven man with a crown of chestnut curls pacing up and down the pier. We drew up alongside, and he came toward us, the breeze ruffling his hair, his eyes alight with love. The babe leaped in my womb.

"It is only I, Mari," he smiled, when he had pulled me up by my hands so I stood before him, " not my brother. I promised to protect with my life the holy vessel of his blood."

"Oh, I have brought it for you!" I cried in delight. "It is in my baggage."

He raised a single eyebrow. "What is in your baggage?"

"The silver chalice from which we drank at our last supper together."

"Sweet Mari, you have brought it for me?"

I nodded, unable to look away from his face.

"Know you not that you yourself are the holy vessel of which he spoke to me?" Seth asked softly.

Slowly, I understood. "But I thought . . . Then you will stay with me?"

"Will you marry me, Mari?"

"After all that has happened? Why would you marry me now, and not before?"

"Now," he said firmly, "it is my destiny."

"Destiny!" I cried, "Destiny! Don't you ever throw that word up to me again!" Seth covered his face with his arms in mock terror and ran, but slowly, seeing I was too heavy for a game of tag. I squealed with laughter, and the unaccustomed sound felt good in my throat. I caught him and held him, aiming my lips at his smiling mouth. We kissed hungrily and joyfully; he lifted me in his arms and bore me from the pier, while our little boys and Salome danced after us shouting their delight.

Later, when I brought out the chalice from its wrapping in a cloth of softest wool and placed it in his hands, Seth wept aloud, and I with him. As we held each other, I realized more than ever how deep his love for his brother had been. For myself, I think I could not have borne my own suffering without the comfort of being with Seth. "I have something else to show you," he said, wiping his face with his sleeve and going to the chest where his belongings were stored. From the very bottom, he took out a package wrapped in a fitted bag of the heaviest purple woolen felt. I drew in my breath, for the woolen case was itself a gorgeous work, but he drew from it a polished coffer, exquisitely carved from the fragrant wood of a tamarack tree. He pressed on a square ingeniously hidden in the carved design, and the lid sprang open. He had carved the inside to hold five stacks of six silver coins — Greek tetradrachms, the most common of currency. "These were the price of my brother's life," he said hoarsely. He covered his face with his arms and sobbed.

We were married at the autumn solstice by Nina, the only priestess on Scarios besides myself qualified to perform the rite. Miriam served as mother of both the bride and the groom, and Lucius and Lysander and our children stood up with us. Since everyone present was in the wedding, we had no guests but ourselves and Miriam's well-appointed household. We feasted, however, for the three days accorded by custom, at the insistence of Miriam, whose hospitality knew no limits. Nor did her wisdom, for the festivities marked a turning away from our mourning toward the celebration of life, from the past sorrow toward the promise of the future.

We settled down to endure the winter storms and await the birth of Yeshua's child. Being with Seth again began to heal the sharpness of my loss of Yeshua, though tears still came for no apparent reason at times, and the sense of Yeshua's presence — or absence — still rushed over me unexpectedly like chill winds off the gray sea. But sometimes, and this is curious and difficult to explain, yet I must tell it: at times it seemed to me that Seth *was* Yeshua, that we were together again, and that he understood this himself and felt no reproach. There was no loss of Seth when I felt this; we continued to share all the memories and concerns of the life and children we had together. It is most strange, and I cannot explain it.

But the child grew. The only living issue of Yeshua's flesh grew daily within my body. I was struck with awe at the realization of it one day as Nina and I sat before the warm hearth in our pleasant sitting room, and she, reading my thoughts, looked up with tears starting to her eyes.

"A holy child, to be sure," she exclaimed, "a child of destiny."

"Oh, Nina! Yes, I feel it too." Yeshua had been so careful for the safety of this little one. The "holy vessel of his blood," he had called me when he had sworn our protection from Joseph of Arimathea. So I wondered and pondered, and as the birth grew nearer, the memory of other births began to push into my mind.

I had never had difficulty in childbed. The smallness and flexibility of my bones and my wide hips made it easier for me than for many women, but even the easiest birth is an anxious and painful ordeal. Besides, my last memory of childbirth had not been in this world, but under the baleful eyes of the Annanaki where I had given birth in the stead of the terrible Goddess of the Netherworld. And to whom? To myself. Nina had not been allowed to share that experience with me as she did my waking thoughts, but now she caught the flashes of it that pushed into my mind as my time approached, and when this happened her eyes would narrow and a worried frown would cloud her face.

"What is it, Mari? What do you fear?" she insisted one day, when the image of grinning demons waiting to devour my child drifted into my conscious memory from that other place.

"The terrors of the Netherworld return to me now because it was there I last experienced giving birth. I know there is nothing to fear, yet the memory comes unbidden," I explained.

I remembered how sick I had been after that, how tormented by the dark fears and imaginings I had brought back with me, until the day I went to Yeshua at the home of Simon the Pharisee and anointed his feet with myrrh and bitter tears. Yeshua healed my soul. He drove out the demons and opened my heart again to the delight of living in this world.

"Yeshua, my beloved," I whispered. Yeshua. And he could do it again. Just the thought of him sent them away. But I knew I was supposed to remember something else. Only a few days earlier, the Goddess had sent me a marvelous realization. As though in a vision I foresaw Yeshua's own descent to the Netherworld. I foretold his death, and his harrowing of Hell, his marriage with the Dark Goddess; and I had understood the meaning of it all, as though I dreamed a vivid dream.

"You have not believed your own vision," I heard Almah say again, and alongside all of this, around and behind it, I could hear the familiar voice of Isis calling and feel her tears on my own cheeks as so often before, while she searched and sorrowed through the ages for her lost Osiris. In my descent to the Netherworld, I had become one with its Dark Queen, and so even in the joy of this coming birth, a part of me remains, remembers my rejected sister, bitter Ereshkigal, howling and comfortless in the endless travails of death and rebirth.

But there is only *one* Goddess, of Heaven, Earth, and Hell. That sweet knowledge stole over me softly as a kiss—I, Mari, am brave Inanna too, for I have dared to seek wisdom in the Netherworld; and I am *She*, Isis, She whose voice I have always heard and whose grief I have always shared.

"In my body She bore and nurtured him, and in yours She wed him in the holy rite," Almah's voice said again. Isis calling to Osiris—Osiris, his perfect being fragmented into little lives and little deaths in flesh and time. She had called him home, back to herself, but not before he had sanctified the world of flesh and matter with his life-giving presence. Our marriage was the wedding of body and soul; through Him spirit descended into matter, infusing, informing it, rendering it sacred. The marriage of eternity and time had been celebrated when we Two became One. And the child of that marriage now stretched and strengthened within my womb!

I gasped with the intensity of my realization. Nina wept. She came to me and knelt putting both hands on my belly. "Oh, Mari," she whispered, "What manner of being is this? What will She be?"

It seemed perfectly right to call her "She."

The Goddess brought me to bed on a bright winter day when glistening drops from the just-past storm still clung to the olive trees and the gray clouds parted and fled, turning the sea deep blue as lapis in the sun. And She was kind, so kind that Miriam, bustling about the details of the birth, found little to do, her help all but unnecessary. When she placed the infant on my belly, busy about tying off the cord, the newborn Goddess opened one eye, and we regarded each other.

"Poor wee lady," Nina cooed, "have we surprised thee unawares?" Salome and Seth chuckled at the comical expression of the babe, who opened her other eye, but did not alter her puzzled scowl, seemingly amazed to find herself among strange people.

"From whence, beloved, hast thou come to us?" I asked my child, "From what wondrous dream have we awakened thee?"

"Thou art Hasmonean, for certain," Seth admired. "I mark thy red hair."

"Aye, red as her great-grandmother Anna's," Miriam agreed.

"Then Anna thou shalt be," I told my solemn daughter, "and a great lady."

"May the boys come in now?" Lysander begged from the doorway.

"What? There is someone who is not already in?" Miriam snorted, as Shaher and Shalem, together with the huge form of Lucius, crowded into the bedchamber.

Little Anna grunted agreeably as I wrapped her in a linen cloth, then she turned her intent gaze on her brother, Shalem, whose face was nearest. He endured her scrutiny for several minutes, staring back, as interested as she. Then he reached out timidly to touch her incredibly perfect, incredibly tiny hand. His round eyes grew rounder as the baby curled her delicate fingers around his own not too clean one.

"Where does she come from?" he wondered in his gruff little boy's voice.

"If she could speak, I believe she would tell us, for I think she knows," Seth answered him softly.

"Can we teach her to talk?" Shaher asked eagerly.

Seth laughed. "She will learn soon enough." His voice turned sober. "But by then she will have forgotten what she now knows—as we all do."

Epilogue

The Holy Grail

I have spoken, but in vain, for what words can tell
Of things that have no yesterday, tomorrow or today?

Takakusu

The infant Goddess proved powerful in her helplessness—she reordered the whole household around her needs and
demands, commanding our willing obedience to her every whim,
rewarding us with luminous looks from her great eyes or the adorable pursing of her pink mouth. Almah arrived on Scarios for her
Naming, and stayed until our departure for the shores of Gaul. She
could barely take her hands from baby Anna, playing with her
whenever she was awake and sitting peacefully silent, holding her
as she slept. I knew she was spoiling the baby and that I would be
sorry for it later, but I could not forbid her, knowing she would probably never again see this sole living descendant of her beloved Yeshua.

We set sail in the fine brisk winds of a fresh morning, after
weeks of exhaustive checking and rechecking of our preparations.
Almah and I had parted many times, but never before had it been
for good. I thought I would die with my own grief and with the
sharing of hers when she placed little Anna in my arms, kissed
me, and turned away.

We no longer had the steady Jason with Geshtinanna and their
daughters to show us the way, but the captain of this much larger
vessel was known to Jason and trusted by him. The journey was
long, but not unpleasant, and we talked many hours with Joseph
and his stewards, making plans for our new life.

Of course, little has turned out as we planned, yet all has been
well. The import business that Joseph and Seth conceived during

the voyage is flourishing beyond their hopes. Besides themselves, it is furnishing employment to some of the villagers as well, and is attracting a trade in goods produced here as well as those from afar.

There are many people of the Goddess here, and among them, what surprised us more, a small group of Yeshua's disciples. They make much of the silver chalice, and have enshrined it in their temple in the ornate case Seth carved for it. But they show little interest in the thirty pieces of silver, perhaps because it does not match with their belief that Seth is not Judas, but really Yeshua. Some think he is risen from the dead, and others that another died in his place. They smile knowingly when we say they were twins. For proof, I have read them a letter from Almah, who has gone to Ephesus, on the other side of the sea from here, where she is safe, though far away. But they do not believe the letter, either, though I let them hold it in their hands and look at the seal. Despite their belief that Seth is Yeshua, and their great curiosity about the dark giant Lucius, they understand our need to live our lives in peace and do not intrude unreasonably. We keep the Sabbath with them and break bread and pass the cup in remembrance.

Only yesterday, little Shalem brought to me a perfect red rose, and tears started to my eyes before I could stop them. Even through the blur I saw his stricken look, and I reached out and held him to me. "Oh, Mamma, please don't cry," he begged. "I thought you would like the flower."

"I do like it, darling," I told him. "You were very sweet and thoughtful to bring me so beautiful a rose. I will tell you why I cried." He sat back and regarded me solemnly. He looked so like the young Yeshua that I had to wait a moment more before I could speak again. "Once I knew another little boy just like you—not my own little son, as you are, but I loved him very much; we loved each other."

Shalem nodded gravely. "Did he die?"

"Yes, my darling."

"I am so sorry, Mamma." He put his round arms about my neck and kissed me, as Yeshua had so long ago.

Salome is soon to become High Priestess of the Goddess in the College of Virgins here, and to be wed to a noble lord. Shaher is studying mathematics and law with his father, and Shalem, music.

Little Anna has huge, blue Hasmonean eyes, and her red curls are a glory on the white pillow where she sleeps. I hear the song of shepherd's pipes and know that my love is near. Life loves life. I am content.

Notes

Full references for works mentioned in Notes may be found in the Bibliography.

Part I: The Temple of Ashera

Chapter 1: The Morning Star

Aethel's reference to the temptation of the angels when she is combing Mari's hair refers to the legend of the fall of the angels as told in the *Book of Enoch*, a first- to third-century Christian text that recounts what must have been oral tradition for several centuries before Mari's time. It makes the beauty of mortal women the cause of their fall, and this belief is echoed by Paul in his admonition that women should cover their heads, 1 Corinthians 11:10: "That is why a woman ought to have a veil on her head, because of the angels."

Ninshubur takes her name from the handmaid and companion to the Goddess Inanna. Geshtinanna was the faithful sister of Inanna's sacrifed and resurrected consort, Dumuzi.

Chapter 2: The Holy Maiden of Israel

The College of Virgins, the convent of the priestesses of Ahsera, is derived from many sources. Merlin Stone, in *When God Was a Woman*, pp. 153–61, writes:

> During Biblical times it was still customary, as it had been for thousands of years before in Sumer, Babylon, and Canaan, for many women to live within the temple complex, in earliest times, the very core of the community. As we have seen, temples owned much of the arable land and herds of domesticated animals, kept the cultural and economic records and generally appear to have functioned as the central controlling offices of the society. Women who resided in the sacred precincts of the Divine Ancestress took their lovers from among the men of the community, making love to those who came to the temple to pay honor to the Goddess. Among these people the act of sex was considered to be sacred, so holy and precious that it was enacted within the house of the Creatress. . . .
>
> I suggest that it was upon the attempt to establish this certain knowledge of paternity, which would then make patriarchal reckoning possible, that these ancient sexual customs were finally denounced. . . .

The custom of eunuch-priests, who sacrifice their manhood to the Goddess, is detailed by Sir James Frazer in *The New Golden Bough*, pp. 369–78, 467.

The legend of Almah Mari, or the Virgin Mary, is told in "The Protoevangelion," Chapters 1–2, in *The Lost Books of the Bible*, pp. 24–25. The name "Almah" means "maiden," or "young woman," but is usually translated "virgin." See Barbara Walker, *The Women's Encyclopedia of Myths and Secrets*, p. 1049. "Mari," see Walker, pp. 584–85, was the most ancient name of the great mother goddess.

The definition of the term *Magdalene* is suggested in Walker, pp. 565, 641. In this same place she documents the belief that Mariamne, the first to bear that title, and wife of Herod the Great, who took Joseph as her lover, was that same Mari, the mother of Jesus (but not in this story).

Joachim's lineage as a prince of Persia descended from Esther and Ahasaurus is from Arnold Michael's *Blessed Among Women*, p. 17.

Chapter 3: Almah-Isis

Both versions of the myth explaining the loss of the earth's fertility are accurate reflections of the beliefs of the time. See Marina Warner, *Alone of All Her Sex: the Myth and Cult of the Virgin Mary*, pp. 206-7. According to Warner, Dumuzi is perhaps the oldest name of the dying and resurrected god.

Stone discusses the significance of the custom of the king's ritual humiliation and beating, pp. 142–43.

Chapter 4: The Sacred Marriage

Stone, in her discussion of the Sacred Marriage custom, pp. 133–37, quotes S. N. Kramer, the eminent Sumerologist:

> The most significant rite of the New Year was the Heiros Gamos, or holy marriage between the king, who represented the god Dumuzi, and one of the priestesses, who represented the goddess Inanna. . . . The idea arose that the king of Sumer, no matter who he was or from what city he originated, must become the husband of the life-giving goddess of love, that is, Inanna of Erech. . . . The kings of Sumer are known as the "beloved husbands" of Inanna throughout the Sumerian documents from the time of Enmerkar (about 2600 B.C.) down to the post-Sumerian days, since they seem to have been mystically identified with Dumuzi.

J. J. Bachofen, in *Myth, Religion, and Mother-Right*, p. 215, writes of the dependence of kingship on marriage with the representative of the Goddess. Also see Walker, pp. 501–8.

The ancient Sumerian poem quoted throughout the chapter is taken from the translation by Diane Wolkstein and S. Noah Kramer, "The Courtship of Inanna and Dumuzi," in *Inanna, Queen of Heaven and Earth*, pp. 30–49.

Chapter 5: The Sacrifice

Frazer details the ritual of putting to death of the king by various means, including that of decapitation, pp. 273–328.

On the subject of putting to death a substitute in place of the king, Frazer writes:

> When kings were bound to suffer death, whether at their own hands or at the hands of others, it was natural that they should seek to delegate the painful duty, along with some of the privileges of sovereignty, to a substitute who would suffer vicariously in their stead.

Margaret Alice Murray, in her book *The God of the Witches*, details the practice of ritual regicide, spending several chapters on the discussion of historical cases that she believes were instances of the sacrifice of a substitute.

Chapter 6: The Seeker

The war and unrest that followed Herod's death and the division of his kingdom among his three surviving sons is told in detail by Josephus, in *The Jewish War*, pp. 120–90.

Chapter 7: Queen Isis

The story of Isis and Osiris appears in many sources; however, for the account from Herodotus and the analysis of it that inspired this book, see William Irwin Thompson, *The Time Falling Bodies Take to Light*, chapter 5, pp. 209–343.

Seth, the brother of Isis and Osiris, is treated here as the personification of the principle of limitation and particularly, creator of material existence, the Gnostic Yaltabaoth. For the Gnostic account, see Robinson, p. 98. In the version that applies here, the creator then mistakes himself for the highest god. The coffin in which he imprisons Osiris symbolizes the entrapment of the soul in space and time, and the tree that grows round it, the spinal column, the body. See Thompson, also, pp. 232–33, who writes:

> That Seth is an archon and a power from the days before civilization is clear, for he is presented as a hunter in the night. In finding the body of Osiris and cutting it into fourteen pieces, he is dismembering the moon and its fourteen pieces from the full to the new moon. Seth not only kills the spirit by imprisoning it in space and time, but he also dismembers it into the fragmentary bits that are the incarnations of little personalities that live their fragmentary lives one after another in the sublunary world. To gather up the bits and pieces of our lives on the astral plane and fuse them into one integral being who sees beyond the limits of the life of one ego is the task for both Isis (the soul) and Osiris (the self imprisoned in the particularity of time and space).

The ancient religious practice of using snake venom to induce visions is discussed by Stone throughout chapter 10, but especially pp. 212–13.

For an informative discussion of the serpent as a symbol of wisdom and immortality, see Joseph Campbell, *The Masks of God: Occidental Mythology*, pp. 9–41, 259–375. Originally identified with the Great Goddess herself, the ageless serpent was also the Kundalini, the inner female soul of man in serpent shape, coiled in the pelvis, induced through the proper use of yoga to mount to the head, bringing infinite wisdom. See Thompson also, pp. 18–20, 112–17.

Part II: Caesarea Philippi

Chapter 8: The Harem of the Tetrarch

For a history of Paneas, see Josephus, p. 155.

Chapter 9: The Stranger

The history of the Jewish wars Mari mentions is told in the First and Second Books of the Maccabees, pp. 2210–2275 in the New English Bible, and by Josephus, in Book I.

References to the matrilineal inheritance of property by the farming peoples is thoroughly documented in numerous sources. See Stone, pp. 64–69. Graves writes on p. 7:

It will be noticed that the bride in the Canticles does not depend on a father, but speaks only of her mother, and with the greatest reverence. In her sword dance as Anatha, she honors her mother Ashera, without any mention of her father El, and arranges her bride-price through intermediaries, which is in keeping with the ancient matriarchal practice of bringing the bridegroom to the mother's house, rather than bringing the bride to the father's house as in Genesis xxiv, 67. It will be noted that according to the Canticles, it was Solomon's mother, representing the priestess of Ashera, who crowned him.

Mari's reference at dinner to Yeshua's stay in the East is supported by an enduring legend recently researched by Elizabeth Clare Prophet in *The Lost Years of Jesus*, and by Janet Bock in *The Jesus Mystery*. The story that Jesus's "hidden years" were spent in studying with the masters of wisdom in Indian Tibet, and Egypt exists in both Indian and Tibetan versions of "The Legend of Issa" that are reprinted by both authors. The legend has also been documented in a film by Richard Bock entitled *The Hidden Years*, produced by the Claremont School of Theology, Claremont, California. A similar version is told in Levi's *The Aquarian Gospel of Jesus the Christ*.

Mari's association of dying-resurrected gods with eucharistic rites of wine or ale and bread is an integral part of that whole mythology. See Campbell, *The Masks of God: Primitive Mythology*, pp. 180–83.

Gallus's reading of Plato is correct; see *Phaedo* 68b, *Meno* 81c.

Chapter 10: Palace Intrigue

Much testimony appears in the Old Testament to corroborate Mari's account of the prevalence of goddess worship among the Jews and their Canaanite neighbors, who taught the nomadic shepherds the worship of the Mother along with the rudiments of farming. Robert Graves, in his own translation of the Song of Songs, p. 2, writes:

Dr. Raphael Patai, in his carefully documented works *Man and Temple* and *The Hebrew Goddess*, shows that out of the 360 years that Solomon's temple-complex lasted at Jerusalem, the matriarchal Canaanite goddess Ashera, who represented the old farming population of Israel, had been worshipped there for 240 as Jehovah's bride and sister with her wooden image publicly displayed. The tribe of Ahser had originally been named in her honor. Dr. Patai points out that when Elijah slaughtered the 400 priests on Mount Carmel he left the priests of Ashera unmolested; Baal was then Jehovah's rival male deity and therefore like Molech, Milcom, Chemosh, (I Kings XI, 7) and all the other male gods, had to be suppressed.

The hymn to Isis is from Sir E. A. Wallis Budge, *Gods of the Egyptians*, vol. 1, p. 519, vol. 2, p. 90, quoted in Walker, p. 45.

Chapter 11: The Holy Birth

Miriam's account of the holy birth is consistent with the most widely accepted chronology, placing the death of Herod the Great between three and five years A.D. See Joseph B. Tyson, *The New Testament and Early Christianity*, pp. 55–56.

NOTES

The slaughter of the innocents is told in Matthew 2:16–18. Miriam's reference to Seth's escape in a basket of reeds is part of the traditional mythology surrounding Judas. See Otto Rank, *The Myth of the Birth of the Hero*, pp. 21–22.

Chapter 13: Philip the Tetrarch

Herod Antipas became tetrarch of Galilee and Perea at the same time his half-brother Philip was given his tetrarchy, following the death of their father, King Herod (Josephus, pp. 138–39).

Chapter 14: Nazareth

Joseph's description of Antipas's situation follows Campbell, *The Masks of God: Occidental Mythology*, pp. 269–72. The fabulous palace at Jerusalem is described in detail by Josephus, p. 344, and illustrated, p. 345.

Chapter 15: The Temple

For a description and drawings of Herod's Temple, which Josephus attests had no rival for grandeur in the world at that time, see Josephus, pp. 346–65. Also see Mier Ben-Dov's *In the Shadow of the Temple*, pp. 72, 98–9, 126–27, 128.

The sacredness of women's blood, its significance in Near Eastern creation myths, taboos, etc., referred to in Mari's story to Seth follows Walker, p. 645. Mari recites fragments of "The Courtship of Inanna and Dumuzi," from Wolkstein and Kramer, pp. 39–47.

Part III: The Descent into Hell

Chapter 16: Magdalene

The story of Herod and Mariamne is told by Josephus, pp. 93–96.

Chapter 17: Judas of Scarios

Asamonius, or Hasmonius, was the father of the Hebrew royal line, according to Josephus, Book I, pp. 13–80, in his detailed history of the reign of the Hasmoneans and their overthrow by Herod with the support of Rome. For a more concise and modern account, see Tyson, pp. 48–53.

Chapter 20: Sita

Sita's story points to the Hindu tradition. Denise Carmody writes in *Women and World Religions*, p. 46:

> Widows in the classical Hindu scheme were prohibited from remarrying. They were supposed to shun men completely, and they were conditioned to think that they had caused their husband's deaths, devouring them through their *karmic jaw* (their own bad karma). In strict Hindu families, the widow was a tragic figure. She was forced to an ascetic life—sleeping on the ground, eating only one meal a day, going without honey, meat, wine, or salt, using no ointments, perfumes, or colored clothing. By medieval times, she was expected to shave her head. Since any laxity would endanger not only her own auspicious rebirth, but also her husband's, his family was rigorous in enforcing her asceticism. . . . All this was applied even to child brides whose marriage had never been consummated. . . . Small wonder that so many brides chose to jump on their husband's

funeral pyres, an action which, as a further bind, was only meritorious if done from pure conjugal love.

Yeshua's presence in India is part of the "Legend of Issa"; see note for chapter 9.

Chapter 21: Inanna, the Morning Star

The hymn to Inanna and the first half of the poem are taken from S. N. Kramer's translation in "Sumerian Mythology," in *Memoirs of the American Philosophical Society*, vol. 21, 1944, pp. 88–89 reprinted and abridged in Joseph Campbell, *The Masks of God: Primitive Mythology*, p. 413. The balance of the poem beginning with "Inanna was about to ascend from the netherworld,/When the Annanaki seized her" is from Wolkstein and Kramer, *Inanna, Queen of Heaven and Earth*, pp. 68–89.

Walker, citing interpretations by Graves in *The White Goddess* and Angus in *The Mystery Religions*, pp. 885–886, writes:

> The Bible presents the Dance of the Seven Veils as a mere vulgar striptease performed by Salome to "please Herod" (Matthew 14:6–8). Actually, the Dance of the Seven Veils was an integral part of the sacred drama, depicting the death of the surrogate-king, his descent into the underworld, and his retrieval by the Goddess, who removed one of her seven garments at each of the seven underworld gates. The priestess called Salome, or "Peace" (Shalom) impersonated the descending Goddess, passing through seven gates. . . .
>
> Salome represented Ishtar as the third of her three high priestesses or "Marys". . . . She may have been identical with the sacred harlot Mary Magdalene, or Mary of the Temple, whose so-called "seven devils" were the same underworld gatekeepers to whom the temple dancer gave her veils. These veils, like the rainbow veils of Maya, signified the layers of earthly appearances or illusions falling away from those who approached the central Mystery of the deeps. Isis too had seven stoles with the same mystical significance.

Chapter 24: The Mirror Image

Mari's reference to Herod's madness at his death is from Josephus, p. 124, and pp. 90–93.

The twinship of Jesus and Judas is a version of the myth of the warring opposites; see Walker, pp. 481–82.:

> The Syrian *Acts of Thomas* declares that Judas was Jesus' twin brother, whose full name was Judas Thomas, i.e., "Judas the Tammuz." Passages in the Koran insist that Judas had the same face as Jesus and was crucified in his stead. (Walker cites Rudolf Augstein, *Jesus, Son of Man* (New York, Urizen Books, 1977), pp. 151, 183.)

Chapter 26: The Demons

The words of the Star Goddess to Mari, p. 291, are paraphrased, not quoted, from *The Spiral Dance*, by Starhawk.

The Dark Goddess, the despised "other self," represents the "fallen" or mortal self, the body, which is doomed to death and decay. Yeshua-Osiris, the pure spiritual being, in Mari's envisioned Harrowing of Hell, and later in his marriage to her (because through her descent she has taken the identity of the Dark Goddess), unites with and takes to himself all that is mortal, this elevating flesh and matter by recognizing her as the Goddess, Mother of all things. Their marriage is the recognition that divinity, which is a unity, can only express itself in the particular; i.e., a mortal body at a certain time in a specific place. The converse of the myth is also working through Isis, the soul, searching for her beloved Osiris, who has been trapped in the succession of mortal, bodily, lives. Both movements seek a unity between matter and spirit.

The story of Mari's anointing of Yeshua's feet is told in Luke 7:36–50. Popular myth holds that the woman in the story was also the woman taken in adultery, and that he cast from her seven devils.

Part IV: The Anointed One

Chapter 29: Lazarus

Yeshua's chant as he leads the Round Dance is from The Acts of John, 94–96, translation following Montague Rhodes James, *The Apocryphal New Testament* (Oxford: The Clarendon Press, 1953), p. 251; reprinted in Campbell, *The Masks of God: Occidental Mythology*, pp. 371–73.

The raising of Lazarus is told in John 11.

Chapter 30: The King of the Jews

John Hyrcanus II was the last of the Hasmoneans, who had taken the priesthood as well as the crown (Tyson, pp. 55).

The fortress of Antonia is described with illustrations in Josephus, p. 345.

The love poetry in this instance of the Sacred Marriage is from the Song of Solomon, believed by many scholars to have originated as a liturgy for the Sacred Marriage and later sung at regular weddings. See Graves, *The Song of Songs*, pp. 3–4.

Chapter 32: The Cross

The rites of the scapegoat, recalled by Antipas's scourging and mocking of Jesus, clothing him in a red robe, etc., are associated with killing the old king and devouring his sacrificial body. This was the ancient rite of purging the tribe by expelling a scapegoat, on whose head were heaped the sins of the past year. This ancient death and resurrection rite seems to have had a double meaning: the killing of the god or king to save him or the people from the sterility of age, and the expulsion of evils (or devils) amid rejoicing of a people who were redeemed by the sacrifice of a hero-victim. See Frazer, pp. 588–628.

Chapter 33: The Third Day

The account of Easter morning begins with John 20:1.

The grave wrappings alone remain is from John 20:4–7.

The vision in the tomb is from John 20:11–13.

Jesus is first seen by Mary, John 20:14–17.

Mary is sent to the disciples with a special message, but they do not want to hear it from a woman. The story is told in a Gnostic text, *The Gospel of Mary*, cited in Pagels, *The Gnostic Gospels*, pp. 77–88.

Epilogue: The Holy Grail

The European myth of the coming of Mary Magdalene to France (Gaul) with the holy grail is treated in Marjorie Malvern's *Venus in Sackcloth*, where she claims that the Magdalene exceeded the Virgin Mary in popularity, and that many medieval cathedrals were in fact dedicated to her, not the virgin.

The same ideas are developed in the psuedo-documentary *Holy Blood, Holy Grail*, by Baigent, Leigh, and Lincoln, who write, p. 374:

> If our hypothesis is correct, the Holy Grail would have been at least two things simultaneously. On the one hand, it would have been Jesus' bloodline and descendents—the "Sang Raal," the "Real" or royal blood of which the Templars, created by the Prieure de Sion, were appointed guardians. At the same time the Holy Grail would have been, quite literally, the receptacle or vessel which contained Jesus' blood. In other words, it would have been the womb of the Magdalen—and by extension, the Magdalen herself. From this the cult of the Magdalen, as it was promulgated during the Middle Ages, would have arisen—and been confused with the cult of the Virgin. It can be proved, for instance, that many of the famous "Black Virgins" or "Black Madonnas" were early in the Christian era shrines not to the Virgin, but to the Magdalen—and they depict a mother and child. It has also been argued that the Gothic cathedrals—those majestic stone replicas of the womb dedicated to "Notre Dame"—were also, as *Le Serpent Rouge* states, shrines to Jesus' consort rather than to his mother.

Bibliography

Adler, Margot. *Drawing Down the Moon*. Boston: Beacon Press, 1981.

Allbright, William Powell. *Yahweh and the Gods of Canaan*. New York: Doubleday, 1968.

Bachofen, J. J. *Myth, Religion, and Mother-Right*. Princeton, N. J.: Princeton University Press, 1967.

Baigent, Michael, Richard Leigh, and Henry Lincoln. *Holy Blood, Holy Grail*. New York: Delacorte Press, 1982.

Ben-Dov, Meir. *In the Shadow of the Temple*. New York: Harper and Row, 1985.

Bhaghavad Gita. Translated by Franklin Edgerton. New York: Harper and Row, 1944.

Blavatsky, H. P. *Isis Unveiled*. 2 vols. Pasadena, CA: Theosophical University Press, 1976.

Bock, Janet. *The Jesus Mystery*. Los Angeles, CA: Aura Books, 1980.

Brandon, S. G. F. *The Trial of Jesus of Nazareth*. New York: Stein and Day, 1979.

Book of the Dead. Translated by E. A. Wallis Budge. New York: Bell Publishing, 1960.

Gods of the Egyptians. Translated by E. A. Wallis Budge. New York: Dover Publications, 1969.

Campbell, Joseph. *The Masks of God: Primitive Mythology*. New York: Viking Press, 1959.

———. *The Masks of God: Oriental Mythology*. New York: Viking Press, 1962.

———. *The Masks of God: Occidental Mythology*. New York: Viking Press, 1964.

———. *The Masks of God: Creative Mythology*. New York: Viking Press, 1970.

Carmody, Denise Lardner. *Women and World Religions*. Abington, 1979.

Davis, Elisabeth Gould. *The First Sex*. New York: G. P. Putnam's Sons, 1971.

Dinnerstein, Dorothy. *The Mermaid and the Minotaur*. New York: Harper Colophon Books, 1977.

Eliade Mircea. *The Myth of the Eternal Return*. Princeton, N. J.: Princeton University Press, 1954.

———. *Shamanism*. Princeton, N.J.: Bollingen Series, 1964.

Endo, Shusaku. *A Life Of Jesus*. New York: Paulist Press, 1973.

Frazer, Sir James G. *The Golden Bough*. New York: Macmillan, 1922.

Goldburg, B. Z. *The Sacred Fire*. New York: University Books, 1958.

Goldenburg, Naomi. *The Changing of the Gods*. Boston: Beacon Press, 1979.

Graves, Robert. *King Jesus*. New York: Farrar, Strauss, & Giroux, 1946.

———. *The White Goddess*. New York: Farrar, Strauss, & Giroux, 1948.

———. *The Song of Songs*. New York: Crown Publishers, 1973.

Graves, Robert, and Raphael Patai. *Hebrew Myths*. New York: Doubleday, 1964.

Holy Bible, New English Version. New York: Oxford University Press, Cambridge University Press, 1970.

Holy Bible, Revised Standard Version. Cleveland: World Publishing Company, 1962.

Hooke, S. H., *Middle Eastern Mythology*. Harmondsworth, England: Penguin Books, 1963.

Jonas, Hans. *The Gnostic Religion*. Boston: Beacon Press, 1963.

Josephus. *The Jewish War*. Edited by Gaalya Cornfeld. Grand Rapids, MI: Zondervan, 1982.

Jung, Carl Gustav. *Man and His Symbols*. New York: Doubleday, 1964.

Jung, Carl Gustav, and Kerenyi, C. *Essays on a Science of Mythology*. New York: Bollingen, 1949.

Kinsley, David R. *The Sword and the Flute*. Berkeley: University of California Press, 1975.

Kramer, Samuel Noah. *History Begins at Sumer*. New York: Doubleday, 1959.

Larousse Encyclopedia of Mythology, London: Hamlyn Publishing Group, 1968.

Larsen, Martin A. "The Great Osiris." *Michigan Alumnus Quarterly Review* 5 (Dec. 1960).

Levi. *The Aquarian Gospel of Jesus the Christ*. Los Angeles: Devorss, 1907.

Lost Books of the Bible. New York: Bell Publishing, 1979.

Malvern, Marjorie. *Venus in Sackcloth*. Carbondale, IL: Southern Illinois University Press, 1975.

Michael, Arnold. *Blessed Among Women*. Los Angeles, CA: Scrivener, 1971.

Murray, Margaret Alice. *The God of the Witches*. New York: Oxford University Press, 1973.

Neumann, Erich. *The Origins and History of Consciousness*. Princeton, N.J.: Princeton University Press, 1954.

———. *The Great Mother: An Analysis of the Archetype*. Princeton, N.J.: Princeton University Press, 1963.

O'Flaherty, Wendy Doniger. *Women, Androgenes, and Other Mythical Beasts*. Chicago: University of Chicago Press, 1980.

Pagels, Elaine. *The Gnostic Gospels*. New York: Random House, 1979.

Pfeifer, Charles F. *The Dead Sea Scrolls and the Bible*. New York: Weathervane Books, 1969.

Platt, Rutherford H. *Forgotten Books of Eden*. New York: Bell Publishing, 1980.

Pritchard, James B. *The Ancient Near East*. 2 vols., Princeton, N.J.: Princeton University Press, 1958.

Prophet, Elizabeth Clare. *The Lost Years of Jesus*. Malibu, CA: Summit University Press, 1984.

Robinson, James M., ed. *The Nag Hammadi Library in English*. San Francisco: Harper and Row, 1977.

Rank Otto. *The Myth of the Birth of the Hero*. New York: Vintage Books, 1959.

Schurer, Emil. *The Literature of the Jewish People in the Time of Jesus*. New York: Schocken Books, 1972.

Starhawk, *The Spiral Dance*. New York: Harper and Row, 1979.

Stone, Merlin. *When God Was a Woman*. New York: Dial Press, 1976.

Suzuki, D. T. *On Indian Mahayana Buddhism*. New York: Harper Torchbooks, 1968.

Sypher, Wylie. "THe Meanings of Comedy." In *Comedy*, by George Meridith. New York: Doubleday, 1956.

Thompson, William Irwin. *The Time Falling Bodies Take to Light*. New York: St. Martin's Press, 1981.

Tyson, Joseph B. *The New Testament and Early Christianity*. New York: Macmillan, 1984.

Upanishads. Translated and edited by Swami Nikhilananda. New York: Harper Torchbooks, 1964.

Walker, Barbara G. *The Women's Encyclopedia of Myths and Secrets*. San Francisco: Harper and Row, 1983.

Warner, Marina. *Alone of All Her Sex: The Myth and Cult of the Virgin Mary*. New York: Alfred A. Knopf, 1976.

Watts, Alan. *Myth and Ritual in Christianity*. New York: Beacon, 1968.

Wolkstein, Diane, and Samuel Noah Kramer. *Inanna, Queen of Heaven and Earth*. New York: Harper and Row, 1983.

Zimmer, Heinrich. *Myths and Symbols in Indian Art and Civilization*. Princeton, N.J.: Princeton University Press, 1946.